T0305396

New Global Economic Architecture

ADBI SERIES ON ASIAN ECONOMIC INTEGRATION AND
COOPERATION

Previous titles published in association with ADBI include:

Infrastructure and Trade in Asia
Edited by Douglas H. Brooks and Jayant Menon

Infrastructure's Role in Lowering Asia's Trade Costs
Building for Trade
Edited by Douglas H. Brooks and David Hummels

Trade Facilitation and Regional Cooperation in Asia
Edited by Douglas H. Brooks and Susan F. Stone

Managing Capital Flows
The Search for a Framework
Edited by Masahiro Kawai and Mario B. Lamberte

The Asian Tsunami
Aid and Reconstruction after a Disaster
Edited by Sisira Jayasuriya and Peter McCawley

Asia's Free Trade Agreements
How is Business Responding?
Edited by Masahiro Kawai and Ganeshan Wignaraja

Monetary and Currency Policy Management in Asia
Edited by Masahiro Kawai, Peter J. Morgan and Shinji Takagi

Implications of the Global Financial Crisis for Financial Reform and Regulation
in Asia
Edited by Masahiro Kawai, David G. Mayes and Peter J. Morgan

Infrastructure for Asian Connectivity
Edited by Biswa Nath Bhattacharyay, Masahiro Kawai and Rajat M. Nag

A World Trade Organization for the 21st Century
The Asian Perspective
Edited by Richard Baldwin, Masahiro Kawai and Ganeshan Wignaraja

New Global Economic Architecture
The Asian Perspective
Edited by Masahiro Kawai, Peter J. Morgan and Pradumna B. Rana

The Asian Development Bank Institute (ADBI), located in Tokyo, is the think
tank of the Asian Development Bank (ADB). ADBI's mission is to identify effective development strategies and improve development management in ADB's
developing member countries. ADBI has an extensive network of partners in the
Asia and Pacific region and globally. ADBI's activities are aligned with ADB's
strategic focus, which includes poverty reduction and inclusive economic growth,
the environment, regional cooperation and integration, infrastructure development,
middle-income countries, and private sector development and operations.

New Global Economic Architecture
The Asian Perspective

Edited by

Masahiro Kawai

Project Professor, Graduate School of Public Policy, University of Tokyo, Japan

Peter J. Morgan

Senior Consultant for Research, Asian Development Bank Institute, Japan

Pradumna B. Rana

Associate Professor, S. Rajaratnam School of International Studies, Nanyang Technological University, Singapore

Edward Elgar
Cheltenham, UK • Northampton, MA, USA

Published by
Edward Elgar Publishing Limited
The Lypiatts
15 Lansdown Road
Cheltenham
Glos GL50 2JA
UK

Edward Elgar Publishing, Inc.
William Pratt House
9 Dewey Court
Northampton
Massachusetts 01060
USA

A catalogue record for this book
is available from the British Library

Library of Congress Control Number: 2014941550

This book is available electronically in the ElgarOnline.com
Economics Subject Collection, E-ISBN 978 1 78347 220 8

ISBN 978 1 78347 219 2

Typeset by Servis Filmsetting Ltd, Stockport, Cheshire
Printed and bound in Great Britain by T.J. International Ltd, Padstow

Contents

Contributors

Akkharaphol Chabchitrchaidol is Economist, ASEAN+3 Macroeconomic Research Office (AMRO) in Singapore.

Andrew F. Cooper is Professor, Balsillie School of International Affairs and Department of Political Science at the University of Waterloo, Canada. He is also Distinguished Fellow at the Centre for International Governance Innovation.

Hal Hill is H.W. Arndt Professor of Southeast Asian Economies in the Arndt–Corden Department of Economics, Crawford School, College of Asia and the Pacific, The Australian National University.

Masahiro Kawai is Project Professor, Graduate School of Public Policy, University of Tokyo. He was formerly Dean and CEO, Asian Development Bank Institute, Tokyo, Japan.

Jayant Menon is Lead Economist, Asian Development Bank, Manila, Philippines.

Peter J. Morgan is Senior Consultant for Research, Asian Development Bank Institute. He was formerly Chief Economist, HSBC, Hong Kong, China.

Vikram Nehru is Senior Associate and Bakrie Chair in Southeast Asian Studies, Carnegie Endowment for International Peace, Washington, DC, USA. He was previously Chief Economist for East Asia and the Pacific at the World Bank.

Michael G. Plummer is Director, SAIS Europe, and ENI Professor of International Economics, Johns Hopkins University, Bologna, Italy and (non-resident) Senior Fellow, East-West Center, Honolulu, USA.

Fernando Prada is Associate Researcher at FORO Nacional Internacional, Lima, Peru.

Pradumna B. Rana is Associate Professor, International Political Economy, S. Rajaratnam School of International Studies, Nanyang Technological University, Singapore. He was formerly Senior Advisor of the Office of Regional Economic Integration, Asian Development Bank, Manila, Philippines.

Reza Siregar is Group Head and Lead Economist, ASEAN+3 Macroeconomic Research Office (AMRO) in Singapore.

Ganeshan Wignaraja is Director for Research, Asian Development Bank Institute, Tokyo, Japan. He was formerly Principal Economist, Asian Development Bank, Manila, Philippines.

Preface

In the postwar period, the global economic architecture was dominated by the advanced economies in the West. They designed the international monetary system, international development financing frameworks and global trade liberalization schemes. They also dominated the leadership of key global institutions, such as the International Monetary Fund (IMF), the World Bank and the World Trade Organization (WTO). They were successful in sustaining long-term economic growth through the provision of global public goods to promote international economic and financial stability, economic reconstruction and development, and open, non-discriminatory trade. The so-called Washington consensus was the supporting philosophy behind these efforts.

Today, however, the balance of economic and financial power is shifting toward the emerging economies, especially those in Asia, and both global governance and economic policy thinking are beginning to reflect this shift. One notable example is the move away from the G7 to the G20 as the premier forum for international policy cooperation. Another is the recent recognition by the IMF that free capital flows may not be always desirable for developing and emerging economies, and by the World Bank that the role of the state is essential in facilitating sustainable and inclusive economic development. Perhaps the most striking development was the appeal from European countries for financial assistance from major emerging economies, such as the People's Republic of China (PRC), to help ease the eurozone sovereign debt and banking sector crisis. Another development has been the rise of aid flows from major emerging economies, such as the PRC, Brazil and India, to lower-income developing economies.

In addition to this shift in economic balance, the recent global financial crisis and the eurozone financial crisis have highlighted the shortcomings of the current global economic architecture and international monetary system, and have sparked an international debate about possible remedies for them. Significantly, the global financial crisis began in the United States, which is the largest and most central economy in the world and home to the world's most sophisticated and developed financial system and the most dominant global reserve currency – the dollar. It is still the home of the theories of self-regulating financial markets and free capital flows even though they have fallen into disrepute.

This book addresses the important question of how a regional architecture can induce a supply of regional public goods that can complement and strengthen the global public goods supplied through the global architecture. A related question is how much global and regional public goods Asian emerging economies will be able to provide in order to help maintain global financial stability, open trading regimes, and sustainable economic development. A further question is what and how much intellectual input these economies can offer to influence the global debate on these issues.

The global financial crisis and the eurozone sovereign debt and banking crisis highlighted the risks that emerging economies, including those in Asia, face even if their own macroeconomic and financial fundamentals are sound. The awareness of this risk is stimulating the search for policies and arrangements to reduce these economies' vulnerability to such external shocks. The eurozone crisis also raised important policy questions about regional financial cooperation and architecture. Although Asia is much less integrated than Europe, one important lesson is that regional cooperation can play a critical role in achieving macroeconomic and financial stability. This includes: improving the effectiveness of regional macroeconomic and financial surveillance; creating a macroeconomic and financial policy coordination mechanism; and strengthening regional financial safety nets.

One area of current debate surrounds the issue of how the IMF as a provider of global financial safety nets can work with regional financing arrangements. Several Asian emerging economies, such as the Republic of Korea and Indonesia, faced shortages of US dollar liquidity in the aftermath of the Lehman collapse in the fall of 2008 even though they had pursued sound economic and financial policies. The Republic of Korea and Singapore were able to secure international liquidity from the US Federal Reserve in the form of currency swap arrangements, but not all countries were able to enjoy such a privilege. At the same time, the problem of the so-called IMF "stigma" remains a major barrier to the activation of an IMF safety net in emerging Asia. The Chiang Mai Initiative Multilateralization has emerged as the financial safety net in Asia, but many issues remain in terms of how it can coordinate its activities with those of the IMF.

Other areas covered in this book include the interplay of global and regional financial regulation, the role of the World Trade Organization versus those of bilateral and regional trade agreements, and finally the parts to be played by the World Bank and regional development banks.

The chapters in this book were originally presented at the conference on "The Evolving Global Architecture: From a Centralized to a Decentralized System", which was jointly sponsored by the Asian Development Bank Institute (ADBI) and the S. Rajaratnam School of International Studies, Nanyang Technological University in Singapore on 26–27 March 2012. The papers have been updated to reflect recent changes and developments. We hope that they can contribute in a significant way to the debate about how to reform the global economic architecture and to develop an infrastructure for creating regional public goods.

Masahiro Kawai
Peter J. Morgan
Pradumna B. Rana

Abbreviations

ACMF	ASEAN Capital Markets Forum
ADB	Asian Development Bank
AEC	ASEAN Economic Community
AFAS	ASEAN Framework Agreement on Services
AFC	Asian Financial Crisis
AfDB	African Development Bank
AFMGM+3	ASEAN+3 Finance Ministers and Central Bank Governors' Meeting
AFMM+3	ASEAN+3 Finance Ministers' Meeting
AFSB	Asian Financial Stability Board
AFSD	Asian financial stability dialogue
AMF	Asian Monetary Fund
AMRO	ASEAN+3 Macroeconomic Research Office
APEC	Asia-Pacific Economic Cooperation
AREM	ASEAN+3 Regional Economic Monitoring
ASA	ASEAN Swap Arrangement
ASEAN	Association of Southeast Asian Nations
AU	African Union
BFSN	bilateral financial safety net
BIS	Bank for International Settlements
BOP	balance of payments
BRICS	Brazil, Russian Federation, India, People's Republic of China, South Africa
CABEI	Central American Bank for Economic Integration
CAF	Andean Corporation of Finance
CAF	Development Bank of Latin America
CAFTA	Central American Free Trade Agreement
CDB	Caribbean Development Bank
CEPEA	Comprehensive Economic Partnership for East Asia
CMI	Chiang Mai Initiative
CMIM	Chiang Mai Initiative Multilateralization
DDA	Doha Development Agenda
EAFTA	East Asian Free Trade Area
EBA	European Banking Authority

ECB	European Central Bank
EFSF	European Financial Stability Facility
EFSM	European Financial Stabilization Mechanism
EFTA	European Free Trade Association
EIOPA	European Insurance and Occupational Pensions Authority
ELDMB	Executive Level Decision Making Body
EMEAP	Executives' Meeting of East Asia-Pacific Central Banks
ERPD	Economic Review and Policy Dialogue
ESA	European Supervisory Authority
ESFS	European System of Financial Supervision
ESM	European Stability Mechanism
ESMA	European Securities and Markets Authority
ESRB	European Systemic Risk Board
EU	European Union
FCL	Flexible Credit Line
FOMIN	Multilateral Investment Fund
FONPLATA	Financial Fund for the Development of the River Plate Basin
FSB	Financial Stability Board
FSF	Financial Stability Forum
FTA	free trade agreement
G20	Group of Twenty
GATS	General Agreement on Trade in Services
GATT	General Agreement on Tariffs and Trade
GCC	Gulf Cooperation Council
GDP	gross domestic product
GEA	global economic architecture
GEC	global economic crisis
GECC	Global Economic Coordination Council
GFC	global financial crisis
GPA	Government Procurement Agreement
GSM	Global Stabilization Mechanism
IBRD	International Bank for Reconstruction and Development
IDA	International Development Association
IDB	Inter-American Development Bank
IEI	international economic institution
IFC	International Finance Corporation
IIC	Inter-American Investment Corporation
IMF	International Monetary Fund
IOSCO	International Organization of Securities Commissions

IPR	intellectual property rights
ITA	Information Technology Agreement
Lao PDR	Lao People's Democratic Republic
MDB	multilateral development bank
MERCOSUR	*Mercado Comun del Sur* (Southern Common Market)
MFN	most-favored nation
NAFA	North American Framework Agreement
NAFTA	North American Free Trade Agreement
NBW	New Bretton Woods
NEPAD	New Partnership for Africa's Development
OECD	Organisation for Economic Co-operation and Development
OFC	offshore financial center
PCL	Precautionary Credit Line
PLL	Precautionary and Liquidity Line
PRC	People's Republic of China
RCEP	Regional Comprehensive Economic Partnership
RFI	Rapid Financing Instrument
ROO	rules of origin
RTA	regional trading agreement
SBA	Stand-By Arrangement
SEACEN	South East Asian Central Banks
SME	small and medium-sized enterprise
SRDB	subregional development bank
TPP	Trans-Pacific Partnership
UN	United Nations
WFO	World Finance Organization
WTO	World Trade Organization

1. Asian perspectives on the evolving global architecture

Masahiro Kawai, Peter J. Morgan and Pradumna B. Rana

1.1 INTRODUCTION AND SUMMARY

The global economic architecture which evolved out of the historic 1944 Bretton Woods Conference comprised various international economic institutions (IEIs): the International Monetary Fund (IMF) established to promote macroeconomic stability; the General Agreement on Tariffs and Trade (GATT) – the predecessor of the World Trade Organization (WTO) – to ensure an open trading system; and the World Bank, to provide development finance for poverty reduction. The G7/G8 was established in the mid-1970s to oversee the IEIs and subsequently the Financial Stability Forum (FSF) was established in 1999 in response to the Asian Financial Crisis to promote financial stability and develop best practices for financial regulation and supervision.

This relatively simple architecture, which worked well for a few decades, has now come under severe strain. One important reason is that the governance system of the old architecture does not reflect the move from a uni-polar to a multi-polar world. This process accelerated after the global financial crisis (GFC) of 2008–09, most notably the increased economic power of Asia, especially the People's Republic of China (PRC) and India. Another is that policies of IEIs (e.g. charters, quotas and voting rights) were designed in the interests of the like-minded members in 1944 and are strongly protected by the original members. Third, the context in which the IEIs operate has also changed dramatically, particularly in the area of globalization of finance. Finally, many observers argued that the current architecture actually contributed to the development of the GFC.

At the height of the global financial crisis, a number of academics and politicians had made calls for a "New Bretton Woods (NBW)", meaning a comprehensive reform of the old architecture. While the recent upgrading of the Group of Twenty (G20) Finance Ministers process into a

G20 Summit of Leaders and the FSF into the Financial Stability Board (FSB) are encouraging, those hoping for a NBW are likely to be disappointed. This is mainly because the rebound from the GFC turned out to be faster than expected: instead of a Global Depression we had a Great Recession.

It is, therefore, likely that in the future we will not have a NBW. Instead the global architecture will move incrementally towards a more network-based decentralized/multi-layered system where national, bilateral and regional institutions work closely with a "senior" global institution.

While the global architecture is moving towards a more decentralized system, the G20, which has declared itself as the "premier forum for international economic cooperation", suffers from both "input" legitimacy – its exclusive nature and lack of broader representation – and "output" legitimacy – its ability to strengthen international cooperation and come up with effective solutions. Its agenda is also quickly becoming overcrowded. How can we make the G20 more effective? How can we promote greater complementarity between global, regional and national institutions? Is the world economy governable?

The objectives of this book are: (i) to review key issues in reforming the global architecture including the roles of the oversight bodies such as the G20; (ii) to identify evolving trends in the global architecture including developments at the regional and the national levels; and (iii) to develop ideas and principles to ensure that national and regional efforts complement global institutions and do not try to supplant them. The book focuses on the following five sub-topics and comprises ten chapters:

(i)   G20 effectiveness and reforms;
(ii)   global financial safety nets and regional safety nets;
(iii)   global and regional financial architecture;
(iv)   trade architecture: WTO and regionalism;
(v)   World Bank and regional development banks.

1.2   G20 EFFECTIVENESS AND REFORMS

The first two chapters focus on the move from the G7/G8-led to the G20-led architecture and how this architecture is becoming more decentralized. Chapter 2 by Pradumna B. Rana sets the stage for the rest of the book, and argues that the relatively simple architecture created at Bretton Woods faces a number of challenges. First, the governance system of the old architecture does not reflect the move from a uni-polar to a multi-polar world: it reflects the dominance of the US and Europe and does not reflect the economic rise and political power of emerging markets, particularly those in Asia (PRC and India) and, therefore, it lacks legitimacy. Second, as predicted by the theory of clubs, policies of IEIs (e.g. charters, quotas and voting rights) were designed in the interests of the like-minded members in 1944 and are strongly protected by the original members. Third, the context in which the IEIs operate has also changed dramatically. Of particular note is globalization, especially financial globalization, which has increased the incidence of financial crisis and the need for regional and national actions to complement global ones (Kawai and Rana 2009).

Also, since the rebound from the GFC has turned out to be faster than expected, Rana argues that complacency has set in and it is unlikely that the calls for a NBW will be realized. It is, therefore, likely that in the future the global architecture will move incrementally towards a more network-based decentralized/multi-layered system where national, bilateral and regional institutions work closely with a "senior" global institution.

A decentralized architecture is not hypothetical. It already exists in the development architecture, where the World Bank is complemented by four major regional development banks. Also the IMF has been working fairly closely with the European Central Bank and the recently established European Stability Mechanism (ESM) in trying to resolve the sovereign debt crisis affecting the region.

Rana argues that at the present level of political will, an incremental and a more decentralized process is what can be envisaged in terms of global economic architecture (GEA) reform. If in the future, however, the incidence of financial crises was to increase and political will among countries and cooperation were to strengthen, one could then perhaps see a move towards a more rules-based and centralized system. Rana concludes that Asia could support this evolving architecture by building robust regional institutions to complement global ones.

In Chapter 3, Andrew Cooper argues that, in a break from past situations of crisis, a new form of collective action comprising an old elite of states and a cluster of emerging powers, namely the G20, emerged from the global financial crisis of 2008–09. While laudable, the G20 is still an awkward institutional arrangement, with some innovative qualities and some serious gaps in terms of efficiency and representation. He credits this reformist model of governance to Paul Martin, successively Finance Minister and Prime Minister of Canada.

Cooper observes that, in contrast to the BRICS, selected middle-income powers have used the opportunity to take a leadership role in the G20: the Republic of Korea had hosted the G20 in 2010, Mexico in 2012, Australia in 2014, and Turkey will host it in 2015 and possibly Indonesia in 2016. The Republic of Korea had been very active in the G20 from the very outset and it had introduced two new agenda items in the Seoul summit: a global financial safety net and development assistance for poor countries.

Despite its successes, the G20 continues to suffer from problems of "output" and "input" legitimacy. Cooper argues that, in contrast to the successes of initial summits, the Toronto summit of June 2010 and the Seoul summit of November 2011 presented more mixed if not completely pessimistic experiences. This loss of momentum does not mean the collapse of the G20 project, argues Cooper. As a crisis committee, the G20 is still moving on a number of fronts including on issues related to global imbalances.

In terms of "input legitimacy", Cooper notes that there were two issues. The first was the absence of the United Nations in the design. Hence, there was a UN-oriented backlash against the G20 and Joseph Stiglitz was requested to convene another panel. This backlash has now eased and the UN has endorsed that the two institutions are different and complementary not competitive. The other criticism was from non-member countries. This had also been addressed to some extent at the Seoul summit when the G20 settled on a formula for non-member participation, enabling the summit to invite up to five guests. Further efforts must be made to make the G20 more inclusive.

1.3   GLOBAL FINANCIAL SAFETY NETS AND REGIONAL SAFETY NETS

As mentioned above, formation of an effective global financial safety net to deal with global systemic crises has become an important agenda item of the G20. In Chapter 4, Reza Siregar and Akkharaphol Chabchitrchaidol make the case for further strengthening the Chiang Mai Initiative Multilateralization (CMIM) and the ASEAN+3 Macroeconomic Research Office (AMRO). The CMIM crisis fund of US$240 billion remains a mere fraction of the amount committed to the European Stability Mechanism. Complementarity between the regional and the global safety net should also be promoted in order to ensure the CMIM's success.

According to the authors, the CMIM faces a number of challenges. First, should the CMIM package be part of the bilateral swap arrangement among the ASEAN+3 economies or should these two approaches be kept independent? Second, is there a need to develop conditionalities for the CMIM to safeguard from moral hazard while providing flexible and timely support? Third, is there a need to eventually de-link the CMIM from IMF conditions, which would be contingent on the surveillance capacity of AMRO?

Siregar and Chabchitrchaidol highlight the major tasks of AMRO. AMRO prepares quarterly reports on the macroeconomic situation of ASEAN+3 countries collectively as well as individually. During crisis periods, AMRO: (i) prepares an analysis of the economic and financial situation of the swap-requesting country; (ii) monitors the use and impact of the funds disbursed under the CMIM Agreement; and (iii) monitors the compliance by the swap requesting country with any lending covenants to the CMIM Agreement. They also mention that although AMRO is a new institution, it has made good progress in recruiting staff and strengthening its capacity.

In Chapter 5, Hal Hill and Jayant Menon note that the need for regional safety nets (surveillance and financing arrangements) arose from the Asian Financial Crisis of 1997–98 when there was some disillusionment with IMF programs and policies. The three components of regional safety nets in Asia were the regional economic review and policy dialogue process (ERPD), the Chiang Mai Initiative (CMI), and the Asian Bond Markets Initiative (ABMI). All three components were interrelated. Subsequently, the CMI was upgraded to CMIM and the AMRO was established.

Hill and Menon then ask the question whether ASEAN+3 has all the elements of a strong regional financial safety net. The answer is, not yet. During the recent global financial crisis, the CMIM was not used. This was perhaps because the size of the CMIM was too small and/or because of the "stigma" attached to IMF conditions in the Asian region. They recommend that the CMIM's size be expanded and the linkage with IMF be reduced.

1.4 GLOBAL AND REGIONAL FINANCIAL ARCHITECTURE

In the wake of the global financial crisis of 2007–09, the G20, together with the FSB, has been at the forefront of global efforts to develop a standard approach to financial reform, and to develop an international architecture to deal with surveillance and regulation of global systemic risks and global systemically important financial institutions (SIFIs). Many nations have implemented financial reforms as well. However, the authors in this part of the book argue that, in view of the progress of regional financial integration, especially in Europe and Asia, there is a significant role for regional cooperation to bridge the gap between global and national initiatives.

In Chapter 6, Masahiro Kawai and Peter Morgan: (i) outline the case for regional-level financial regulation in Asia; (ii) compare the experiences of Europe and Asia; (iii) identify the challenges; and (iv) offer recommendations for enhancing regional financial regulation in Asia. They argue that the recent global financial crisis heightened the urgency of financial regionalism in Asia – which had taken off in response to the Asian Financial Crisis of 1997–98 – and that financial regionalism in the region could benefit from increased regulatory harmonization and mutual recognition. An increasingly economically and financially integrated Asia needs more intensive financial cooperation, including harmonized financial regulation and supervision.

They observe that financial integration in Europe has been supported by a large number of supra-national institutions including the three European Supervisory Authorities (ESAs) established for microprudential supervision and the European Systemic Risk Board for macroprudential supervision. But still there is an absence of an EU-wide framework for resolution of cross-border banks (although legislation for this is now being considered) and national insolvency laws have not been harmonized in the region.

Kawai and Morgan argue that Asia does not have an over-arching political structure comparable to that of the EU. Nonetheless, progress is being made in promoting financial cooperation under the auspices of ASEAN Economic Community; ASEAN, ASEAN+3 and EMEAP surveillance processes; CMIM and AMRO; and the Asian Bond Markets Initiative. A weaker institutional arrangement in Asia requires a different approach from that of Europe. They recommend a number of measures to strengthen regional financial regulation in Asia, including: (i) accelerating the ASEAN Economic Community process; (ii) strengthening the CMIM and AMRO to eventually evolve into an Asian monetary fund; (iii) embarking on an Asian Bond Fund-3; and (iv) creating an Asian financial stability dialogue to monitor regional financial markets, facilitate macroeconomic and financial policy dialogue and cooperation, and secure regional financial stability.

1.5　TRADE ARCHITECTURE: WTO AND REGIONALISM

Asian economies have benefited hugely from the liberalization of trade in recent decades. Earlier, trade liberalization efforts had focused on unilateral and various multilateral agreements achieved by the WTO. However, with the failure to complete the Doha Round, attention has shifted to bilateral or plurilateral free trade agreements (FTAs). This shift has been criticized by Bhagwati and others as potentially trade diversionary, and the debate since then has focused on the issue of whether such agreements are "building blocks" or "stumbling blocks" to a new multilateral round.

Masahiro Kawai and Ganeshan Wignaraja in Chapter 7 observe that, although Asia was a latecomer in developing FTAs, it has now emerged at the forefront of global FTA activity. The number of FTAs concluded by countries in the region has increased from just three in 2001 to 76 in 2013. Amid slow progress in the Doha negotiations and the global and eurozone crisis, they conclude that Asian regionalism is here to stay. Policymakers should therefore focus on how to maximize the benefits of FTAs while minimizing their costs. Their firm-level survey resulted in a more nuanced view of FTAs.

Kawai and Wignaraja note that FTAs pose a number of challenges. The first challenge is the limited coverage of agricultural goods and services trade in Asian FTAs. They argue that WTO-plus provisions, such as competition policy, investment provisions, trade facilitation and government procurement, among others, must also be considered in future FTAs. A second challenge is limited services trade liberalization in Asian FTAs. Services account for more than half the GDP of most Asian countries and trade in services has grown rapidly. Studies suggest that impediments to trade in services, particularly regulatory restrictions on foreign services and service providers, exist across Asia. Such impediments may occur in ownership rules, technical regulations, licensing, and qualification requirements.

A third challenge relates to insufficient coverage of Asian FTAs of new issues which go beyond the WTO framework. The WTO system that emerged from the Uruguay Round in the mid-1990s consisted of substantive agreements on goods and services. So-called "WTO-plus" elements include liberalization in agricultural and non-agricultural market access, competition policy, investment, trade facilitation, and government procurement. WTO-plus agreements and "new age" FTAs, which are comprehensive and address the Singapore issues, are becoming more common globally.

The fourth challenge is how to improve the utilization of FTAs. In addition to the information gap, the provisions of FTAs were complex and could not be fully understood by small and medium-sized enterprises (SMEs). There was, therefore, a need to improve business support services. The fifth challenge is tackling the "Noodle Bowl" effect, for example overlapping rules of origin (ROOs) in FTAs which increased transaction costs for firms. With the rapid spread of FTAs throughout Asia, multiple ROOs in overlapping FTAs posed a serious burden on SMEs in particular.

Kawai and Wignaraja argue that these challenges require responses at the national, regional and global levels. At the national level, policy-makers need to increase efforts to address the above-mentioned challenges. At the regional level, they identify two competing tracks that could lead to an Asian region-wide FTA: the Regional Comprehensive Economic Partnership (RCEP) among the ASEAN+6 countries (the 10 ASEAN economies plus Australia, the PRC, India, Japan, the Republic of Korea and New Zealand) and the Trans-Pacific Strategic Economic Partnership (Trans-Pacific Partnership, or TPP). At the global level, important initiatives in areas such as global supply chains may be of greater use than plurilateral agreements (which focus on rule making and liberalization on a single trade issue) within the WTO framework.

In Chapter 8, Mike Plummer argues that although the WTO system is functioning well, with the rule-based system being respected and an improved dispute settlement mechanism in place, the multilateral liberalization process has stalled with the deadlock in the Doha Development Agenda (DDA). The consensus view is that North–South economic tensions were the main cause of the deadlock. Plummer believes that this view is only partially correct: another important reason for the DDA deadlock is intra-BRICS rivalry and competition. As intra-regional trade among BRICS had steadily grown, political interests in these economies have become sensitive to competition from fellow BRICS members and protectionist policies were utilized.

Plummer then argues that, with the stalling of the DDA, regionalism is the only way forward. After reviewing the "building bloc" vs. "stumbling bloc" aspects of FTAs, he concludes positively that regional trading agreements in Asia are serving as the "building bloc" of multilateral trade liberalization. First, regionalism could enhance the negotiating power of smaller economies. The process of structural adjustment unleashed by a regional trading arrangement could also make multilateral trade initiatives easier. Finally, regional integration could push member economies to be more efficient, competitive and market friendly, preparing them to effectively participate in multilateral trade agreements.

1.6 WORLD BANK AND REGIONAL DEVELOPMENT BANKS

The World Bank and various regional multilateral banks, including the Asian Development Bank (ADB) and the Inter-American Development Bank (IDB) have a long and complex relationship including both competitive and cooperative aspects. The G20 has called on the multilateral banks to increase their efforts to support the development objectives of emerging economies. At the same time, the proliferation of other aid-related organizations calls for a re-examination of the role of the multilateral banks.

Vikram Nehru in Chapter 9 focuses on the World Bank–ADB relationship. He observes that the "foreign aid architecture" has become a lot more complicated in the present globalized environment. On the supply side, there has been an explosion of bilateral and multilateral agencies, and multiple new private donors. On the aid delivery side, the explosion has become even more dramatic. There have been an increasing number of international NGOs receiving money from bilateral agencies and thousands of private sector groups involved in aid. Modalities of efficient aid delivery had to be found and implemented. Also, the issue of donor coordination had become more important so that donors did not work at cross-purposes and add to the administrative burden of the recipients. Implementation of the Paris Declaration on Aid Effectiveness had to be accelerated and expanded to cover non-traditional donors. National development agencies must also insist on rigorous evaluation methods to identify successful projects.

Nehru then adds that there is a need to promote coordination between the World Bank and ADB. In Asia, the World Bank and ADB face a very challenging situation. First, the rapid growth of the Asian countries means that many had moved from low-income status to middle-income status and consequently needed fewer financial resources from the World Bank and ADB. Consequently, there is a need to provide more knowledge resources instead. The second issue is governance reform which is more acute at the World Bank. The recent increase in shares of developing countries, particularly the PRC, had raised the share of developing countries from 42.6 per cent to 47 per cent, but this was still short of what is needed to obtain parity with the advanced countries. The third challenge confronting the World Bank and ADB in Asia was their relationship with each other in operational matters and in advising clients on development policies and strategies.

Nehru argues that the two institutions need to coordinate on all these issues in order to reduce the cost of operations and the burdens on client countries. Where the two institutions have cooperated (for example, to carve out "areas of primacy"), results have been encouraging, but there remain areas of friction between the two institutions. He recommends several modalities for enhancing coordination between the World Bank and ADB. One is that the World Bank focus on global public goods – trade, climate change, international migration, global financial stability and disaster management – and ADB focus on regional public goods and services such as regional integration, regional financial stability, and regional infrastructure development. The other modality is to merge the two institutions, with the center mobilizing resources, and operations being decentralized at the regional level. The final modality is for the two institutions to muddle along much as they have done in the past.

In Chapter 10, Fernando Prada focuses on the relationship between the World Bank and the IDB. He argues that the IDB has been successful in promoting sustainable growth in Latin America by striking a balance between its three main functions, namely the provision of: (i) financial assistance; (ii) capacity-building (institution building and knowledge generation and dissemination); and (iii) international public goods (infrastructure for regional integration).

Prada argues that the "aid architecture" in Latin America is already fairly decentralized. While the World Bank and IDB have focused their assistance on the social sector, public sector reform and capacity-building, sub-regional development banks (such as the Corporacion Andina de Fomento, Caribbean Development Bank and the Central American Bank for Economic Integration) have focused on infrastructure, capital market development and private sector operations. An important difference between Asia and Latin America, he notes, is that, unlike the latter, the former does not have sub-regional development banks. Asia can, therefore, benefit from Latin America's experience with sub-regional development banks.

REFERENCE

Kawai, M. and P.B. Rana. 2009. The Asian Financial Crisis revisited: Lessons, responses, and new challenges. In R. Carney (ed.) *Lessons from the Asian Financial Crisis*. New York: Routledge, pp. 155–97.

2. From a centralized to a decentralized global economic architecture: an overview

Pradumna B. Rana

2.1 INTRODUCTION

The Asian Financial Crisis of 1997–98 led to calls for a new international financial architecture and discussions focused on crisis prevention, crisis management and crisis resolution efforts (see Kawai and Rana, 2009). The global economic crisis (GEC) of 2008–09, which was initially expected to be the worst crisis since the Great Depression of the 1930s, likewise led to calls for a New Bretton Woods (NBW) system – a wider and much more comprehensive set of reforms of the global governance system and international economic institutions (IEIs), similar to the remarkable 1944 Bretton Woods conference where the World Bank, the International Monetary Fund (IMF) and the General Agreement on Tariffs and Trade (GATT), the predecessor of the World Trade Organization (WTO), were established.

In the post-global economic crisis (GEC) period, a number of academics and politicians have made calls for an NBW. These include Stiglitz (cited in Bases 2008) and Sarkozy and Brown (cited in Kirkup and Waterfield 2008). The central bank governor of the People's Republic of China (PRC), Zhou (2009), has also made a pitch for a new reserve asset; and the World Bank President, Zoellick (2010), has called for a return to a modified gold standard. Supporting the need to return to a modified gold standard, Mohamad (2012) has called for an NBW with poor countries well represented. So far, a number of proposals to reform the global economic architecture (GEA) – the configuration of institutions for global economic governance – have been implemented. These include the upgrading of the Group of Twenty (G20) finance ministers and central bank governors group to the G20 Summit of Leaders and designating it the "premier forum for our economic cooperation" (European Commission 2009), and the upgrading of the Financial Stability Forum

11

to the Financial Stability Board by expanding membership. But could post-GEC reforms of the GEA disappoint like those discussed under the new international financial architecture? If so, cycles of crises, talk of architecture reform, and complacency in reforms could continue without significantly enhancing the resilience of the GEA. How could the global economic architecture evolve?

The objectives of this chapter are to answer three questions:

(i)   Will we have an NBW in the post-GEC period, as called for by several academics and policymakers?
(ii)   How has the GEA evolved and how could it look in the future? Will it be more rules-based or informally network-based? Will it be more centralized or decentralized?
(iii) What is the role of Asia in this new architecture and how can it contribute?

Section 2.2 of the chapter argues that it may be too optimistic to expect an NBW or a radical set of reforms of the GEA in the future. It argues that reforms are expected to be more incremental. Section 2.3 reviews the pre-GEC architecture, essentially the one established at Bretton Woods, which was led by the G7 and G8, and highlights its shortcomings. Section 2.4 highlights the post-GEC G20-led architecture. Section 2.5 focuses on the move to a more decentralized GEA where regional institutions are linked together to a more senior global organization by rules and regulations. Such a system would be more flexible in terms of membership, governance, representation and agenda. Section 2.6 argues that Asia can contribute to the evolving GEA by establishing institutions to enhance regional economic integration and by trying to make sure that regional institutions are complementary to global ones.

2.2   NEW BRETTON WOODS IN THE FUTURE?

Helleiner (2010) has argued that the creation of a new GEA is not an outcome of a single event or meeting but a long-drawn-out process involving a legitimacy phase (thinking that the old regime needs to be replaced), interregnum phase (experimental and discussion phase), and a constitutive phase (formal negotiation phase). In this typology, as discussed later in the chapter, it is appropriate to conclude that the GEC has led to a view that the pre-GEC architecture needed to be changed and that the G20 has successfully implemented some of the changes. We are, therefore, in the interregnum phase of a new architecture where various ideas for reforms are being discussed. The question is whether we will ever go to the constitutive phase and have an NBW. The answer is, probably not, for two reasons. First, the application of the theory of clubs leads to the conclusion that IEIs are relatively inflexible institutions that are difficult to reform in response to the demands of a rapidly changing world because of the vested interests of the original members of the club (section 2.3). Second, as is usually the case, with the adverse impacts of the GEC being less serious than expected – instead of the Great Depression II we had the Great Recession – complacency has set in on the reform agenda, and the commitment and urgency to reform IEIs seen during the crisis has decreased. For example, representatives of the finance industry have successfully resisted and diluted the reform agenda.[1] Only if the euro area were to collapse and the world were to experience the Great Depression II, which it avoided in 2008 and 2009, could we expect the commitment to reform to become urgent once again. This probably is the only chance for those who call for an NBW.

2.3 PRE-GLOBAL ECONOMIC CRISIS G7 AND G8-LED GLOBAL ECONOMIC ARCHITECTURE

The pre-GEC economic architecture was very similar to the one created in Bretton Woods, under which the IMF was to promote macroeconomic and financial stability,[2] the GATT was to ensure an open trading environment globally, and the World Bank and later the regional development banks (e.g. the Asian Development Bank (ADB)) were to provide development finance for poverty reduction (Table 2.1). The G7 was created in the mid-1970s from the G5 to oversee the process of provision of international

Table 2.1 Pre-GEC G7- and G8-led architecture

	G7 and G8
Macroeconomic and financial stability	IMF
Financial stability	FSF
Open trading system	WTO
Development finance and poverty reduction	World Bank, ADB and other regional development banks

Notes: ADB = Asian Development Bank; FSF = Financial Stability Forum; IMF = International Monetary Fund; WTO = World Trade Organization.

Source: Author.

public goods by various IEIs. The Russian Federation joined the group in 1997 to form the G8. In response to the Asian Financial Crisis, the Financial Stability Forum was established in 1999 with a small number of staff to help coordinate the development of standards and codes and best practices for policy and transparency, financial sector regulation and supervision, and market integrity. Another institution established that year was the G20 finance ministers and central bankers group, comprising both G8 members and systemically important emerging markets; this body had existed in the shadow of the G8 since its creation. In 1995, the GATT was folded into the World Trade Organization (WTO) with a proper organizational and staffing arrangement.

While the pre-GEC G7 and G8-led GEA worked well for a number of decades, it had many shortcomings. First, its governance did not reflect the move from a unipolar to a multipolar world. It represented the dominance of the United States (US) and Europe, and did not reflect the economic rise and political power of emerging markets, particularly those in Asia (the PRC and India), so it lacked legitimacy. Emerging markets had no representation at the G7 and their voice in the IEIs was limited. According to long-term projections made by Goldman Sachs, emerging markets will continue to grow rapidly over the next 40 years. In 2003, the three largest economies in the world by 2050 were predicted to be the PRC, the US and India (Wilson and Purushothaman 2003). In 2007, the 2003 ranking was revised to the PRC, India and the US (Poddar and Yi 2007). More recently, it has been projected that the 2007 ranking could be obtained even earlier – within the next 30 years or so (ADB 2009). Despite their economic dynamism, however, the PRC and India will be far behind the US in terms of per capita incomes, poverty reduction and military power.

Kawai et al. (2009) have examined the evolution of the shares of developing and emerging markets in IMF quotas, and in global trade and gross domestic product (GDP, in terms of purchasing power) – two rough indicators of their importance in the world economy. They have found that the trade shares of developing and emerging economies have risen more rapidly than their share in IMF quotas. This contrast was even clearer for their share of world GDP. Quotas that also determine voting power at the IMF are especially low for rapidly growing emerging markets such as Brazil, the PRC and India. Kelkar et al. (2005) found that these three countries had 19 per cent fewer votes than Belgium, Italy and the Netherlands collectively, although they had 21 per cent more nominal GDP, 400 per cent more purchasing power GDP, and 2800 per cent greater population. On the other hand, Europe controls directly or indirectly 10 chairs out of 24 on the IMF Executive Board, even though it has a common monetary policy and about 30 per cent of quota and voting rights.

Second, IEIs are relatively inflexible institutions and cannot change even if they wish to. Kawai et al. (2009) have applied the theory of clubs to explain this phenomenon. IEIs are clubs in the sense that they produce goods that are at least partially non-rivalrous (more than one user can consume) and at least partially excludable (users can be denied access to them). Their most important services include order and predictability in international trade and finance. The application of club theory to IEIs leads to the conclusion that IEIs tend to be relatively inflexible institutions: club charters are usually designed to maintain firm control in the hands of founding members and those who share their preferences.

The charters, quotas and voting rights of IEIs were designed in the interest of like-minded original core members in 1944 and are inflexible and difficult to change as membership expands. In comparison with the 44 countries that participated in the Bretton Woods conference, membership of the IMF and World Bank now stands at 188. This inflexibility has led to frictions on various occasions. The membership of the WTO is more than 150 but an additional 30 countries have applied to join or are in accession negotiations. At a recent Asia-Pacific Economic Cooperation (APEC) Summit in Honolulu, US President Obama demanded that the PRC "play by the rules" of international trade (Nakamura 2011). The PRC reacted with speed: "First, we have to know whose rules we are talking about. . .If the rules are made collectively through agreement and China is a part of it, then China will abide by them. If rules are decided by one or even several countries, China does not have the obligation to abide by that" (Eckert 2011).

Third, with globalization, especially financial globalization, the environment in which the IEIs have operated has also changed dramatically and this has reduced their effectiveness. The number and types of global and regional public goods have increased. Policymakers were wary of uncontrolled financial flows during the Bretton Woods era and permitted capital controls. In the 1980s and 1990s, under the Washington Consensus,[3] they embraced financial liberalization and deregulation – ushering in an age of highly integrated financial markets and capital flows that have dwarfed the operations of IEIs. As early as the 1960s, the United Kingdom (UK) was promoting financial globalization through its support of deregulated Euromarkets for London. But the momentum accelerated when Thatcher took political office in the UK in 1979 and Reagan in the US in 1980. IMF management even launched an initiative in 1995 to overturn the commitment to capital controls by amending its articles of agreement to gain a liberalization mandate with respect to capital movement. This initiative was only withdrawn after the recent global economic crisis.

With financial globalization, a new type of crisis called a capital account crisis or "generation three" crisis (Dornbusch 2001) – associated with large inflows and sudden reversals of capital flows, the bursting of asset bubbles, and a banking crisis – has started to hit emerging markets. Such a crisis tends to affect an economic entity's balance sheets and solvency positions. The costs of balance sheet recessions tend to be higher, and recovery from such a crisis takes longer. They also tend to be systemic, affecting most or all sectors of the economy, with strong contagion to neighboring countries (which may be innocent bystanders). Based on their experience with the Asian Financial Crisis, Kawai and Rana (2009) argued that efforts to prevent and manage a capital account crisis required actions at the global, regional and national levels or a multilayered global financial safety net.

Fourth, IEIs face a "governance trilemma" (Kawai et al. 2009, p. 13). There is broad agreement that IEIs need to become: (i) more democratic; (ii) more effective in delivering public goods; and (iii) universal by accepting all countries that apply for membership. These requirements add up to a trilemma; achieving any one or two objectives makes achieving the other more difficult. For example, the United Nations (UN) is democratic and universal, but suffers on effectiveness. Similarly, the IMF and World Bank are universal and effective but not democratic.

2.4 POST-GLOBAL ECONOMIC CRISIS G20-LED GLOBAL ECONOMIC ARCHITECTURE

After the GEC, dominant powers moved quickly and created the G20 Summit by upgrading the G20 finance and central bank officials' forum, which started in 1999 but was kept under the shadow of the G7 and G8. The leaders labeled the forum the "premier forum for our international economic cooperation" and in September 2009 President Obama categorically announced that G20 would replace the G7.[4] The leaders also upgraded the Financial Stability Forum into the Financial Stability Board, with wider membership of all G20 members. The post-GEC G20-led GEA is depicted in Table 2.2.

Raising the profile of the G20 to a leaders' level forum was no doubt enormously significant. For the first time, systemically important emerging markets were brought into the core of global economic governance. It was an historic event that partially addressed the inclusiveness and legitimacy problems of the pre-GEC G7 and G8-led architecture. But problems remain. The G20 represents 4.2 billion people of the world but not the other 2.6 billion people. How can their views be incorporated and the legitimacy of the G20 enhanced?

The G20's approach of making the grouping more inclusive beyond the 19 member countries and groupings has been to invite representatives of

Table 2.2   Post-GEC G20-led architecture

	G20: "Premier forum for international economic cooperation"
Macroeconomic and financial stability	Strengthened IMF but legitimacy still questioned
Financial stability	FSF to FSB
Open trading system	WTO: no changes yet
Development finance and poverty reduction	Strengthened World Bank with some enhanced legitimacy

Notes: FSF = Financial Stability Forum; FSB = Financial Stability Board; IMF = International Monetary Fund; WTO = World Trade Organization.

Source: Author.

various regional groupings. Initially, this process was ad hoc at the discretion of the host country. For example, the UK invited the Association of Southeast Asian Nations (ASEAN) and the New Partnership for Africa's Development (NEPAD), Canada added the African Union, the Republic of Korea brought in the Global Governance Group (3G), and France brought in the Cooperation Council for the Arab States of the Gulf (GCC) for the November 2011 Summit. Since the Seoul Summit, however, it has been decided to invite no more than five non-member invitees, of which at least two are to be from Africa.[5]

However, enhancing the inclusiveness of the G20 is only a first step. Individual countries can collectively decide on the global policy changes needed but the relevant IEIs have to implement these changes. Thus, an effective global governance system requires additional governance reforms in the IEIs implementing the reforms. This is the second area where progress has been slow.

At the 2006 annual meeting of the IMF and World Bank in Singapore, the members had increased the quotas of the PRC, Mexico, the Republic of Korea and Turkey on an ad hoc basis by small amounts. At that time, several other reforms were also proposed (including a new quota formula and the second round of quota increases) that were to be completed over a two-year period. This resulted in the April 2008 quota and voice reform which was labeled by the IMF Board of Governors as "far-reaching reforms of the institution" (IMF 2008) aimed at rebuilding its credibility and legitimacy. Again in November 2010, as part of the 14th General Review of Quotas, the IMF Management announced what it labeled as the "most fundamental governance overhaul in the Fund's 65-year history" (IMF 2010). This comprised, among others, a proposal to shift 6 per cent of the quota to dynamic emerging markets and developing countries and to reduce European representation at the IMF Board by two chairs. But neither the 2008 reform nor the 2010 one have yet been ratified.[6] Even with their ratification, the shift in quotas to developing countries will be relatively small and misalignments will remain.[7]

2.5   FUTURE GLOBAL ECONOMIC ARCHITECTURE: LIKELY SCENARIO

In this context, how could the post-GEC GEA evolve? A likely scenario is a series of incremental moves to a more decentralized GEA where national, bilateral and regional initiatives work closely with a senior global institution. This would mean complementing monolithic IEIs with a multilayered decision-making structure along the lines of "functional federalism" advocated at the national level (Kawai et al. 2010). It also involves the application of the principle of subsidiarity, which means that decisions should be made at the lowest possible administrative level. Decentralization would make international decisions more flexible and accountable, making them more like decisions within countries, which typically involve several layers of government. The value of decentralization lies in its ability to produce public goods that are important to some, but not for all, countries. Regionally decentralized decision-making also has the advantage of inducing large emerging economies to take leadership in providing regional public goods, even before they take leadership of global bodies.

Decentralized decisions create new challenges: regional decisions need to be made globally coherent to act as building blocks of a global system. This requires paying close attention to connections within a decentralized system to make sure they complement each other and the global system.

Such a decentralized architecture is not hypothetical. It already exists in the development architecture, where the World Bank is complemented by four regional development banks (Figure 2.1).[8] The decentralization trend is evident in other types of architecture as well. In the trade architecture, the WTO coexists at the global level with the European Free Trade Association (EFTA), the proposed Free Trade of the Americas and the proposed East Asian Free Trade Area (EAFTA) and the Regional Comprehensive Economic Partnership (RCEP) which is being negotiated in East Asia (Figure 2.2). The inter-regional Trans-Pacific Partnership and the Trans-Atlantic Trade and Investment Partnership are also being negotiated. In the financial architecture, we have the Financial Stability Board at the global level and the European Systemic Risk Board, the three European bodies for banking, insurance and securities market, and the

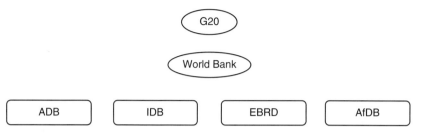

Notes: ADB = Asian Development Bank; AfDB = African Development Bank; EBRD = European Bank for Reconstruction and Development; IDB = Inter-American Development Bank.

Source: Author.

Figure 2.1   Decentralized development architecture

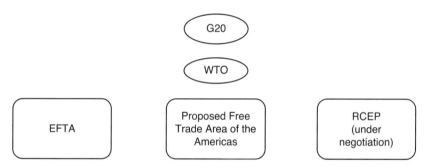

Notes: RCEP = Regional Comprehensive Economic Partnership; EFTA = European Free Trade Association; WTO = World Trade Organization.

Source: Author.

Figure 2.2   Decentralizing trade architecture

proposed Asian Financial Stability Board (AFSB) at the regional level (Figure 2.3).

The international monetary architecture has a number of layers (Figure 2.4; Rana 2012). The G20 is at the apex, with various multilateral safety nets at the IMF: the new Flexible Credit Line (FCL) and the Precautionary Credit Line (PCL). Then we have the bilateral financial safety nets (BFSNs) among central banks that were triggered when Singapore and the Republic of Korea faced liquidity problems in late 2008.

In Asia, about a dozen and a half bilateral swaps were established between central banks of the region under the Chiang Mai Initiative

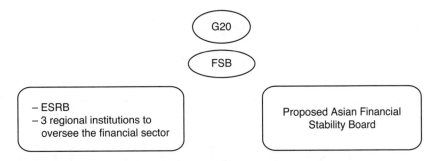

Notes: ESRB = European Systemic Risk Board; FSB = Financial Stability Board.

Source: Author.

Figure 2.3   Decentralizing financial architecture

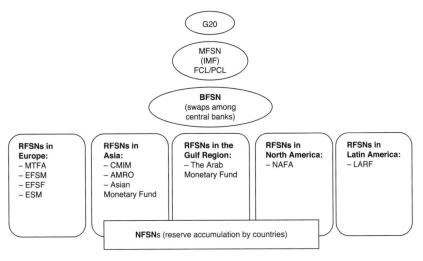

Notes: AMRO = ASEAN+3 Macroeconomic Research Office; BFSN = Bilateral Financial Safety Nets; CMIM = Chiang Mai Initiative Multilateralization; EFSF = European Financial Stability Facility; EFSM = European Financial Stabilization Mechanism; ESM = European Stability Mechanism; FCL = Flexible Credit Line (IMF); LARF = Latin American Reserve Fund; MFSN = Multilateral Financial Safety Nets; MTFA = Medium Term Financial Assistance; NAFA = North American Framework Agreement; NFSN = National Financial Safety Nets; PCL = Precautionary Credit Line (IMF); RFSN = Regional Financial Safety Nets.

Source: Author.

Figure 2.4   Decentralizing monetary architecture

in the aftermath of the Asian Financial Crisis. In March 2010, these were combined and expanded to become the Chiang Mai Initiative Multilateralization (CMIM) or the US$120 billion "self-managed reserve pooling arrangement". All ASEAN+3 members[9] (plus Hong Kong, China) contribute to this fund and are eligible to borrow from it in case they face payment problems. Under this arrangement, foreign exchange is earmarked for crisis prevention but held in separate national accounts. The CMIM retains the provision of the Chiang Mai Initiative (CMI) that only 20 per cent of the amounts can be withdrawn without an IMF program in place. In May 2012, the size of the pool was doubled to US$240 billion and the 20 per cent limit increased to 30 per cent. The IMF link and the lack of an independent surveillance unit to conduct due diligence inhibited the use of these arrangements during the recent global economic crisis. In April 2011, the ASEAN+3 Macroeconomic Research Office (AMRO), an independent surveillance unit for the CMIM, was established in Singapore. AMRO's mandate is to "monitor and analyze regional economies, which contributes to the early detection of risks, swift implementation of remedial actions, and effective decision-making of the CMIM" (ASEAN+3 Finance Ministers Joint Media Statement 2 May 2010).[10] AMRO became fully operational in October 2011, with 10 staff, and more are being recruited. AMRO is to produce quarterly reports and table them biannually for discussion by the ASEAN+3 finance and central bank deputies. In the event that the CMIM is activated, AMRO will assume the key role of providing an objective assessment of swap requesting countries and make a recommendation to the CMIM parties. If the application is approved, AMRO will then monitor the use and impact of swap funds.

At the present level of political will, an incremental and more decentralized process is what we can envisage in terms of GEA reform. However, if the incidence of financial crises were to increase and political will and cooperation among countries were to strengthen in the future, one could then perhaps see a move toward a more rules-based system. In such a context, as discussed below, it is possible that the G20 could be replaced by the Global Economic Coordination Council (GECC) and the Financial Stability Board by a World Finance Organization (WFO).

Despite the plethora of IEIs, the Stiglitz Commission (UN 2009) recommended the establishment of a globally representative forum to be called the GECC at a level equivalent to the UN General Assembly and the Security Council. The GECC could meet annually at the heads of state and government level to assess developments and provide leadership in economic, social and ecological issues. It would promote development, secure consistency and coherence in the policy goals of the major international organizations, and support consensus building among governments on efficient and effective solutions for global economic governance issues. Such a council could also promote the accountability of all IEIs, identify gaps that need to be filled to ensure the efficient operation of the global economic and financial system, and help set the agenda for global economic and financial reforms.

The case for establishing a WFO analogous to the existing WTO has also been made (Eichengreen 2009). In the same way that the WTO establishes principles for trade policy without specifying outcomes, the WFO would establish principles for prudential supervision (capital and liquidity requirements, limits on portfolio concentrations and connected lending, adequacy of risk measurement systems, and internal controls) without attempting to prescribe the structure of regulation in detail. The WFO would define obligations for its members, who would be obliged to meet international standards for supervision and regulation of their financial markets. Membership would be mandatory for all countries seeking access to foreign markets. The WFO would appoint an independent panel of experts to determine whether countries were in compliance with those obligations, failing which the authorities would be able to impose sanctions against countries that fail to comply. The WFO would not dictate regulatory conditions on countries.

2.6 THE ROLE OF ASIA

Although the pace of regional integration has picked up considerably after the Asian Financial Crisis of 1997–98, Asia is very much behind Europe in terms of building supranational institutions. What are the institutions that Asia needs to develop to support such a decentralized architecture? In the area of macroeconomic stability, as already mentioned, the region has the CMIM and AMRO, the independent surveillance unit for the CMIM. In the medium term, the two institutions should be merged to form the Asian Monetary Fund (AMF). In a perception survey of ASEAN+3 opinion makers conducted by a team from Nanyang Technological University (NTU), two-thirds of the respondents felt that the AMF should be established some time during 2016–20 and that the CMIM and AMRO should be combined to form the AMF (Rana et al. 2012). In the meantime, a more structured approach of promoting complementarity between CMIM/AMRO/IMF, similar to the "troika" model being used in Europe, should also be considered in Asia (Rana, 2014).

In the area of international trade, early steps are being taken to establish an Asia-wide free trade agreement (FTA). With the implementation of the ASEAN+1 FTAs between ASEAN and the PRC, Japan, the Republic of

Korea, India, Australia and New Zealand, the RCEP comprising 16 Asian nations is being negotiated.

In the area of financial stability, less progress has been made. But since the newly established Financial Stability Board does not include all Asian countries, as in Europe, Asia could consider establishing the proposed Asian Financial Stability Board (AFSB) by involving the region's regulators and supervisors. The AFSB would, among others, promote capital market rules and regulations (micro-prudential monitoring) and promote the stability of the financial system throughout the region through early warning systems (macro-prudential monitoring). It could also coordinate Asia's participation in the Financial Stability Board and represent the region in relevant international forums to ensure that the Asian context is adequately understood in financial policies and regulatory reforms.

In addition to establishing the institutions mentioned above, in an environment of decentralized architecture, Asian countries should strive to make national and regional decisions coherent globally in order to prevent races to the bottom and more generally to make national and regional institutions and agreements complementary or the building blocks of an efficient global system. Regional institutions should focus on regional public goods and global institutions on truly global public goods. The G20 is also in the process of developing best practices to promote complementarity between national, regional and global institutions.

2.7 CONCLUSIONS

One of the questions this chapter sought to answer was: will we have an NBW, as called for by academics and politicians, in the post-GEC period? The chapter finds that, while the establishment of the G20 Summit is encouraging since for the first time systemically important emerging markets have been given a voice in international economic issues, those hoping for an NBW, like those hoping for a new international financial architecture in the post-Asian Financial Crisis period, will probably be disappointed. We are at an interregnum phase of the NBW, but the constitutive phase could fizzle out. This is for two reasons. First, as predicted by the theory of clubs (discussed in section 2.3), policies of IEIs have been relatively inflexible. In particular, the slow progress in governance reforms of the IEIs or the so-called "chairs and shares" (voting rights, management and Board representation) reform to give greater voice to emerging markets – particularly those in Asia, the PRC and India – commensurate with their growing economic and political power has led to questions regarding their legitimacy. Second, the recovery from the Asian Financial Crisis as well as the recovery from the GEC turned out to be faster than expected. Faster-than-expected recovery has led to complacency in implementing reforms and in some cases dilution of the reform agenda.

It is, therefore, likely that in the future we will not have an NBW but an architecture that will move incrementally toward a more decentralized system where national and regional initiatives will work closely with the existing IEIs. In this context, Asia has an important role to play in this architecture by building institutions for regional integration (such as the AMF, Asia-wide FTA, and AFSB). Asia also has to make sure that regional initiatives complement global ones and that there is no duplication. Additionally, Asia needs to take various actions to enhance the legitimacy of the G20 process.

NOTES

1. For example, the implementation of Basel III has been adversely affected by the resistance of the industry.
2. Originally, the IMF's mandate was to promote macroeconomic stability. As the incidence of financial crisis increased with financial globalization, it started to focus on crisis prevention and crisis management as well.
3. The prevailing thinking at the time was that governments were the problem and markets the solution.
4. The G7 continues to meet, albeit with much less fanfare. More recently, it has been meeting to try to resolve the euro area crisis.
5. See Rana (2011 and 2012) on how the G20's inclusiveness could be enhanced from the Asian perspective.
6. As of 10 September 2012, 124 members having 73.38 per cent of the total quota had ratified the 2010 reform (IMF, 2012). Although this meets the required threshold for effectiveness (which is the consent of membership accounting for over 70 per cent of the total quota), the quota increase cannot be effective until the Board Reform Amendment – which, among others, proposes that Europeans give up two chairs at the IMF Board – also enters into force. As of 10 September 2012, 105 members having 66.14 per cent of total quota had accepted the latter amendment, well short of the required 85 per cent.
7. Even with the ratification of the April 2008 quota reform, the quota share of emerging markets and developing countries will increase by only 1.1 per cent. Another 2.8 per cent reallocation will occur when the 2010 agreement is ratified (Virmani and Patra 2011). Quota misalignments will therefore remain, but at a lower level.
8. The development architecture is quite complex, with over 200 multilateral agencies and bilateral and private foundations (Kharas 2007).
9. ASEAN plus the PRC, Japan and the Republic of Korea.
10. AMRO's purposes are to: (i) conduct macroeconomic and financial surveillance of members; (ii) provide members with policy recommendations to mitigate economic and financial crisis; and (iii) assist members if they are utilizing financial resources of CMIM (*The Economist*, 10 December 2011, Job Description).

REFERENCES

Asian Development Bank (ADB). 2009. *India 2039: An Affluent Society in One Generation*. Manila: ADB.
Bases, D. 2008. World faces new Bretton Woods moment: Stiglitz. Reuters. 6 November, available at: http://www.reuters.com/article/2008/11/06/us-financial-stiglitz-interview-sb-idUSTRE4A58BI20081106 (accessed 28 October 2012).
Dornbusch, R. 2001. A primer on emerging market crises. National Bureau of Economic Research Working Paper 8326. Cambridge, MA: National Bureau of Economic Research.
Eckert, P. 2011. Obama's Pacific aspirations strain US ties with China. *Jakarta Globe*. 14 November, available at: http://www.thejakartaglobe.com/world/obamas-pacific-aspirations-strain-us-ties-with-china/478474 (accessed 28 October 2012).
Eichengreen, B. 2009. Out of the box thoughts about the international financial architecture. International Monetary Fund Working Paper 09/116. Washington, DC: International Monetary Fund.
European Commission, 2009. Leaders' statement: The Pittsburgh summit, available at: http://ec.europa.eu/commission_2010–2014/president/pdf/statement_20090826_en_2.pdf (accessed 28 October 2012).
Helleiner, E. 2010. A Bretton Woods moment? The 2007–2008 crisis and the future of global finance. *International Affairs* **86**(3): 619–36.
International Monetary Fund (IMF). 2008. IMF Board of Governors adopts quota and voice reforms by large margin. Press release, available at: http://www.imf.org/external/np/sec/pr/2008/pr0893.htm (accessed 28 October 2012).
International Monetary Fund. 2010. Factsheet: IMF quotas. November 2010, available at: http://www.imf.org/external/np/sec/pr/2010/pr10418.htm (accessed 28 October 2012).
International Monetary Fund. 2012. Proposed amendment on the reform of the IMF Executive Board and the 14th general review of quotas: Status of acceptances and consents. 10 September 2012, available at: http://www.imf.org/external/np/pp/eng/2012/091012.pdf (accessed 28 October 2012).
Kawai, M. and P.B. Rana. 2009. The Asian financial crisis revisited: Lessons, responses and new challenges. In R. Carney (ed.) *Lessons from the Asian Financial Crisis*. New York: Routledge, pp.155–97.
Kawai, M., P. Petri and E. Sisli-Ciamarra. 2009. Asia in global governance: A case for decentralized institutions. Asian Development Bank Institute (ADBI) Working Paper 157. Tokyo: ADBI.
Kawai, M., P. Petri and E. Sisli-Ciamarra. 2010. Asia in global governance: A case for decentralized institutions. In M. Kawai, J.-W. Lee and P. Petri (eds) *Asian Regionalism in the World Economy: Engine for Dynamism and Stability*. Cheltenham, UK and Northampton, MA, USA: Edward Elgar Publishing.
Kelkar, V.L., P.K. Choudhry, M. Vanduzer-Snow and B. Bhaskar. 2005. The International Monetary Fund: Integration and democratization in the 21st century. Paper presented at the G24 Technical Group Meeting. Manila. 17–18 March.
Kharas, H. 2007. Trends and issues in development aid. Wolfensohn Center for Development Working Paper 1. Washington, DC: Brookings Global Economy and Development.

Kirkup, J. and B. Waterfield. 2008. Gordon Brown's Bretton Woods summit call risks spat with Nicolas Sarkozy. *The Telegraph*. 15 October, available at: http://www.telegraph.co.uk/news/worldnews/europe/france/3205033/Gordon-Browns-Bretton-Woods-summit-call-risks-spat-with-Nicholas-Sarkozy.html (accessed 28 October 2012).

Mohamad, M. 2012. West needs to go back to the capitalist basics. *Financial Times*. 11 January, available at: http://www.ft.com/cms/s/0/9f60aff2–3ba8–11e1-bb39–00144feabdc0.html#axzz25hY5FsV4 (accessed 28 October 2012).

Nakamura, D. 2011. Obama at APEC summit: China must 'play by the rules'. *The Washington Post*. 13 November, available at: http://www.washingtonpost.com/world/obama-at-apec-summit-china-must-play-by-the-rules/2011/11/12/gI QALRu2FN_story.html (accessed 28 October 2012).

Poddar, T. and E. Yi. 2007. India's rising growth potential. Global Economics Paper 152, available at: http://www.usindiafriendship.net/viewpoints1/Indias_Rising_Growth_Potential.pdf (accessed 28 October 2012).

Rana, P.B. 2011. A proposal to enhance the G20's 'input' legitimacy. VoxEU.org. 22 October, available at: http://www.voxeu.org/article/proposal-enhance-g20-s-input-legitimacy (accessed 28 October 2012).

Rana, P.B. 2012. The evolving multi-layered global financial safety net: Role of Asia. S. Rajaratnam School of International Studies (RSIS) Working Paper 238. Singapore: RSIS.

Rana, P.B. 2014. Conflict between US-led and China-led architecture. VoxEU. org, 5 August.

Rana, P.B., W.M. Chia and Y. Jinjarak. 2012. Monetary integration in ASEAN+3: A perception survey of opinion leaders. *Journal of Asian Economics* 23(1): 1–12.

United Nations. 2009. Report of the Commission of Experts of the President of the United Nations General Assembly on reforms of the international monetary and financial system. New York: United Nations (Stiglitz Commission Report).

Virmani, A. and M.D. Patra. 2011. IMF Reforms 2010: Do they mirror global economic realities? *Economic and Political Weekly*, **XLVI**(30), 23 July, available at: http://www.epw.in/special-articles/imf-reforms-2010-do-they-mirror-global-economic-realities.html (accessed 28 October 2012).

Wilson, D. and R. Purushothaman. 2003. Dreaming with BRICs: The path to 2050. Global Economics Paper No. 99. New York: Goldman Sachs.

Zhou, X. 2009. Reform the international monetary system. *BIS Review* 41/2009, available at: http://www.bis.org/review/r090402c.pdf (accessed 28 October 2012).

Zoellick, R. 2010. The G20 must look beyond Bretton Woods II. *Financial Times*. 7 November.

3. The Group of Twenty: input and output legitimacy, reforms and agenda

Andrew F. Cooper

3.1 INTRODUCTION

The elevation of the Group of Twenty (G20) to the leaders' level anticipated a new form of collective action at the apex of the global system. In a break from past situations of economic stress, whether the 1930s or early 1980s, key countries from both the old elite of states and a cluster of emerging powers were able to act together within a multilateral crisis committee process via the G20 and attendant institutions. In terms of form, speed and scope of agenda this process allowed an unprecedented degree of cooperation. Yet shared anxiety about a massive rupture of the system did not translate into an embedded set of shared interests or norms (Rachman 2010). Cooperation even in a concentrated forum via the G20 is not the same as consensus. Hanging together in a sustained fashion still faces enormous obstacles due not only to differences over outputs in terms of policy delivery but some serious gaps in terms of input legitimacy as well. The result is an awkward institutional arrangement, with some important innovative qualities (including an extension of insider status to an enhanced cluster of Asian countries including not only the People's Republic of China (PRC) and India but also the Republic of Korea and Indonesia) but also some serious gaps in terms of efficiency and representation.

It should be recognized at the outset that such flaws have a paradoxical flavor to them given that the push for the G20 in the first place was to enhance the legitimacy of an expanded summit at the center of power beyond the institutional status quo with lessons learnt from previous crises. The recognized champion of this reformist model was Paul Martin, successively Finance Minister and Prime Minister of Canada between 1993 and 2006. In an April 2004 speech, at the Woodrow Wilson Center in Washington DC, Prime Minister Martin articulated the genesis and the framework he had in mind:

an approach I believe to be worthwhile would be to look at the lessons learned from the G-20 Finance Ministers that was formed in the wake of the Asian Financial Crisis that began in 1997. We foresaw an informal gathering of finance ministers, representing established and emerging centres of influence, and coming from very different political, economic, cultural and religious traditions. We wanted to bridge the 'us' versus 'them' mentality that bedevils so many international meetings, and it has worked remarkably well – because peer pressure is often a very effective way to force decisions. We believe a similar approach among leaders could help crack some of the toughest issues facing the world. (Martin 2004)

Ideally, therefore, the G20 contained elements of advances towards a cosmopolitan order, in which countries from most of the major regions and cultures would obtain representation. Not only could the G20 offer instrumental delivery, it could do so explicitly as a forum of "un-like" actors, fully reflective of a diversity of voices. Instrumentally, although continuing to come up against serious barriers pertaining to competitive national interest, the G20 could be situated in the wider conceptual literature as a forum in which participants possessed the potential to make a genuine effort to find solutions that could be accepted by others on the basis of openness to learning and deliberation (Woods 2010; Koenig-Archibugi 2010). The logic of bringing in emerging economic powers to the "high table" of international affairs seemed unassailable. In the words of Timothy Garton Ash in January, 2008, prior to the financial crisis:

The dangers of climate change, nuclear proliferation, disease and poverty – not to mention the fragile state of globalized capitalism – demand a more credible and representative cast at the annual intergovernmental summit. As Asia rises, it is ever more absurd that the world's unofficial top table has a seat for Italy but not for China. (Garton Ash 2008)

As the G20 moved from concept to practice, galvanized by the financial shocks of late 2008, many of these claims became embedded in the project. As David Held has signified, the G20 featured "an unprecedented successful attempt by developing countries to extend their participation in key institutions of global governance" (Held 2010, p. 204).

This cosmopolitan image was strengthened by the presence of key regional drivers within the G20. All members of NAFTA were included, each of the European Union (EU) 4 (the United Kingdom, France, Germany and Italy), plus Japan and the BRICs (Brazil, Russian Federation, India, and the PRC). Additional space was made available for Turkey, Saudi Arabia, South Africa, Australia, as well as Indonesia and the Republic of Korea, making the forum global in its reach.

Such a diverse membership also opened the way for connections of different forums with a wide number of regional organizations – the Association of Southeast Asian Nations (ASEAN) as well as the African Union (AU) and MERCOSUR, the Gulf Cooperation Council (GCC) and the Economic Cooperation Organization (ECO). To give just one example of how this connection was made at the level of declaratory language, Saudi Arabia defended its position in the G20 not by referencing its leadership position in the Middle East but because of its role in the GCC (Zawya 2009).

Yet, over time, it is clearly the contested nature of the G20 that has come to the fore. One type of criticism is that the G20 is an explicitly top-down, executive mode of institutional reform. Not only is the initiative state-centric in origin, it is leader-centric with a sharp differentiation between the role of heads of government and ministers and/or bureaucrats. From another angle the G20 appears to constitute an extended form of insider–outsider discrimination via a self-selected club. Such criticisms, although justified to some considerable extent, also require some nuancing in order to privilege both the sources of reform and status quo orientation in the G20.

3.2 RE-FRAMING THE G20 AS BOTH A SOURCE OF REFORM AND STATUS QUO ORIENTATION

The first component of reform orientation that must be showcased is the degree of institutional engagement with challengers – or potential rivals – located in the G20. Traditionally, concerts have been formed with "like-minded" countries as in 1919 or (in terms of an anti-revolutionary ethos) in 1814–15. In cases of concerts formed with "unlike-minded" countries, most notably at the end of World War II, their existence has been limited in terms of time period and agenda. The more common approach of the relationship between ascending and dominant powers has been conflict oriented, not cooperative practices, featuring a mix of balance of power and unilateral strategies. Prussia under Bismarck/Kaiser Wilhelm performed as a classic realist power, with the goal of enhancing national interest and national capabilities through the acquisition of territory (Kennedy 1987). The Soviet Union's behavior was quite similar, with an emphasis on bipolarity and proxies on a regional basis. Concert power as played out in the United Nations (UN) was secondary to the great game, and usually centered on the use or non-use of veto power in the UN Security Council.

Moreover, the United States (US) operated in much the same manner with a low priority on cooperation in the international system before World War II. As a result of congressional objections, the US walked away from the League of Nations post-World War I. During the inter-war period, the US adopted a spoiler role in times of crisis – as witnessed by its willingness to torpedo the 1933 World Economic Conference in London (Foss and Austin 1933).

But the US's ambivalence towards multilateral cooperation resurfaced during its moment of US uni-polarity in the post-Cold War period, as featured by the American reliance on informal "coalitions of the willing" as opposed to formal institutions such as the UN or the North Atlantic Treaty Organization (NATO). Situated in this version of a hub and spoke matrix the US as the central pivot is accorded full power of agency with an enormous amount of autonomy provided for its commitments and capabilities (Cooper 2008).

The collective challenge of the "Third World" in the 1970s and early 1980s provided a different lens to the cooperative/conflict dynamic. As opposed to individual rising states the G77/Non-Aligned Movement (NAM)/UN Conference on Trade and Development (UNCTAD) challenge of the "Third World" put a heavy emphasis on solidarity by countries from the global South. This challenge was cast in an oppositional, or even counter-hegemonic, framework with the aim of transforming the system (Cox 1979; Ruggie 1983).

This approach had a potentially constructive element, the trade union oriented approach for a more equitable deal on commodity sales, for example. But it also contributed to an ossification of diplomacy, with a sharp division between North and the global South. There was little or no space for mixed coalitions.

The established powers were challenged explicitly due to their privileged role in systemic terms, as expressed in their veto status inside the UN, the directorate role assumed by the G7/8, the longstanding debate over votes and shares in the International Financial Institutions, the globally-directed initiatives (such as those dealing with Offshore Financial Centers or OFCs) from the Organisation for Economic Co-operation and Development (OECD), and the existence of exclusive small groups such as the "green room" process through the World Trade Organization (WTO).

The intensity of the challenge was magnified by a psychological sense of being outsiders in the multilateral system, kept away from these privileges. The only redress was therefore through solidarity, maximizing the use of weight of numbers. Attempts to negotiate around these differences (and images of bias in the system) met with repeated failure. The classic case of this dilemma was the 1981 Cancun conference, a creative attempt to break out of the North/South standoff inspired by the Brandt Commission report under the leadership of Mexico, Canada and Austria.

However, notwithstanding the record of conflict, a strong case can be made that cooperation has been on an upward trajectory since the economic ruptures in 2008. Key multilateral forums are opening up in a more equitable fashion. As highlighted by the pivotal institutional response – the G20 – to the financial crisis there is some considerable recognition at the heart of the system that the G7/8 or any other small exclusive club is not a legitimate or effective means of problem solving.

The dynamics – and the context – around the G20 are very different. Even with the flaws of "output" and "input" legitimacy that will be discussed in this chapter the fundamental claim that cooperation is overtaking competition as the dominant mode of behavior in the aftermath of the 2008 financial crisis must be taken seriously. Although some commentators do make analogies to historical patterns of behavior, presenting the image of a rising PRC as the twenty-first century equivalent of Prussia (Goldstein 2003), the structural rationale for viewing cooperation rather than competition as the dominant trend at the apex of the international system is substantial. The PRC and the US have certainly built up a deep and intricate form of interdependence, dubbed Chimerica by Niall Ferguson (Ferguson 2007). Although not without controversy and stress, the PRC has massive holdings of US treasuries. US multinationals have invested heavily in the PRC, and companies such as Walmart and Costco (and American consumers) continue to rely heavily on made-in-PRC goods. Statistics collected by the US–PRC Business Council (2011) highlight the measure of interdependence, with PRC exports to the US amounting to a US$1 billion a day in 2010 (just under 25 per cent of PRC exports) (see Table 3.1).

Diplomatically, both the symbolic and instrumental advantages for emerging/ascending powers participating in new forums with the old

Table 3.1   The PRC's trade with the United States, 2001–10 (US$ billion)

	01	02	03	04	05	06	07	08	09	10
US exports	19.2	22.1	28.4	34.7	41.8	55.2	65.2	71.5	69.6	91.9
% change*	18.3	14.7	28.9	22.2	20.5	32.0	18.1	9.5	−2.6	32.1
US imports	102.3	125.2	152.4	196.7	243.5	287.8	321.5	337.8	296.4	364.9
% change*	2.2	22.4	21.7	29.1	23.8	18.2	11.7	5.1	−12.3	23.1
Total*	121.5	147.2	180.8	231.4	285.3	343.0	386.7	409.2	366.0	456.8
% change*	4.5	21.2	22.8	28.0	23.3	20.2	12.8	5.8	−10.6	24.8
US balance	−83.0	−103.1	−124.0	−162.0	−201.6	−232.5	−256.3	−266.3	−226.8	−273.1

Notes: * Calculated by the United States–China Business Council (USCBC).

Source: US Department of Commerce; US International Trade Commission (ITC).

establishment were confirmed by the experience of the G20 finance in the late 1990s in the aftermath of the Asian/International Monetary Fund (IMF) crisis. The extent of this institutional advance on non-G20 countries generally and key Asian economies – being at the table on an equal basis – should not be minimized. The establishment of the G20 set a precedent by opening up membership on a procedural basis to pivotal countries in the global South. Not only did a large group of countries from all quadrants of the globe enter the G20, these countries gained some significant forms of ownership of the forum. The distribution of the hosting function showed that the G8 was willing to share elements of power. The scope and magnitude of the GFC also illustrated that a nuclear, G7-centric governance response was not sufficient: liquidity was needed from high-savings countries. The functional option was to enact a G20 leaders' economic summit.

To highlight the similarities between the two crises that created the G20 finance and the G20 at the leaders' level is not to exaggerate the parallels to an unwarranted degree. The shocks triggering the G20 finance became largely identified with a specific region as witnessed by the common usage of the label, the "Asian" crisis. And even this label is misleading as the crisis hit hardest a particular cluster of countries, namely Thailand, Republic of Korea, Indonesia and Malaysia (Wade 1998). The strong reaction at the global institutional level was generated not by the Asia (or more precisely an East Asian or ASEAN plus) crisis per se, but by the fear that the symptoms would spread via a contagion effect.

By contrast the 2008 crisis was an authentic global phenomenon. Although a school of thought had developed that the big rising states and/ or emerging markets were decoupled from the reverse contagion (with the economic shocks spreading from the established industrial countries to the global South) (Oakley 2009), the dominant scenario was considered a return to the global or great depression of the 1930s. It was this scenario that concentrated the minds of policymakers in the PRC, India and Brazil as well as the Group of Eight (G8) countries, in other words those outside the G8 but in the G20 finance.

Because of these differences in scope the academic responses from a critical perspective to the two episodes of institution building have been very different. Given the magnitude of the crisis, there was little in the way of immediate negative reaction about the intensity of the response. The main source of disagreement was about the cause of the crisis (Cooper and Subacchi 2010), and the implications in terms of concert power (Åslund 2009).

Alternatively the reform process animated through the G20 finance was interpreted by its critics as a consolidation – not a loosening – of power by the G8 and by the ideology of neo-liberalism more generally. Notwithstanding the signs that the G20 was operated through a culture of formal equality, and that the non-G8 members developed an enhanced comfort zone within this ambit, this forum was commonly portrayed as a process not signifying a new mode of global governance but a more concerted form of discipline emanating from the traditional core of the international system (Beeson and Bell 2009; Bailin 2005).

Yet, notwithstanding this critical perspective, the creation of the G20 finance had attractions, especially for a country such as the PRC, without having many defects. It allowed "an informal mechanism for dialogue among systematically important countries" but did so "within the framework of the Bretton Woods institutional system", a theme that has continued to be emphasized. The PRC thus received greater status and access without moving away from the rest of the rising states/emerging countries on its own. As one prominent PRC economist commented: "Broader representation is crucial. The G20 is designated to fulfill this need for representation from emerging countries" (Yu 2005, p. 6).

Without a catalyst, however, the reform project designed to bring about an expanded forum at the apex of power could not overcome the formidable obstacles of political/diplomatic interests. The status quo remained more attractive to most of the G7/8 members than a leap into the unknown. The US, under George W. Bush, was reluctant to share power unless there was a fundamental rationale for doing so. Reinforcing these instincts, there were concerns that such a revamped summit could be used to "gang up" on the US. Smaller members of the G8 worried about a possible loss of status.

3.3 MOVING BEYOND THE BRICS

Another source of reform orientation – often overlooked in the focus on the BRICS – is the space for additional countries, including those from Asia. Through the dominant lens, associated with the image of concert power, global affairs are moving towards an accentuated form of multipolarity, in which power coalesces around a small number of dominant poles (the established G7/8 and BRICS). Such a perception is consistent with past eras in which a group of big, dominant countries would come together at the time of decisive ruptures, as witnessed in 1814/15, 1919 and 1945.

Notwithstanding these signs of commonality with past eras, though, there are other scenarios that point to a very distinctive alternatively framed environment. At odds with the impression of a new concert of powers is the relatively large number of countries involved in the G20, as featured both in the late 1990s with the establishment of the G20 finance and in the elevated G20 at the leaders' level. In 1814/15 the concert was made up of five core countries – Britain, Prussia, Russia and Austria plus France. Although other countries participated, unlike at the G20, there was no illusion of equality. The same basic formula was utilized at the 1919 Paris Treaty negotiations, where there was a "Big Four", or arguably a "Big Three" with the United Kingdom (UK), the US and France. Moreover, in similar fashion, there was a Big Three at Yalta and Potsdam, although of course five countries received permanent veto-bearing seats at the UN. By way of contrast, the members of the G20 are quite numerous and diverse. There is neither the image of allies or victors in war, nor is there the sense of ideological uniformity or anti-revolutionary ethos. In the G20, as the hub of the new order, there are countries from every quadrant of the globe plus some implicit (although not initially formalized) regional representation.

Under such conditions there is space for different – although perhaps not mutually exclusive – components to form within the G20 at the leaders' level. As rehearsed, most of the attention here focuses on the interaction between the established G7/G8 and the rising BRICS group (Cooper 2010). What provides the BRICS with its distinct character is the impressive economic performance by the entire cluster of countries that can be considered emerging or rising states. All of the original BRIC countries – Brazil, Russian Federation, India and the PRC – have their annual gross domestic product (GDP) at over US$1 trillion each.

Yet beyond the core trilateral G8 countries and the BRICS is another key, albeit largely unanticipated, component within the G20. The gap between the largest of the BRIC states and middle powers comes out clearly in terms of nominal GDP. As compiled by the IMF (2011) the comparative data for 2011 put the PRC's economy at US$6988.470 billion, the highest amongst the BRIC states, followed by Brazil at US$2517.927 billion, and India at US$1843.382 billion. By way of comparison, the GDP of middle powers, while impressive, lag behind. The Republic of Korea's GDP is calculated at US$1163.847 billion and Indonesia at US$834.335 billion (IMF 2011).

If in a different economic category, however, some of these middle powers have a combination of resources, diplomatic opportunities and skills that mark them out as a privileged cluster. This opportunity has been reinforced by a number of factors. The first major opening was the choice to take the G20 model "off the shelf" from the G20 finance as opposed to alternative designs around a smaller group such as a G12/G13/G14 favored by many EU states, including President Nicolas Sarkozy of

France. At a meeting held in Washington on 18 October 2008, President Sarkozy (accompanied by President of the European Commission José Manuel Barroso and the French Finance Minister Christine Lagarde) tried to move President Bush towards an enlarged G8 with pivotal emerging states, albeit significantly not a fully-fledged G20. President Bush might have been a "lame duck", but on this issue he did not act as one. Fearful that the Sarkozy approach would gain traction, he made it clear that he wanted the summit to be bigger and more inclusive than the G7/ G8-plus model. Significantly, the Treasury Secretary Hank Paulson writes in his memoirs that he had proposed a G20 meeting before Sarkozy's visit in an effort to deflect the French approach which the "White House suspected [was an effort] to pull off a publicity coup on our home turf" (Paulson 2010, p. 373).

The second opening for reform came as a result of the attitude of the BRICS to the G20. By way of contrast there was an enormous buy-in from the emerging powers for the G20, at least in the initial stages. When the call came for the G20, all of the ascending states not only took part but energetically participated in the preparation. As the Brazilian Finance Minister (Mantega 2008) indicated, the call from these countries was for a new form of institutional improvisation:

> there is no agile structure prepared to deal with emergency economic problems. That is what we have seen at this time. . .We have to turn this G20 into a forum or a tool of some kind that can provide answers to immediate problems and coordinate its actions better amongst many countries. We are facing the most serious financial crisis perhaps since the crisis of 1929, and as this crisis is getting more serious it demands quick answers, immediate answers. It must be monitored day by day, hour by hour, so that the necessary measures can be taken to handle the problems that arise. So, there must be very agile instruments available for that to happen.

Further, all the emerging powers bought into the coordinated approach, as can be seen most emphatically in the manner by which the PRC and other countries embraced the stimulus program both individually and collectively. To be sure, this buy-in was facilitated by the way that the G20 finance evolved as a problem-solving forum. However, this image was reinforced in turn by the opening up of other institutions to the ascending states, the prime example being the reform of the Financial Stability Forum into the Financial Stability Board. In so doing, a number of the traditional anomalies disappeared, most notably the presence of Hong Kong, China and not the PRC in this institution.

Up to the June 2010 Toronto G20 summit there were ample signs of success in terms of the building of "input" legitimacy. Momentum built up through the initial Washington summit in November 2008, London in April 2009, and especially Pittsburgh in September 2009. The dominant message through this process was that governments needed to "finish the job" by implementing the stimulus measures they promised before putting on the brakes, which if done too abruptly or sharply, could push many economies back into recession.

Diplomatically, this concentrated approach also had the advantage of not going too far in disturbing the consensus established through the G20 process. At the time of Pittsburgh in late September 2009, there did appear to be the prospect that the agenda could open up in a more ambitious manner. Most notably, the issue of global "imbalances" was placed on the agenda along with a renewal of the drive for IFI reform (Nelson 2010, p.10)

Since Pittsburgh, any such prospects for an enlarged consensus have eroded considerably. The relationship between the PRC and the US has been severely tested amidst charges of heightened protectionism and currency manipulation. More generally, the G20's willingness and/or ability to expand its mandate have been curtailed by the immobilization of issues such as finance for climate change.

More specifically, the opening for middle powers came about through gaps in alternative forms of leadership via the BRICS. Certainly, the extent to which the BRICS want to embrace this institutional main game, as opposed to national self-insurance and/or alternative global/regional institutional options in which they have more autonomy, is still unclear (Barma et al. 2007). Put another way, it is unclear whether the preference of the big rising states from the global South is to work through core inter-governmental forums or to utilize other parallel forms of international coordination. One argument points towards the emergence of "an ambiguous new order . . . in which multilateral institutions . . . have only a limited role to play alongside emerging national and regional strategies" (Woods 2010).

Signs of this parallelism were further accentuated by the move to formalize the BRICs/BRICS as a grouping with a concern with equity and justice for the less powerful and those intended to curtail the restrictive unilateral or plurilateral/coalitional activity by the most powerful. The Yekaterinburg Joint Communiqué declared that:

> We are committed to advance the reform of international financial institutions, so as to reflect changes in the world economy. The emerging and developing economies must have greater voice and representation in international financial institutions, and their heads and senior leadership should be appointed through an open, transparent, and merit-based selection process. We also believe that there is a strong need for a stable, predictable and more diversified international monetary system. (Yekaterinburg Joint Communiqué 2009)

By way of contrast, select middle powers have grabbed the opportunity to take a leadership role within the G20. In overall terms, it must be appreciated that a middle power hosted the G20 in 2010 (Republic of Korea), 2012 (Mexico), and 2014 (Australia), and will host it in 2015 (Turkey), and 2016 (possibly Indonesia). In specific terms, much of the credit for maintaining the output legitimacy amid policy differences must go to the Republic of Korea and Australia. The Republic of Korea and Australia both worked hard after the London summit to institutionalize the G20. A joint op-ed column that the leaders of the Republic of Korea and Australia, Lee Myung-bak and Kevin Rudd, contributed to the *Financial Times* urging the G20 leaders to agree on a framework for macroeconomic policy coordination in Pittsburgh was one of the highlights of their joint action (Lee and Rudd 2009). Both countries felt that their efforts paid off when G20 leaders in Pittsburgh decided to designate the G20 as the premier forum for international economic cooperation and to make it an annual meeting.

The Republic of Korea, as the 2010 chair country, took the forum through two G20 summits in 2010, Toronto in June and Seoul in November. As *The Economist* points out, the Republic of Korea's energetic leadership helped turn the G20 into "a talking-shop worth having" (*The Economist* 2010). The Republic of Korea has been active at the G20 from the very beginning. President Lee Myung-bak decided early on to contribute to global discussions on ways to fight the global financial crisis as the Republic of Korea was one of the hardest hit victims in the 1990s Asian Financial Crisis. He called for a standstill on trade protectionism at the first G20 summit in Washington in November 2008. The Republic of Korea's contributions have been particularly noteworthy in the areas of common interests both for the emerging and developed countries, as it defines its role as a bridging power between the two camps. Korean initiatives at the Seoul summit included global financial safety nets and development assistance for poor countries.

The idea of the financial safety net attracted strong interest from emerging market economies that are vulnerable to sudden changes in international capital flows. Before the 2008 crisis, emerging markets in need did not want to turn to the IMF for help because an IMF bailout brought a stigma effect, destroying the credibility of borrowers. What they needed in the IMF was a pre-crisis prevention insurer, not just a post-crisis bailout fund. During the Seoul summit, the G20 decided to strengthen the IMF's crisis prevention role by expanding the IMF's Flexible Credit Line and introducing a new Precautionary Credit Line. G20 leaders hoped that these new sources of funding would reduce the need for emerging countries to accumulate foreign reserves as self-insurance against volatile global capital flows. The Republic of Korea also sought ways for the IMF lending facilities to link up with various regional arrangements such as the Chiang Mai Initiative (CMI) in Asia.

The Republic of Korea's presidency of the G20 also presented an opportunity to bring development issues to the table. With its vivid memories both of development successes and failures, the Republic of Korea pushed for a development agenda and multi-year action plan, including a pledge for duty-free, quota-free market access for low-income countries. The initiatives could make the G20 summit a much more inclusive and relevant event for the entire world as it can bring more than 173 non-member countries into the G20's sphere of influence.

The Seoul summit also aimed to achieve macroeconomic coordination with detailed policy recommendations for each individual member country to develop the Framework for Strong, Sustainable and Balanced Growth. The uneven and slowing global economic recovery sparked a currency war, with the US, the PRC and Japan beefing up the battle to grow through exports. The PRC's currency policy in particular was the target of major concern among its trading partners. Believing that the PRC government keeps its currency undervalued, the US and others called for the appreciation of the PRC currency at the Seoul summit. Identification and correction of macroeconomic imbalances were another thorny issue. The US wanted to set numerical targets on current account surpluses and deficits but major surplus countries such as Germany and the PRC strongly opposed proposals to quantify limits on them. In the end, no breakthrough on currency and imbalance issues was reached at the Seoul summit. But the Republic of Korea managed to broker significant agreements. On currency levels, the leaders agreed to move toward market-determined exchange systems, and on macroeconomic imbalances they set the deadline of June 2011 for coming up with "indicative guidelines" of what constitutes an over-the-top deficit or surplus. There are media reports that President Lee threatened not to end the meeting until the PRC and other opponents agreed to the deadline (Mo and Seo 2010).

Another key agenda was to overhaul the IMF, especially the shift of 6 per cent in quota to under-represented members from the over-represented countries. The Republic of Korea as the chair worked hard to hammer out agreements on most of the controversial issues by the November 2010 summit. Most agree that the apparent breakthrough in the reform of IMF governance, even subsequent stalling, counts as a major achievement of the G20.

In addition to agenda-setting and coordination, the Korean government in Seoul demonstrated its commitment to input legitimacy by way of effective consensus-building and global communication in the run-up to the

G20 Seoul summit. It hosted the World Bank and IMF conferences along-side the meetings of finance ministers and central bank governors in the Republic of Korea and invited most top government officials from Africa to hear their opinions about the G20 agenda and build up a consensus on the development issue. The Seoul Development Consensus was advanced as a means that integrated countries from the global South into the global economy, while retaining an emphasis on political autonomy. The Republic of Korea also organized a gathering of more than 100 chief executive officers from Fortune 250 companies during the Seoul Summit in a bid to reflect private-sector views when political leaders discuss global issues and concerns. Indeed the "business summit" has become a regular event as wit-nessed through the 2011 Cannes summit and subsequent meetings.

3.4 ONGOING PROBLEMS OF "OUTPUT" AND "INPUT" LEGITIMACY

Notwithstanding the infusion of the G20 with middle power diplomatic creativity and commitment, the constraints on the G20 have become enormous. In contrast to the successes of the initial summits, the Toronto summit in June 2010 and the Seoul summit in November 2010 present more mixed if not completely pessimistic experiences. As the urgency of the economic crisis diminished, the sense of common purpose that united the G20 leaders seemed less present. As noted above, at the time of the Seoul summit in particular, the G20 became caught up in a number of bitter disputes such as those over the "currency war", both in terms of US charges of PRC manipulation of the yuan and US quantitative easing, and global imbalances and the debate over current account targets. With the erosion of urgency, due to perceptions that the global crisis was easing, these policy differences became embedded in the G20 process. The media increasingly adopted a much more skeptical view than their earlier glowing reviews of the G20's role as a crisis committee. The new mood was summed up by the *Financial Times*, which concluded that the Seoul G20 demonstrated "how not to run the world" (*Financial Times* 2010).

At Cannes, in November 2011, the impact of the euro-crisis situation was palpable. Instead of being able to move forward to the function of steering group, the G20 crisis reverted to the role of crisis committee. The dominant theme was a concern with firewalls and buffers against conta-gion and the need for a sustainable path of economic development for Europe.

Such a restricted outcome was exacerbated by the tensions in French leadership. In style the real deficiency was due to over-promising by

President Sarkozy. Instead of concentrating on a manageable agenda, President Sarkozy declared that progress could be garnered on a wide number of fronts: an ambition that combined state-centrism with elements of innovative networking with non-state actors. The most notable illustration of the trajectory towards the network approach was the elevation of Bill Gates to a privileged position within the G20 as a powerful champion for a financial transaction tax. Although provided with insider status, nevertheless, Mr Gates was marginalized at Cannes amid the preoccupations with the euro area crisis.

In terms of agenda, this loss of momentum does not translate into a collapse of the entire G20 project. And these constraints should not be exaggerated to the point where the G20 is viewed as having lost its capacity to act as a hub of global governance. As a crisis committee the G20 is still moving forward on a number of points. One is to put emphasis on IMF surveillance inside Europe itself, with the push to have Italy accept "voluntary" oversight over its austerity measures. Such a move is designed to create an effective instrument that would allow these austerity measures to be implemented to a clear timetable without any slippage. The fact that the final declaration says that this surveillance will be carried out with public verification with respect to policy implementation on a quarterly basis shows the extent of the anxiety.

As a nascent steering committee, there is also progress toward an agenda beyond the immediate ambit of the financial crisis. One illustration emerged at the 2013 Russian G20 with the engagement of foreign ministers on the Syrian issue.

Yet the formidable constraints on the G20 should not be ignored. Due to the embedded constraints of collective action, as Stephen Krasner predicted, the Seoul G20 "stumbled" over a wide number of the impediments that it faced (Asian Institute for Policy Studies 2010). In the face of such impediments there is a need to look at the G20 not only as the hub of a new mode of cooperation but alternatively as both an accommodative/functionally cooperative and a political/conflict-oriented institutional design.

In terms of "input" legitimacy two flaws in the original G20 design stand out. The first flaw was the absence of the UN in the design. Although Secretary-General Ban Ki-moon did attend the Washington G20, some considerable distance appeared between the UN and the G20 approach on the eve of the initial summit. In a news conference on 11 November (the G20 being on 14–15 November), Ban focused his attention on the need for "inclusive multilateralism", with a focus on protecting the well-being of the developing countries, as well as major UN development goals, including climate change, food crisis issues and financing for development. Ideationally, the main source of contest came from the move by the GA President to convene a panel of experts, chaired by Joseph Stiglitz, in contradistinction to the G20. Organizationally, the main alternative focal point became the UN Conference on the Global Economic Crisis at the end of June 2009.

Having grabbed the spotlight as the dominant site of criticism during the formative stages of the G20 at the leaders' level, however, the UN-oriented backlash against the G20 has eased. As the G20 has expanded its agenda the UN has endorsed the credo that the two institutions are different and complementary, not competing and contradictory (Kim 2010b). UN Secretary-General Ban Ki-moon has accepted de facto a subordinate role, in which he attends the G20 summit as the world's top civil servant but plays a secondary role to the leaders seated at the world's top table.

The other criticism is from a non-member perspective. While acknowledging the innovative design for global governance through the establishment of the G20 for new multilateralism, the self-selective nature of the G20 (and the bias toward bigness) exposes the Achilles heel of the G20 in terms of its representational gaps. The G20 in principle and in practice has been animated by an instrumental – with attendant "output" legitimacy – purpose. In the rush to find solutions, nonetheless, there is a need to catch up in terms of "input" legitimacy about the balance between member and non-member countries and the regions they come from. If cognizant of the forum's strengths, sophisticated observer-participants of the Korean summit recognized "membership composition" as the G20's glaring weakness (Lee 2010, p. 43).

The regional/smaller state criticism of the G20 can be put into three broad categories. The first is the group of countries that reject the G20 in an outright fashion, most notably the ALBA (Bolivarian Alliance for the Americas) countries. Due to India's presence in the G20, Pakistan is the one Asian country that falls squarely into this category. It is interesting from this perspective, therefore, that at least one task force (chaired by Richard Armitage and Samuel Berger, top aides to Presidents George W. Bush and Bill Clinton) proposed that Pakistan be given at least observer status in the G20 (Iqbal, 2010). Still, such overtures have not blunted Pakistan's opposition, cast not in a regional-representation but defense of universal multilateralism mode. This view was made explicit in the run-up to the Toronto G20 summit, when Pakistan's UN ambassador, Abdullah Hussain Haroon, warned against any formal relationship of the UN with the G20:

> Frankly, what we do not want to see, is for the UN Secretary-General or the UN and by implication, its membership to own or be associated with any decisions in whose finalization it has no voice or participation. . . Any global

economic architecture must, in our view, ensure inclusiveness, transparency and full representation of all developing countries and promote full complementarities and coherence. (*The Nation* 2010)

A second category is the cluster of countries that are potential additional members of the G20 if the design expanded in one way or another. Some of these countries have been quite vocal in their demands. In Europe, the early position of Norway stands out in this category. Norwegian Foreign Minister Jonas Gahr Støre offered a robust critique of the G20, labeling it as "a grouping without international legitimacy" or without a "mandate" concerning "its functions" (*Der Spiegel* 2010). Yet the focus of his instrumental proposals was directed at broadening the G20, not replacing it. His prime objective was that the members of the Nordic Council – Norway, Sweden, Denmark, Finland and Iceland – should share a rotating seat together with the Baltic States. Extending this line of thought, the suggestion was also made that similar arrangements could be made for other under-represented groups, such as African and Arab countries (Government of Norway 2009).

In the African context, Nigeria used regional gatherings to exert its own candidacy for entry into the "high table" of the G20. Having been left out at the summit, Nigeria reasserted its claims for membership at a meeting of African finance ministers (on the sidelines of the IMF annual meeting), with its own Finance Minister, Mansur Muhtar, arguing that: "We have been clamouring for a greater role . . . For us the key concern is to see that the principle [of enhanced representation] gets accepted" (Reuters 2009).

Here the lack of a visible campaign by Asian countries, notably Malaysia and Thailand, is salient. Both of these countries had been members of the G22 that also emerged from the Asian/IMF crisis in 1998, and had been considered for membership for the G20 finance. But in neither case did these countries make a high-profile public claim to a seat at the top table on a national basis.

The third group of "outsider" countries expressed concern that decisions were being taken within the G20 without their representation or consent, but rather than outright rejection, the preference has been a pursuit for inclusion. The G20 is viewed as having some positive features but remains in need of refinement in order to maximize its benefits to a greater range of countries.

This orientation is showcased above all in the Asian context through ASEAN. This was a robust claim at the outset with ASEAN advocating for a formal seat at the table of the G20, as opposed to simply representation by its chair. This way forward was advocated at Davos in January 2010 by the Vietnamese Prime Minister, Nguyen Tan Dung

(ASEAN Secretariat 2010), as he pushed the notion that there should be an "increase [in] the representation of G20", stating "I think that it is important to institutionalise the participation of regional organisations like ASEAN". Over time, however, ASEAN demonstrated considerable flexibility. The leaders' statement from the 2010 ASEAN summit declared: "ASEAN strongly believes that it can contribute to the deliberations of the G20 through the continued participation of the ASEAN Chair and the ASEAN Secretary-General" (Rana 2010; 2011).

3.5 REGIONALISM AS A CATALYST FOR FURTHER REFORMS

It is the dynamic surrounding the G20 as an elevated form of new multilateralism that continues to be subject to scrutiny. Although the coordination problems have become more difficult as its agenda has evolved, the quality of the G20 entrepreneurship and technical readiness continues to stand out. Taking account of the fundamental power change taking place in the global economy (Alexandroff and Cooper 2010; Chin 2010), the G20 serves as the hallmark signal that the multilateral system can not only adapt but serve as a catalytic agent for other forms of institutional reform, notably in the transition from the Financial Stability Forum to the Financial Stability Board and the redistribution of voting rights and seats in the IMF.

However, notwithstanding its framing as an innovative diplomatic project, it is still a stretch to argue that the G20 broadened out composition and expansive agenda can be equated with the democratization of global governance (Asian Institute for Policy Studies 2010). With the G20's institutional embeddedness has come an intensity of sentiment that the organizational format necessary for a pivotal crisis committee is not the construct appropriate for its elevation to a global steering committee.

Some of the ingredients essential for this modification center on efficiency goals, with the aim of making the G20 work more smoothly. With respect to the G20 preparation process, the main focus has been on the pros and cons with respect to the establishment of a secretariat in order to "provide institutional memory, continuity for monitoring and follow-up of commitments, as well as to support outreach and consultation" (Carin 2010). Champions of the "leaders are different" school resist any big move to over-bureaucratize the forum. Yet both the Republic of Korea and France have expressed support for institutionalizing the G20 forum through the creation of a Secretariat.

The positive image of the G20, nonetheless, lies not only in getting things done but in legitimacy. If the loss of the lifeboat ethos makes it more difficult to maintain institutional coherence on an issue-specific basis it makes it more contingent to address the G20's governance deficiencies. Looking inwards, the priority is on introducing order to the G20 hosting functions. As a crisis committee, the G20 as a leaders' summit broke with the sequencing established by the G20 finance. Rather than choosing hosts according to a group or bucket system, these duties were distributed on an ad hoc basis, with the US up to the Pittsburgh G20 doing most of the orchestration. Confirmed by the selection of Mexico to host in 2012, however, the G20 appears to be moving back to the legacy model of the G20 finance.

Looking outwards, the focus concerns the closing of the regional representation gap largely on behalf of small countries. Some significant progress has already been made, albeit in an ad hoc fashion. In terms of substance, the main attraction offered for non-members via the evolving G20 agenda has been on the Republic of Korea's proposals on the Global Financial Safety Net and Development Issues. According to Dr Junkyu Lee, senior advisor to the Korean Ministry of Strategy and Finance, in talks with the Vietnamese Ministry of Finance officials (as host of the G20 and the Presidency of ASEAN 2010 respectively), in the near term, the G20 could set up a regional-scale cooperation regime or mutual agreement on financial safety assistance (Vietnam Business News 2010) that would help insulate developing countries from the ill-effects of global economic crises.

As witnessed by this type of interaction, ASEAN has proved receptive to greater inclusion in the G20 process. Outreach efforts to regional organizations such as ASEAN in turn offer the G20 an opportunity to enhance inclusion and address legitimacy concerns (Bhattacharya 2010). ASEAN participation at the June 2010 summit in Toronto (Xinhua 2010) followed this model, via the participation of the ASEAN Chair and Secretary-General. This approach bolstered both the G20's input and output legitimacy function along with its capacity of the forum to act as a network hub.

The big remaining question rests on whether these types of fluid adjustment reach the boundary of what is viable, or whether they provide a staging ground for further reforms. At the Seoul summit the G20 settled on a formula for non-member participation, enabling the summit host to invite up to five guests. On the face of it this went a long way to settling the regional representation, as it was reported at the time that the Sherpas "set a tradition that the invitations should be made on a consensus of G20 members, not in the host country's own desire" (Cho 2010). On closer look, though, this formula does not end the debate.

The most ambitious means of meshing efficiency with legitimacy is to temper the original model for a G20. Rather than allowing further EU representation, as has happened through the presence of Spain and to some extent the Netherlands, a process of rollback and contraction should be implemented. This single big move will help build legitimacy for the G20 outside the EU. But just as importantly, it will encourage more innovative forms of coordination inside the EU, the instrumental rationale for which has been revitalized by the difficulties with addressing the euro area crisis. As highlighted by a Brookings Institution publication, therefore, the ongoing governance stalemate in Europe is creating gridlock for wider global governance reform (Bhattacharya et al. 2010).

To be sure, the political and diplomatic pressures to add, not subtract, will continue to be intense. A case in point is the treatment of the Netherlands at the Toronto G20. Having initially signaled that the Dutch would not be invited, Canada relented (not just out of a sense of like-mindedness, but as a result of good personal chemistry at the leadership level) and allowed the Netherlands in with a cluster of other countries (Ethiopia, Malawi and Viet Nam) implicitly under the banner of regional representatives. Whatever political or diplomatic advantage gained by this supplementary move, nonetheless, was offset by the problematic logic of letting in another EU claimant. Instead of lending credence to the notion that the G20 represented a shift of global governance for a world that was realigning its power and normative foundations, it reinforced the image of the G20 as having an arbitrary "club" design (MacCharles 2010).

Yet the logic of balancing EU representation with other forms of regional representation has been acknowledged by the Republic of Korea as the host of the November 2010 G20 summit. With the formula negotiated by the G20 Sherpas in place, the door opened to Ethiopia, Malawi, Viet Nam and Singapore as the representatives of alternative organizations, but closed to further EU representation beyond the case of Spain (in its anomalous position as a permanent guest). In justifying the introduction of the "G20 plus five" approach, the Korean preparatory committee explicitly stated that this decision had been made because "we finally agreed that we needed to have a better geographical balance" (Cho 2010).

Moreover, as witnessed by the mode of the engagement of both France and Mexico with small countries, this culture is becoming ingrained in the G20. Before the formation of the G20, France pushed the idea of a Group of 14 (G14) privileging the PRC, India, Brazil, Mexico and South Africa along with Egypt. For the Cannes G20 in November 2011, by way of contrast, France invited another group of countries, all but one of which fits into the category of small states: Ethiopia as chair of NEPAD, the UAE as chair of the Gulf Cooperation Council, and Equatorial Guinea as chair of the AU, along with Spain and Singapore, representing the 3 Group (3G). Mexico invited Chile, a key member of the 3G, and Colombia along with Spain with the explicit representation of the 3G still open.

3.6 MOVING THE ENGAGEMENT OF SMALL STATES BEYOND REGIONAL REPRESENTATION

The role of the 3G and the specific role of Singapore merit special attention in an analysis of the push to facilitate greater legitimacy of the G20
by integrating it more closely with small and medium states as well as
the UN. This initiative featured a specific form of entrepreneurial and
technical leadership and a diverse coalition of 28 small and medium-
sized economies around the world: six from Southeast Asia and Asia-
Pacific (Singapore, Malaysia, Brunei Darussalam, the Philippines, New
Zealand and Viet Nam); three from the Middle East (Bahrain, Qatar
and the United Arab Emirates); three from Africa (Rwanda, Senegal and
Botswana); eight from Europe (Sweden, Belgium, Ireland, Luxembourg,
Switzerland, Liechtenstein, Monaco and San Marino); two from Latin
America (Uruguay and Chile); and six from Central America and the
Caribbean (Costa Rica, Guatemala, Panama, Jamaica, Barbados and
Bahamas). Instead of a rejectionist stance, the 3G was oriented towards a
bridging and integrationist effort in world politics.

As with other small countries there was a strong element of instrumental self-help attached to this effort, especially on the issue of Offshore
Financial Centers (OFCs). The US become far less tolerant of OFCs in the
wake of the UBS scandal, in which Swiss banking officials stood accused of
facilitating tax evasion by US citizens. During the presidential campaign,
President Obama often cited frustration on "tax havens", often refer-
ring to a single office building in the Cayman Islands that houses 12 000
US-based corporations. The UK – facing a marked decline in the role of
London as a financial hub – is trying to repatriate some of the big pools
of money, not only from tax evaders but from tax avoiders (with Labour
Prime Minister Gordon Brown pledging to have Britons pay the "right
amount of tax"). Germany mounted a concerted drive against the culture
of secrecy found in Liechtenstein, especially when so many rich Germans
have taken advantage of that secrecy. And French President Sarkozy has
stated a successful outcome relating to the regulation of "tax havens", one
of his "red lines" in which the G20 summit must deliver results.

The issue of OFCs as viewed through the lens of efficiency has become
one of the unanticipated markers of the success of the G20. At the first
Washington DC summit in November 2008, Sarkozy lamented the lack of
success in this agenda area. Yet, as pushed by the Paris-based OECD, the
G20 has moved to send a strong signal to those OFCs that have refused to
sign tax information exchange deals.

If a sign of efficient action, however, the issue of OFCs raises the question of input legitimacy to a very different level. Can the G20 not only speak for the rest of the world but impose its will on countries that do not belong to the group? This issue of fairness of representation came to the fore in some of the declaratory statements by the organizers of the 3G. As Singapore's Foreign Minister George Yeo put it very bluntly in one interview:

> At the London meeting [of G20], financial centers became a major issue and countries like Singapore and Switzerland unexpectedly found themselves in the grey list and came under some pressure to alter the way we operate. This was without prior consultation with us, we were not involved in the discussions but we had to react to the decision taken by the G20 and we have reacted. That doesn't seem to me to be the right way to get things done. Hong Kong [,China] which had a situation very similar to Singapore, had [the PRC] to look after its interests so it is not on the grey list but Singapore was, and other countries too. So I think it is important that on issues that concern others, those who have major interest, should also be brought into the discussion. That is a matter of process; it would improve legitimacy and the sense of fairness. (Chowdhury 2010)

Still, if a catalyst for action, the 3G could not have extended its scope of membership if it was only directed to a single issue. What the 3G did was to tap into the same sense of exclusion driving the regional critics but to re-configure this resentment into a larger campaign directed at engagement with the G20 under the banner of variable geometry. Using this device, the 3G could make the argument that small countries should have access to the G20 on a functional basis – very much the same argument that middle powers have made throughout the post-1945 era.

A full analysis of the 3G – especially in terms of impact as opposed to process – lies beyond the ambit of this chapter. However, some key points can be made. First, the 3G allowed a solid platform for those countries that sought inclusion, not resistance to the G20. Second, the 3G offers a means by which the UN can be brought back into the debate about financial decision-making. Indeed much of the mobilization work for the G20 was conducted at UN HQ in New York by Ambassador Vanu Gopala Menon of Singapore.

3.7   EXPANDING THE G20 AGENDA IN ORDER TO MAXIMIZE LEGITIMACY

The most ambitious means of meshing efficiency with legitimacy is to temper the original model for a G20 with some element of the model to "regionalize" the forum. This search is not entirely novel. Just as former

Prime Minister Paul Martin of Canada advocated a shift from the G8 to the G20 as the pivotal forum for dealing with global problems, former Belgian Prime Minister Guy Verhofstadt has been a champion to "regionalize" the G8: the core of his idea being that this traditional "club of the rich" could be converted into a "network of the big regional continental organizations". In that framework Prime Minister Verhofstadt conceptualized a forum made up of regional groupings such as the European Union, MERCOSUR, ASEAN, NAFTA and the African Union – all with equal weighting (Van Langenhove 2004).

If more ambition is needed to translate this idea from the G8 to the G20, such thinking goes to the core of the G20's problematique. On the one hand, this approach acknowledges the G20's highly innovative attributes. Far more than an un-reformed UN, or an un-representative G8, the G20 offers a viable organizational update – dealing with the paradoxical situation where "the policy authority for tackling global problems still belongs to the states, while the sources of the problems and potential solutions are situated at transnational, regional or global level" (Thakur and Van Langenhove 2006) – in order to be in tune with twenty-first century realities. On the other hand, it offers one further way of dealing with the G20's legitimacy gaps, with a greater balance between member and non-member countries and the regions they come from.

In instrumental terms a network (as opposed to simply a "club") approach jumps out even on the agenda item that has done most to put a brake on the G20's activities, the euro area crisis. Although the core responsibility for dealing with the euro area crisis will remain with the European economies themselves, the G20 still has an important role in terms of the use of peer pressure. Such techniques in some ways at least can be connected with the culture of peer pressure embedded in other regional forums, above all ASEAN, but only if there is built-in regional representation.

Secondly, the move by the Republic of Korea to embrace a form of host/regional institutional mode of outreach (or to break with G8 terminology, consultation) should be refined and institutionalized. Such a process of consultation could be enhanced by implementing this form of activity through more varied means; for example, in addition to the initiatives taken by the host country, moves along these lines could be taken via a G20 Secretariat (if one is established as proposed by President Sarkozy and the Republic of Korea) or more loosely via a team of Sherpas (in either a troika format or a more ad hoc fashion). In accordance with the principle of variable geometry, the focus would be on select groups of the excluded with a functional orientation being engaged with particular agenda items of the G20.

In terms of the policy agenda the concern of Singapore, in an enhanced position given its leadership role in the 3G and its selection to chair the IMF Monetary and Financial Committee in March 2011, will continue to focus on the G20's main game in terms of financial regulation both directly and indirectly via the Financial Stability Board and the Basel committee on banking supervision. Yet if it can consolidate its place in the G20 via the 3G, there are a variety of other issues that it could contribute to as well: the integrated version of Global Green Growth giving primacy to economic policy measures leading to investment-led and innovation-driven growth, as well as the new agenda item of Livable Cities.

In terms of process, the work of ASEAN could be supplemented by borrowing the approach initiated by South Africa in the African context, a further form of indirect representation in the G20 via a regional committee of finance ministers and governors of central banks under the auspices of the Asian Development Bank and/or other bodies. This initiative has worked well. The scope of the membership for this committee is impressive, including as it does some countries that sought membership (Egypt and Nigeria) in a reformed G8 themselves (C10 2010; All Business 2010).

Although states will retain their primacy within the G20 context, it will also be advantageous if participation could be stretched on a functional basis. A regional dimension could be built into the G20 Business forum, the structure that has become a major embedded constituency for the G20 (Kim 2010a) as has taken place in the International Chamber of Commerce's G20 Advisory Group.

With some supplementary innovative reforms along these lines, it may be suggested, therefore, that the regional dynamics surrounding the G20 could move from a weakness to a source of strength. As emphasized throughout this chapter the "rejectionists" of the G20 have not been many in number, with most regional bodies wanting to find ways to work within the summit process. Moreover, formalistic recipes of dealing with the regional dimension (such as regional elections) have not gained traction beyond the realm of conceptual thinking (Wade and Vestergaard 2010). The feature that inculcates the G20 with so many of its institutional flaws, its ad hoc improvised nature, also provides the trait that allows the forum to move beyond these deficiencies. The G20 can make ample assertions about its position as a model of global governance. To fully justify these claims, however, the forum must be more than a flexible and purposeful diplomatic space for multilateral innovation. It must attend to its most glaring source of contestation, the G20's lack of inclusiveness undermining its legitimacy.

3.8 CONCLUSIONS: IMPERATIVES AND CONSTRAINTS WITH RESPECT TO FUTURE G20 REFORM

The institutionalization of the G20 at the leaders' level, in a similar fashion to the original G20 finance, was "shock activated" (Kirton 2013) in that the forum was erected to carry out a governance response to a serious crisis. This intense, unanticipated nature of the shocks placed the onus on delivery rather than legitimacy for the forum. It was only after the immediacy of the crisis activation eased that legitimacy concerns rose to the top of the policy/diplomatic debate.

As the G20 gains a greater role in the governance architecture, primarily through an expanding "steering group" agenda, the legitimacy concerns of the forum necessarily become more pressing. Accommodating the design issues of legitimacy is a longer-term project that differs from the instantaneous, ad hoc experience of the G20 in terms of the governance agenda. That is to say, legitimacy is a theme that will be accorded greater attention when the forum moves further into the post-crisis period. If legitimacy is deemed to be the advancement of governance by those directly impacted by policy decisions and deliberations, then the G20 in the wake of the current crisis was lacking legitimacy in that the governance decisions were made by and for the very countries that were at the core of the global financial crisis. In contrast to other potential formulas (G7/G8, G8 plus into a G12/13/14) the decision to enact the G20 as the forum for crisis response may even be said to have overcompensated on the legitimacy side.

In answering the important questions about both objective and expectations of G20 reform, it is necessary to ask how we should evaluate the G20 on the whole. As the discussion above articulates, the legitimacy of the G20 must be considered with respect to the G20's stages of development. A clear demarcation must be made between the G20's role as a crisis committee and as a potential global steering committee, as part of a wider transitional phase toward longer-term governance (Angeloni and Pisani-Ferry 2012). As a crisis committee the G20 remains dominated by the big global players, whether in the G7/G8 or BRICS. The summit's role as a steering committee, however, raises very different possibilities about the objective of the reform. Should we hope to see ambitious institutionalized advances in the future, as suggested by the Stiglitz Report, to replace the G20 by a Global Economic Cooperation Council (Stiglitz 2010)? Or, should we just take the current situation for granted, since it is only a self-selected forum and will continue to be a self-selected forum.

In terms of its "input" and "output" legitimacy, there is a dilemma with G20. If it becomes more representative in the future, that is, covering more states, it might be less productive and effective. Determining whether the G20 should sacrifice some legitimacy for greater efficiency, or vice versa, will largely depend on the vision of the forum with respect to the overall constellation of global governance. It can be persuasively argued that regionalization of G20 is a good idea and could be a solution to the dilemma. But the precondition is that each regional body is highly efficient in unifying their policy stances and then making productive proposals. With the deepening impact of the euro area crisis, it is increasingly difficult to see that this is not an easy task even in the EU, so it will inevitably take a long time to realize this goal.

At the macro-structural level of world politics, the G20, as the newest institutional innovation in multilateralism, is a reflection of wider trends taking place within the international system. If, as some observers indicate (Woods 2010; Chin 2010), regionalism and decentralization in the international system are indicative of the trajectory of the international system, then mirroring this trend within the governance structure of the G20 is reasonable.

The main challenge is to preserve the fluidity of the G20, which is underwritten by its informal design. This fluidity, despite some policy disagreements, is among the forum's most significant features for weaving its approaches to core economic governance challenges; whether, for example, on the issues of financial regulation, global imbalances, the possibility of a financial transaction tax, trade and development finance. Informality has worked to facilitate mixed coalitions of established and emerging states within the G20 via ad hoc groupings. It is thus imperative that this institutional design issue not be treated in a fixed manner. If and when the G20 moves beyond its crisis committee orientation, a stage projected most seriously by the euro area dilemmas, and the protracted spillover effect in other regions of the world, a revisiting of the G20's role in global governance will be a vital necessity.

REFERENCES

Alexandroff, A.S. and A.F. Cooper, eds. 2010. *Rising States, Rising Institutions: Challenges for Global Governance*. Washington, DC: Brookings Institution.

All Business. 2010. African Development Bank Group: C-10 to Discuss Development Agenda for G20 Summit in Seoul. 4 October.

Angeloni, I. and J. Pisani-Ferry. 2012. The G20: Characters in search of an author. Bruegel Working Paper 2012/04.

ASEAN Secretariat. 2010. Views of ASEAN Sought for G20 Agenda. Press Release. Jakarta. 10 February.

Asian Institute for Policy Studies. 2010. *The G20 and Global Governance Reform.* Seoul: Yonsei University.

Åslund, A. 2009. The G20 must be stopped. *The Financial Times.* 26 November.

Bailin, A. 2005. *From Traditional to Group Hegemony: The G7, the Liberal Economic Order and the Core-periphery Gap.* London: Ashgate.

Barma, N., E. Ratner and S. Weber. 2007. A world without the West. *The National Interest*, **90**(July–August): 23–30.

Beeson, M. and S. Bell. 2009. The G-20 and international economic governance: Hegemony, collectivism, or both? Following the East Asian crisis of 1997–1998. *Global Governance* **15**(1): 67–86.

Bhattacharya, A. 2010. Enhancing the G20's inclusion and outreach. *East-West Dialogue: Shaping the G20 Agenda in Asia – The 2010 Seoul Summit.* 5 April.

Bhattacharya, A., C. Bradford and J. Linn. 2010. Europe's governance causes gridlock for global governance reform. Brookings Institution. 23 April, available at: http://www.brookings.edu/opinions/2010/0424_ governance_linn.aspx.

C10. 2010. Communiqué of the meeting of the committee of African ministers of finance and planning and Governors of Central Banks. Cape Town: Committee of Ten. 21 February.

Carin, B. 2010. A G20 'Non-Secretariat'. In: C. Bradford and W. Lim (eds) *The New Dynamics of Summitry: Institutional Innovations for G20 Summits, Issue and Essays*, Seoul: Korea Development Institute: pp. 383–91.

Chin, G. 2010. The emerging countries and China in the G20: Reshaping global economic governance. *Studia Diplomatica.* **LXIII**(2–3): 105–24.

Cho, J.-S. 2010. 5 non-G20 nations invited to Seoul summit. *Korea Times.* 24 October.

Chowdhury, I.A. 2010. The Global Governance Group ('3G') and Singaporean leadership: Can small be significant? Singapore: ISAS Working Paper No. 108. 19 May.

Cooper, A.F. 2008. Stretching the model of 'coalitions of the willing'. In: A.F. Cooper, B. Hocking and W. Maley (eds) *Global Governance and Diplomacy: Worlds Apart?* Basingstoke, UK: Palgrave.

Cooper, A.F. 2010. The G20 as an improvised crisis committee and/or a contested 'steering committee' for the world. *International Affairs.* **86**(3): 741–57.

Cooper, A.F. and P. Subacchi. 2010. Overview: Global economic governance in transition. *International Affairs.* **86**(3): 607–17.

Cox, R. 1979. Ideologies and the NIEO. *International Organization.* **33**(2): 280–302.

The Economist. 2010. Running the world economy: Finally, a talking-shop worth having. 4 November.

Ferguson, N. 2007. Not two countries, but one: Chimerica. *The Telegraph.* 4 March.

Financial Times. 2010. G20 show how not to run the world. 12 November.

Foss, W. and A.B. Austin. 1933. *The World Economic Conference, London 1933.* London: Soncino Press.

Garton Ash, T. 2008. One practical way to improve the state of the world: Turn G8 into G14. *The Guardian.* 24 January.

Goldstein, A. 2003. An emerging China's emerging grand strategy. In: G. John Ikenberry and M. Mastanduno (eds) *International Relations Theory and the Asia-Pacific*, New York: Columbia University Press.

Government of Norway. 2009. Norwegian call for Nordic membership in the

G20. Press Release. Oslo: Ministry of Foreign Affairs, available at: http://www.regjeringen.no/en/dep/ud/selected-topics/Trade-policy/membership_G20.html?id=587984&epslanguage=en-GB>.
Held, D. 2010. *Cosmopolitanism: Ideals, Realities and Deficiencies.* Cambridge, UK: Polity Press.
International Monetary Fund. 2011. World Economic Outlook Database, September 2011.
Iqbal, A. 2010. US panel calls for Pakistan membership of G-20. Dawn. 28 November.
Kennedy, P. 1987. *The Rise and Fall of the Great Powers: Economic Change and Military Conflict from 1500 to 2000.* New York: Random House.
Kim, J.-H. 2010a. Seoul Business Summit starts to take shape. *Korea Herald,* 22 August.
Kim, J.-H. 2010b. UN, G20 to work in mutually reinforcing ways. *Korea Herald,* 15 November.
Kirton, J. 2013. *G-20 Governance for a Globalized World.* Aldershot, UK: Ashgate.
Koenig-Archibugi, M. 2010. Understanding the global dimensions of policy. *Global Policy.* 1(1): 16–28.
Lee, D.-H. 2010. From Toronto to Seoul: Evolution of the G-20 process. *Studia Diplomatica.* LXIII(2–3): 35–52.
Lee, M.-B. and K. Rudd. 2009. The G20 can lead the way to balanced growth, *Financial Times.* 2 September.
MacCharles, T. 2010. The expanding G8 adds up to a G20 in Huntsville, while Toronto's G20 will be a G33 or 34. *Toronto Star.* 14 June.
Mantega, G. 2008. Transcript of press briefing, available at: www.imf.org/external/np/tr/2008/tr081011.htm.
Martin, P. 2004. Address by Prime Minister Paul Martin on the occasion of his visit to Washington, DC. 29 April.
Mo, J. and E. Seo. 2010. The Korean G20 Presidency and evolving global governance. HGCY Working Paper Series. Seoul. October.
The Nation. 2010. Pakistan voices opposition to UN yielding economic decisions to G-20. 19 June.
Nelson, R.M. 2010. The G-20 and international economic cooperation: Background and implications for Congress. Washington: Congressional Research Service. 10 August.
Oakley, D. 2009. Decoupling gains new group of cheerleaders. *Financial Times.* June 2011.
Paulson, H. 2010. *On the brink: Inside the Race to Stop the Collapse of the Global Financial System.* New York: Business Plus.
Rachman, G. 2010. America is losing the free world. *Financial Times,* 4 January.
Rana, P.R. 2010. Reform of the international financial architecture: How can Asia have a greater impact in the G20? Singapore: RISI Working Paper No. 201. 9 June.
Rana, P.R. 2011. Make G20-plus transparent. *China Daily.* 1 November.
Reuters. 2009. African FinMins call for G20 voice, more support. 5 October.
Ruggie, J. 1983. Political structure and change in the international economic order: The North–South dimension. In: *The Antinomies of Interdependence.* New York: Columbia University Press, pp. 423–87.
Der Spiegel. 2010. Norway takes aim at G20. 22 June.

Stiglitz, J.E. 2010. *The Stiglitz Report. 2010*. New York: The New Press.

Thakur, R. and L. Van Langenhove. 2006. Enhancing global governance through regional integration. *Global Governance*. **12**(3): 233–40.

US–China Business Council. 2011. US–China trade statistics and China's world trade statistics, available at: https://www.uschina.org/statistics/tradetable.html.

Van Langenhove, L. 2004. Regional integration and global governance. UNU-CRIS Occasional Papers.

Vietnam Business News. 2010. ASEAN's position towards the G20 Seoul summit. 5 September.

Wade, R. 1998. From miracle to cronyism. *Cambridge Journal of Economics*. **22**(6): 693–706.

Wade, R. and J. Vestergaard. 2010. Overhaul the G20 for the sake of the G172. *Financial Times*. 21 October.

Woods, N. 2010. Global governance after the financial crisis: A new multilateralism or the last gasp of the great powers? *Global Policy*. **1**(1): 51–63.

Xinhua. 2010. ASEAN to attend G20 Summit in Toronto. china.org.cn. 22 June, available at: http://www.the PRC.org.cn/world/2010–06/22/content_20322748.htm.

Yekaterinburg Joint Communiqué. 2009. Meeting of the Foreign Ministers of the People's Republic of China, the Russian Federation, the Republic of India and the Federative Republic of Brazil. 16 May.

Yu, Y. 2005. China's evolving global view. In: J. English, R. Thakur and A.F. Cooper (eds) *Reforming from the Top: A Leaders' 20 Summit*, Tokyo: UNUP.

Zawya, M.A.-H. 2009. AMF Chairman: SA not over represented in G20. Dow Jones. 4 October.

4. Enhancing the effectiveness of CMIM and AMRO: challenges and tasks

Reza Siregar and Akkharaphol Chabchitrchaidol

4.1 INTRODUCTION

Recent crises, particularly the sovereign debt crisis in the euro area economies, have provided momentum to greater regional financial cooperation in the region. This is particularly evident among the Association of Southeast Asian Nations (ASEAN)+3 economies.[1] Through the establishment of the Chiang Mai Initiative Multilateralization (CMIM) and the ASEAN+3 Macroeconomic Research Office (AMRO) in March 2010 and May 2011, respectively, substantial headway has been made in this regard.

Despite the advance of regional cooperation among the ASEAN+3 economies, a series of fundamental questions have been raised, above all about the size of the CMIM facility. Although the CMIM was doubled in size to US$240 billion with effect from May 2012, the amount has frequently been criticized as insufficient. The European Financial Stability Facility (EFSF) of 750 billion euros in 2011, for instance, amounted to about 8 per cent of the total gross domestic product (GDP) of the euro area, while the CMIM amounted to only about 1.5 per cent of the total GDP of the ASEAN+3 economies. The question, therefore, is whether the CMIM can be an effective and relevant part of regional financial cooperation given its limited financial resources.

Another fundamental issue is the role of the CMIM and its relation to other available facilities, including bilateral swap lines, as well as global facilities – most notably those provided by the International Monetary Fund (IMF). During the 2008 global financial crisis and the 2011 euro area sovereign debt crisis, some ASEAN+3 member economies had access to bilateral swap facilities from both the major ASEAN+3 economies (the People's Republic of China [PRC] and Japan) and their traditional global trading partner (the United States [US]). Given the availability of other sources of liquidity support, should access to and disbursement of the CMIM's facilities be more precisely defined, and should it play a more systematic role in the region's financial architecture? In addition, the issue of accessibility frequently centers upon the types of conditionality attached to the facility. In order to add value to existing global and regional financial arrangements, many have argued that the CMIM facility must at least be complementary to those arrangements and provide greater flexibility and accessibility for ASEAN+3 member economies. Yet the conditionalities which could be related to potential CMIM lending remained vague, even in mid-2012.

The role of AMRO as a surveillance office for the CMIM is vital to the overall success of regional financial cooperation: without a credible and qualified surveillance capacity, it is difficult to envision an effective CMIM. Yet numerous obstacles face the surveillance work of even well-established global multilateral institutions, such as the International Monetary Fund (IMF), which AMRO will need to overcome going forward. Strengthening AMRO's capacity to fulfill its primary responsibility has been passionately debated by CMIM members at the meetings of the deputies of ASEAN+3 Finance Ministries and Central Banks. Typical discussions centered on key concerns, including how AMRO's regional surveillance work would provide value-added to the surveillance work carried out by the IMF, the Asian Development Bank (ADB), and those prepared by the member economies themselves. Other concerns were about how AMRO surveillance could be distinguished from that of existing global and regional surveillance, as well as the minimum infrastructure and set-up requirements that AMRO would need to be in a position to become a credible surveillance unit for the CMIM.

This chapter makes no attempt to present a comprehensive discussion on the CMIM and AMRO. A number of studies have dwelled upon the rationale and motivation behind the introduction of the CMIM and regional financial cooperation (Sussangkarn 2011; Jomo 2011). Others have also deliberated on various possible frameworks that CMIM and AMRO could adopt based on the experience of other regional and global arrangements (Takagi 2010). The primary task of this chapter is to return to and provide constructive responses to the set of issues and challenges discussed above. In particular, we focus our discussion on two issues concerning the CMIM: its role in the context of global and regional financial cooperation, and the design of the facility's conditionality. Moreover, we will also consider several aspects relating to the surveillance activities of AMRO. In short, the primary aim of this chapter is to suggest possible areas in which the effectiveness of the CMIM and AMRO may be increased, despite numerous constraints and limitations.

The outline of the chapter is as follows. The next section presents a brief history and highlights some of the recent developments and commitments of the CMIM and AMRO. In section 4.3, we discuss the set of latent challenges mentioned above and suggest responses to overcome them. In section 4.4, we briefly discuss the conditionalities espoused by the IMF. In section 4.5, we discuss AMRO's current work and process of economic surveillance and provide suggestions on how to improve AMRO's surveillance capacity. A brief concluding remarks section ends the chapter.

4.2   RECENT COMMITMENTS

4.2.1   The CMIM

Arguably, the most significant outcome of the ASEAN+3 Finance and Central Bank Deputies' Meeting in May 2012 was the enhancement of the ASEAN+3 Finance Ministers' Meeting (AFMM+3) to the ASEAN+3 Finance Ministers and Central Bank Governors' Meeting (AFMGM+3), whereby the central bank governors of the 13 member countries (plus Hong Kong, China) would henceforth be invited to participate in this annual senior-level meeting of the ASEAN+3 economies. In past AFMM+3 meetings, central banks were represented at the deputy governor level, so held a lower-level position in the overall decision-making process. The inclusion of central bank governors marked the beginning of a more comprehensive and integrated approach to the management of regional financial cooperation, whereby both fiscal and monetary policy officials jointly oversee and decide on CMIM matters. Participation of central bank governors in the annual ASEAN+3 Finance Ministers and Central Bank Governors' Meeting would also allow a more meaningful and in-depth discussion on the challenges and vulnerabilities of each economy, and further potential avenues for cooperation. As frequently stressed in past works, such as Takagi (2010), surveillance activities must reach audiences at the highest levels of policymaking to be relevant and effective.

During the Annual AFMGM+3 Meeting in May 2012, several other major new commitments were announced (Table 4.1). Responding to the potential need for a larger swap facility, the CMIM Executive Committee announced the doubling of the swap facility to US$240 billion in May 2012. Given the adjusted contributions, while keeping the "purchasing multiples" unchanged, major ASEAN economies (Indonesia, Malaysia, Philippines, Thailand and Singapore) now have access to approximately US$22.76 billion each, an increase from US$4.55 billion previously (Table 4.2). At the same meeting, an increase in the IMF de-linked

Table 4.1   *Recent developments of the CMIM*

	Announced 3 May 2012	Previous
Size	US$240 bn	US$120 bn
IMF de-linked portion	30% in 2012, up to 40% in 2014 subject to review	20%
Maturity (full amount)	12 months, with 2 renewals	90 days
Supporting period (full amount)	3 years	2 years
Maturity (IMF de-linked amount)	6 months, with 3 renewals	90 days
Supporting period (full amount)	2 years	1 year
Scope of facilities	• Crisis resolution function: renamed as CMIM Stability Facility • Introduction of crisis prevention function: CMIM Precautionary Line	Crisis resolution function

Source: AMRO website.

portion from 20 per cent to 30 per cent was also announced. A number of ASEAN+3 economies in fact proposed a higher de-link portion, but as a group eventually agreed to review the issue in 2014, with the intention of further increasing the de-linked portion to 40 per cent. During their deliberations, it was acknowledged that one of the key factors behind the doubling of the total swap facility and the rise in the de-linked portion is the recognition of the speedy establishment of the ASEAN+3 Macroeconomic Research Office (AMRO) and the timely delivery of well-received AMRO surveillance reports by the Executive Committee during the Deputies' Meeting in Sendai, Japan in December 2011 and in Phnom Penh, Cambodia in March 2012. Furthermore, reflecting their appreciation of the urgency in anticipating and preventing future financial crises, the ASEAN+3 Finance Ministers and Central Bank Governors approved the establishment of an additional function for the CMIM, a crisis prevention function, in addition to the crisis resolution function.

Under the current framework of the CMIM, a detailed set of operational guidelines was established, which would enable any swap requests to be processed efficiently and in a timely manner, typically within seven

Table 4.2   CMIM contributions and purchasing multiples

Economy	Financial contribution (billion US$)	Share (%)	Purchasing multiple	Maximum swap amount (billion US$)
Plus Three	**192.00**	**80.00**		**117.30**
Japan	76.80	32.00	0.5	38.40
PRC*	⎰68.40	⎰28.50	0.5	34.20
PRC	76.80 ⎱	32.00 ⎱		
Hong Kong, China	⎰ 8.40	⎰ 3.50	2.5	6.30
Rep. of Korea	38.40	16.00	1	38.40
ASEAN	**48.00**	**20.00**		**126.20**
Indonesia	9.104	3.793	2.5	22.76
Thailand	9.104	3.793	2.5	22.76
Malaysia	9.104	3.793	2.5	22.76
Singapore	9.104	3.793	2.5	22.76
Philippines	9.104	3.793	2.5	22.76
Viet Nam	2.00	0.833	5	10.00
Cambodia	0.24	0.100	5	1.20
Myanmar	0.12	0.050	5	0.60
Brunei Dar.	0.06	0.025	5	0.30
Lao PDR	0.06	0.025	5	0.30
Total	**240.00**	**100.00**		**243.50**

Note: * Excluding Hong Kong, China; Brunei Dar. = Brunei Darussalam.

Source: CMIM Agreement, available at AMRO website.

days of a request being made. Given that one of the original driving forces behind establishment of the CMIM was to ensure a quick and timely disbursement procedure, this established decision-making framework is an important feature of an effective CMIM. The issue of operational efficiency aside, the main challenge is to assure that lenders are satisfied that various safeguards are in place to ensure that any money lent is repaid. The CMIM Agreement currently addresses this in its most minimal form, through a set of precedent conditions that a member country must comply with prior to swap activation, and a set of covenants it needs to comply with throughout the borrowing period. However, such a framework forms only a basic backbone of the conditions that borrowing countries are expected to adhere to. Arguably, what is lacking is policy guidance or conditionality, such that a country that borrows also undertakes policy adjustments towards a more sustainable path, which in turn can reassure lenders of a capacity to repay. In this regard, it is important that a credible framework for conditionality is established early on, preferably during non-crisis periods. More in-depth discussions on these vital and sensitive matters will be elaborated in section 4.3 of this chapter.

4.2.2 The ASEAN+3 Macroeconomic Research Office (AMRO)

In late May 2012, AMRO welcomed its new director, Yoichi Nemoto, a senior official from the Ministry of Finance of Japan, who became the second director of AMRO, replacing Benhua Wei, a senior official who had previously worked at the State Administration of Foreign Exchange of the People's Republic of China. The transition was a smooth one, as Mr Nemoto had worked with Mr Wei since AMRO's establishment as a counselor. Within less than a year of Mr Wei's appointment, a team of about 20 full-time staff had been assembled. In the process, three teams of economists, each headed by a senior economist, were relocated to AMRO's Singapore office from various ASEAN+3 economies. Each team was assigned and mandated to conduct macroeconomic surveillance on a set of ASEAN+3 economies.

Depending on their past work experience, each economist and senior economist was also assigned to one of three area-focused study units, covering fiscal matters; monetary and exchange rate matters; and financial markets. Each unit was tasked with the responsibility to evaluate and assess each particular area across different ASEAN+3 economies. The fiscal team, for instance, was tasked to study various issues on budget and fiscal policy of each ASEAN+3 economy, and carry out cross-country analyses within the ASEAN+3 economies and, if necessary, with other groups of economies around the world. Ultimately, each group aims to identify a set of key indicators to assess the strengths and weaknesses facing each member economy.[2]

Since December 2011, AMRO has submitted a set of surveillance reports on a quarterly basis.[3] The first set comprises individual economy (bilateral) surveillance reports on all 14 economies of the ASEAN+3 (including Hong Kong, China). In addition, the ASEAN+3 Regional Economic Monitoring (AREM) report is produced quarterly to assess and monitor developments in the global economic environment and its impact on ASEAN+3 economies (multilateral-surveillance perspective). In each of these country surveillance and AREM reports, the emphasis is more on short-term potential risks and vulnerabilities, and less on medium to long-term structural challenges.

In addition to the core team of economists, a team of administrative staff managing financial matters, human resources, and other day-to-day office matters, a legal expert, and a senior official to deal especially with CMIM and ASEAN+3-related matters are also in place. A six-person Advisory Panel, with three persons nominated jointly by the ASEAN countries and three from each Plus-3 country,[4] meets with the AMRO director and senior economists on a quarterly basis. The role of the panel includes providing strategic guidance on AMRO's role and activities, and technical guidance on AMRO's economic and financial surveillance, assessments and analysis.

4.3   SELECTED CHALLENGES AND SCOPE FOR AN EFFECTIVE CMIM FACILITY

Despite the current limitation in size of the available swap facility at US$240 billion, a number of measures can be adopted to enhance the effectiveness of the CMIM framework. This section focuses on two key areas. The first area is the relationship between bilateral and multilateral swap facility arrangements. A number of possible avenues for cooperation between a multilateral swap facility such as the CMIM and other available bilateral swap arrangements could complement each other, and therefore boost their capacity and effectiveness. The second focus is on the design of CMIM disbursement, including some aspects of possible conditionalities attached to the CMIM facility, with particular emphasis on timely disbursement, while at the same time safeguarding against potential moral hazard.[5]

4.3.1   Coordination between Bilateral and Multilateral Swap Facility Arrangements

Over the past few years, numerous bilateral swap arrangements have been established amongst the ASEAN+3 economies (Table 4.3). The PRC and Japan, for instance, have extended swap facilities to Indonesia, Malaysia, Thailand and the Republic of Korea over the years to mitigate potential liquidity concerns facing recipient economies, and also to safeguard and promote bilateral trade activities. It is also interesting to note that in some cases the size of the bilateral swap facilities is well above the maximum swap facility extended by the CMIM. Malaysia, for instance, secured a RMB180 billion (or about US$30 billion) bilateral swap arrangement with the People's Bank of China in February 2012 for a period of three years (until February 2015). This swap facility is indeed larger than the US$22.76 billion maximum swap facility that Malaysia is entitled to from the CMIM facility.

Table 4.3   Recent bilateral swap arrangements involving ASEAN+3 economies

Signing date/ Expiry date	Countries	Type of swap		Amount
2 May 2012/ 3 May 2015	Bangko Sentral ng Pilipinas (BSP) and Bank of Japan (BOJ)	Bilateral Swap Arrangement (BSA)	Under the US$6.5 billion BSA, the BOJ would provide the BSP up to US$6 billion in financial assistance in exchange for a corresponding amount of Philippine currency in case Manila's foreign exchange reserves drop to a level that risks a run on the peso. As a two-way swap arrangement, the BSP also would provide the BOJ up to US$500 million in assistance in exchange for a corresponding amount of Japanese yen if Tokyo similarly were faced with balance of payments difficulties.	US$6.5 billion: BOJ→BSP US$0.5 billion: BSP→BOJ.
19 October 2011/ effective until the end of October 2012	Bank of Japan and the Bank of Korea jointly with Ministry of Strategy and Finance and Japan's finance ministry	Yen–Won Swap Arrangement	Non-crisis situation, to stabilizing regional financial markets through supplying short-term liquidity.	US$30 billion equivalent in Yen.
		Won–US$ Swap Arrangement	Mutual benefits and financial stability to enhance the country's sovereign credit condition.	US$40 billion (from US$10 billion).

Date	Institutions	Type	Description	Amount
22 June 2010/ 3 July 2013	Bank of Japan and the Bank of Korea	Yen–Won Swap Arrangement	Bilateral Yen–Won swap arrangement, for supplying short-term liquidity and to enhance mutual cooperation between the two central banks.	US$3 bn equivalent in Yen and Won.
22 March 2012/ 21 March 2015	People's Bank of China and the Reserve Bank of Australia	Bilateral Local Currency Swap	For the purpose of promoting bilateral financial cooperation, facilitating bilateral trade and investment, and safeguarding regional financial stability.	CNY200 billion or A$30 billion.
20 March 2012/ 19 March 2015	People's Bank of China and Bank of Mongolia	Bilateral Local Currency Swap Supplemental Agreement	The two sides believe that this renewed arrangement will help facilitate bilateral investment and trade and safeguard regional financial stability.	Increased from original CNY5 billion or MNT1 trillion to CNY10 billion or MNT2 trillion.
21 February 2012/ 20 February 2015	People's Bank of China and the Central Bank of the Republic of Turkey	Bilateral Local Currency Swap	For the purpose of promoting bilateral financial cooperation, facilitating bilateral trade and investment, and maintaining regional financial stability.	CNY10 billion or TL3 billion.
8 February 2012/ 7 February 2015	People's Bank of China and Bank Negara Malaysia	Bilateral Local Currency Swap	The two sides believe that this renewed arrangement will help promote investment and trade between the two countries and safeguard regional financial stability.	Increased size from CNY80 billion/ RM40 billion to CNT180 billion/ RM90 billion.

Table 4.3 (continued)

Signing date/ Expiry date	Countries	Type of swap		Amount
17 January 2012/ 16 January 2015	People's Bank of China and Central Bank of the UAE	Bilateral Local Currency Swap	For the purpose of promoting bilateral financial cooperation, facilitating bilateral trade and investment, and maintaining regional financial stability.	The amount of the agreement is CNY35 billion or 20 billion Dirham.
22 December 2011/ 21 December 2014	People's Bank of China and the Bank of Thailand	Bilateral Local Currency Swap	For the purpose of promoting bilateral financial cooperation, facilitating bilateral trade and investment, and maintaining regional financial stability.	The amount of the agreement is CNY70 billion or B320 billion.
23 December 2011/ 22 December 2014	People's Bank of China and the State Bank of Pakistan	Bilateral Local Currency Swap	For the purpose of promoting bilateral financial cooperation, facilitating bilateral trade and investment, and maintaining regional financial stability.	The amount of the agreement is CNY10 billion or PKR140 billion.
26 October 2011/ 25 October 2014	People's Bank of China and Bank of Korea	Bilateral Local Currency Swap	The two central banks have also agreed to explore the possibility of converting some swap currencies into reserve currencies. The two sides believe that this renewed arrangement will help enhance bilateral financial cooperation, promote investment and trade between the two countries, and safeguard regional financial stability.	Increase in size from CNY180 billion/W38 trillion to CNY360 billion/ W64 trillion.

Source: National authorities' websites.

With the multilateralization of the Chiang Mai Initiative, the current challenge is not only to avoid potential conflicts between these two approaches, but also to find ways to create synergy between these two types of facilities. Without concrete coordination there is a real risk that the CMIM is undermined by the bilateral facilities, and vice versa. After all, what would be the incentive for an ASEAN+3 economy to apply for the CMIM facility, especially given the size limitation? How can a multilateral swap facility like the CMIM become an attractive facility given a choice of bilateral swap facilities and IMF funding facilities, without leading to moral hazard, while preventing "facility shopping"?

Bilateral and CMIM swap arrangements can indeed complement each other if they are well coordinated. More importantly, decisions to extend both bilateral and CMIM swap facilities should be taken consistently and, as much as possible, under one general framework. In particular, a common framework for bilateral and CMIM swap facilities among the ASEAN+3 economies can be agreed upon in a joint memorandum of understanding. As part of broad guidelines, any request from a member of the ASEAN+3 economies for a bilateral swap facility from another member of the ASEAN+3 should first be submitted to the CMIM facility for consideration. In other words, the request should go through an evaluation and decision process under the CMIM framework. Should the request be approved by the CMIM's Executive Committee, the requesting member economy will then be entitled to receive its available maximum swap amount listed in Table 4.2. In the event that the available CMIM swap amount is less than the amount requested or needed, the bilateral swap can supplement or top up the difference.

Both parties – the recipient and the lender – can benefit from this proposal. The eligible recipient economy is in a position to receive a swap amount larger than its maximum swap amount under the CMIM; the swap provider can take comfort in the due process of surveillance and approval under the CMIM facility, before having to extend the funds. Without this arrangement, the swap-providing economy would have to rely on its own surveillance process, before the swap takes place and afterwards, to decide on the request. Furthermore, the swap-providing economy must bear the whole amount of the swap requested under the non-cooperative framework. However, under a single contract of multilateral swap facility, the swap provider does not have to shoulder the risk of the full amount, as some of the funds fall under the multilateral facility (see Figure 4.1). Naturally, designing appropriate conditionalities attached to the facility is critical. The viewpoint on conditionalities will be discussed in a greater detail in the next sub-section.

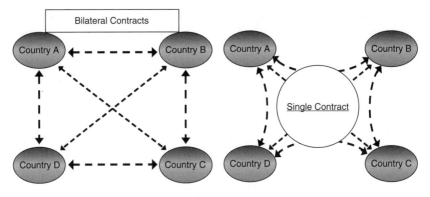

Source: AMRO.

Figure 4.1   From bilateral to multilateral approaches

4.3.2   Conditionality: Accessibility while Safeguarding against Moral Hazard

The legacy and stigma of the 1997 East Asian financial crisis among major East and Southeast Asian economies remains strong. "The conditionalities attached to the 1997–1998 East Asian crisis IMF packages across a number of the East Asian economies were very stringent, involving punitive fiscal and monetary tightening with minimum consideration and understanding of the specific socio-political circumstances of the recipient economies" (Sussangkarn 2011, p. 2). The lack of any request to draw upon the CMI facility at the height of the 2008 global financial crisis following the collapse of Lehman Brothers is a clear reminder of this stigma, given the CMIM's explicit links to the IMF. Yet those links are crucial under the current set-up, as the CMIM will function only if swap providers feel reasonably assured that any funds lent out will be returned. To be relevant to its stakeholders while addressing the legacy and stigma issues, and also to give creditors confidence, conditionalities for the CMIM facility must therefore be designed to be as flexible and accessible as possible, while safeguarding the pool of funds from moral hazard practices.

So far, the simple, quick-fix solution has been to make use of existing mechanisms via the IMF. By linking any drawing beyond 30 per cent of eligible funds (as of May 2012) this implies that countries need to submit to IMF guidelines, which act as a "de facto" conditionality against lax economic policies. While this was acceptable initially for member countries to sign off on their commitments to the CMIM swap arrangement, this is perhaps one of the main reasons why use of the CMIM has so far remained off-limits to its members. This suggests a good case can be made for establishing a framework for conditionality with full CMIM ownership. How then should such a framework be established to make it more flexible and effective, while at the same time not repeating the shortcomings of global lending frameworks? Borrowing the views of Jomo (2011), successful and effective regional arrangements must be flexible but credible, and capable of effective counter-cyclical macroeconomic management as well as crisis prevention management. In other words, facilities under regional financial arrangements must be large enough to be useful, with related conditionalities that are balanced between being strict enough to protect lenders' interests and supporting borrowing countries' economies. Furthermore, such conditionalities would require policy adjustments on the part of the borrowers, which will need to be specified at the outset.

It is useful to draw upon existing models of conditionalities as espoused by the IMF and enhanced over the years. Key characteristics include both the design of the macroeconomic and structural policy recommendations, as well as the tools used to monitor progress towards the goals outlined in those recommendations and plans (IEO 2007). According to the IEO Report, conditionalities should be as streamlined as possible, focus on addressing the cause of crisis, and ensure that lent funds will eventually be repaid. In the case of the CMIM, conditionalities may need to focus on macroeconomic stabilization and balance of payments issues, for instance. Conditionalities may also relate to performance criteria which need to be met, in order for funds to be rolled over once they mature. In cases where conditions are unpopular, mechanisms to lock governments into reform programs may be required, although a balance between enforcement and program ownership by the country in question is also crucial.

Why then, would any conditionality be substantially different from the tried-and-tested IMF conditionality? The CMIM is intended to deal with short-term shocks to the economy and the balance of payments. This is reflected in the nature of the CMIM's facilities, such as shorter activation times and loan maturity. In fact, the CMIM's maturity and supporting period for the IMF de-linked portion is for six months and two years, respectively, or for one year and three years, respectively,[6] for the IMF-linked portion.

Let us briefly consider some of the IMF's lending instruments that share similar objectives to the CMIM facilities, in order to draw lessons from how they are set up and from the experience of their use. The IMF maintains an array of facilities, including concessional lending, as well as a whole range of facilities to address an actual or potential balance of payments need. We consider two types of facilities which correspond most closely to the CMIM's IMF-de-linked portion and the CMIM's

IMF-linked portion: the Rapid Financing Instrument (RFI) and the Precautionary and Liquidity Line (PLL).

The Rapid Financing Instrument is meant to provide rapid financial assistance, with limited conditionality, to any member facing an urgent balance of payments need. The rapid nature of disbursement and limited conditionality means that amounts provided are small; access under the RFI is subject to an annual limit of 50 per cent of quota and a cumulative limit of 100 per cent of quota. In fact, for the IMF's rapid access component (i.e. small emergency loans), low conditionality is the norm, whereas for the high access component (i.e. the bulk of the funds), related conditionalities are needed to focus policies on tackling the underlying shock (Bird 2009), which typically can be resolved only over the medium term. The similarity of the RFI to the CMIM's IMF de-linked portion, both in terms of purpose and characteristics such as maturity, therefore, make the RFI a suitable candidate for comparison. Both facilities are meant to provide rapid financial assistance to members that face an urgent balance of payments need. Table 4.4 compares the available amounts under RFI and the 30 per cent IMF de-linked portion. Taking the case of Indonesia, for example, 100 per cent of IMF quota is equivalent to around US$3.14 billion. If we look at the CMIM's IMF de-linked portion (30 per cent), this amounts to US$6.83 billion. In the case of Thailand, the corresponding numbers are US$2.17 billion and US$6.82 billion, respectively. While the size of the CMIM's IMF-de-linked portion is double the amount of the IMF RFI, it would still only be useful for emergency-situation assistance. Therefore, the conditionalities for the CMIM's de-linked tranche should be no more stringent than the IMF's RFI.[7]

It may be useful to compare a request for disbursement of the full amount of the CMIM swap facility with the IMF's recently revamped Precautionary and Liquidity Line (PLL),[8] rather than the IMF's Stand-By Arrangements (SBAs). Objectives and time horizons of the CMIM and the IMF's SBA are different, with the CMIM focusing on shorter-term adjustments than the SBA. The CMIM was designed to be different from the SBA, to avoid the complex SBA programs that had non-core structural components, which added to perceptions that the programs were too cumbersome and implementation lacked even-handedness. The IMF PLL, on the other hand, attempts not only to address the shortcomings of previous programs, but also to address the inaccessibility of the more recently established FCL – its qualifying criteria being too strict to allow it to be widely utilized. The PLL also has a wider use, that is, for actual and potential balance of payment (BOP) needs. As the PLL is similar to the CMIM in terms of the flexibility and accessibility of its programs, this makes it a useful starting point for designing CMIM conditionality.

Table 4.4 Available funds under the IMF RFI and the CMIM de-linked portion

	IMF Quotas US$ mn	CMIM (US$ mn), total size US$ 240bn	CMIM purchasing multiple	IMF Rapid Financing Instrument		CMIM non IMF-linked	
				50% of quota (per year)	100% of quota (cumulative)	20%	30%
Japan	23 599	76 800	0.50	11 800	23 599	7680	11 520
PRC	14 384	68 400	0.50	7192	14 384	6840	10 260
Hong Kong, China		8400	2.50	0	0	4200	6300
Rep. of Korea	5083	38 400	1.00	2542	5083	7680	11 520
Indonesia	3140	9104	2.50	1570	3140	4552	6828
Malaysia	2679	9104	2.50	1339	2679	4552	6828
Philippines	1539	9104	2.50	770	1539	4552	6828
Singapore	2126	9104	2.50	1063	2126	4552	6828
Thailand	2175	9104	2.50	1088	2175	4552	6828
Viet Nam	696	2000	5.00	348	696	2000	3000
Cambodia	132	240	5.00	66	132	240	360
Myanmar	390	120	5.00	195	390	120	180
Brunei Dar.	325	60	5.00	162	325	60	90
Lao PDR	80	60	5.00	40	80	60	90

Notes:
Brunei Dar. = Brunei Darussalam.
As of June 2012, the official conversion is 1 SDR = 1.51 USD.

Sources: IMF, AMRO, based upon authors' calculations.

The PLL uses both *ex-ante* and *ex-post* conditionalities, which are similar to the CMIM's original concept, based on the need for conditions that were specified in the Chiang Mai Initiative Multilateralization Agreement, as well as the need for monitoring criteria for *ex-post* conditions. Furthermore, PLL qualification hinges upon an assessment that the economy has sound economic fundamentals and institutional policy frameworks; is implementing (and has a track record of implementing) sound policies; and is committed to sound policies in the future. Assessment of qualification for the PLL covers five broad areas: (1) external position and market access; (2) fiscal policy; (3) monetary policy; (4) financial sector soundness and supervision; and (5) data adequacy. It is no coincidence that the CMIM's decision-making board recently announced that qualification criteria for the CMIM's own crisis prevention function is to be assessed in these five areas as well. But more importantly, this concept can also be usefully applied to the Crisis Resolution Function of the CMIM.

Having a fixed set of *ex-ante* criteria (in the five areas listed, for instance) can help improve the timeliness of approval for use of facilities and their disbursement. Setting looser *ex-ante* criteria in these five areas, with gradually tighter conditionalities, can help a larger number of members qualify initially and thus enable them to make use of the CMIM, preventing their exclusion from the beginning. Criteria will need to be economy- and case-specific, given huge divergences in the level of economic development among members. In the case of the PLL, the IMF indicates that in cases where not all criteria are met *ex-ante*, there is a case for using that area of vulnerability in guiding the member's ex-post conditions. Furthermore, limiting conditionalities to these five areas would help them to remain focused and streamlined, and more likely to be relevant to the shocks in question, as these are probably the likely sources of BOP problems. However, as far as the potential use of the CMIM is concerned, the source of shocks can come from other problems as well.

However, there are clear conditions where the PLL will not apply, effectively precluding certain situations. Such conditions are: (1) a sustained inability to access international capital markets; (2) a need for large macroeconomic or structural policy adjustment; (3) a public debt position that is likely to be unsustainable in the medium-term; or (4) widespread bank insolvencies. In the case of the CMIM, while specific conditions may need to be waived in the case of crisis resolution functions, such as the need for sustained access to international capital markets, other situations such as public debt issues may need to be retained. This would be necessary to prevent the facilities from being used beyond their specified mandate of tackling BOP difficulties.

A mix of both *ex-ante* and *ex-post* conditions should be used together in designing the conditionality structure in a holistic and streamlined way. In this case, using *ex-ante* conditionality in the form of pre-qualification criteria can help play a role in reducing potentially complex and unnecessary *ex-post* conditionality. This is one aspect of speeding up the decision-making process, as well as facilitating the follow-up process. The pre-qualification criteria will focus on dealing with the most likely problems and shocks, which by nature should be short-term. These would include conventional macroeconomic conditionalities, as well as other short-term indicators involving financial markets, for instance. As in the IMF PLL, structural targets and structural performance criteria have no role to play in such conditionalities; if they do (requirements for financial sector reform being a case in point), the sources of the problems are likely to be beyond what the CMIM can effectively tackle.

A degree of flexibility in the conditionalities, which can be adjusted according to country performance, should be more conducive to promoting national ownership of strong and effective policies. The argument is that only with national ownership will such reforms be implemented. In the light of concerns about whether the ASEAN+3 community would be able to coerce peers into difficult reforms, national ownership of such policies is vital. To further streamline the process and improve efficiency, the IMF's Independent Evaluation Office (IEO) in its review of IMF conditionalities recommended that a notional cap on the number of conditionalities could be set, at four to five per year, and these should be restricted to areas of core competency (IEO, 2007). This can perhaps be considered in the CMIM context to minimize the number of conditionalities that an economy will need to observe. However, this provision can be subject to caveats that more conditionalities may be added, if required, on a case-by-case basis.

4.4 AMRO: CONDUCTING INTEGRATED SURVEILLANCE

The attainment of an effective CMIM strongly depends on the credible surveillance work of AMRO. This message has been repeatedly pointed out at the numerous semi-annual meetings of deputies. AMRO can learn from other institutions that undertake surveillance, such as the IMF, with its vast experience in global economic and financial surveillance. In this section, we discuss AMRO's current work process on economic surveillance, and make suggestions about how to improve AMRO's surveillance capacity. Takagi (2010) proposes a set of features and characteristics underpinning sound surveillance work. One of them, and arguably the most urgent one for AMRO, is the necessity to establish a centralized and integrated surveillance approach. However, before moving into a detailed discussion on the infrastructure needed to carry out integrated surveillance work at AMRO, the next sub-section presents some of the key features of the ASEAN+3 economies, highlighting their openness and interconnectedness with other economies.

4.4.1 Trade and Financially Integrated Economies

Trade integration of the ASEAN+3 economies with their global partners may vary, but it is clearly significant. On average, between 13 and 14 per cent of total exports of individual ASEAN+3 economies were shipped to traditional markets such as the United States (US) in 2011 (Table 4.5).[9] The emergence of the PRC as a major hub of the production networks in Asia contributed significantly to the rapid rise of intra-regional trade among the ASEAN+3 economies. Major ASEAN economies, such as Indonesia, Malaysia, Thailand and Singapore, sent more of their exports to the PRC than to the US and the European Union (EU) in 2011. Furthermore, Japan continued to be an important trading partner for the emerging markets of the ASEAN+3 economies. In 2011, a resilient intra-regional export performance cushioned the impact of falling exports to Europe and the US on the overall export activities of the ASEAN+3 economies.

Following the intensification of trade integration in the 1980s and 1990s and with the liberalization of the financial sectors in many parts of the ASEAN economies, financial market integration has deepened and widened. There has been an increasing complementarity between foreign direct investment (FDI) and trade, especially as the result of growing fragmentation of production combined with the creation of distribution networks spanning within the ASEAN economies and across to other parts of Asia and the world. As in the case of trade activities, total FDI into the ASEAN economies dropped in 2009, but recovered strongly and grew at a rate of around 100 per cent in 2010 (Table 4.6). A large portion of total FDI came from outside the region. In fact, extra-ASEAN direct investment was nearly five times as high as intra-ASEAN investment. However, intra-ASEAN investment was only second to total investment from the EU, contributing to about 16 per cent of total FDI to the region in 2010 (Table 4.7). This highlights the importance of direct investment between economies within the region. It is also worth highlighting that investment from the Asian economies (ASEAN, Japan, the Republic of Korea, the PRC and India) made up close to 40 per cent of total FDI to the region in 2010.

Table 4.5 Shares of export destinations

(%)

	EU	GIIPS*	France	Germany	Greece	Ireland	Italy	Portugal	Spain	UK	US	PRC	Japan
Brunei Dar.	0.08	0.01	0.01	0.01	0.00	0.00	0.01	0.00	0.00	0.05	0.21	4.62	45.64
Cambodia	26.62	5.16	1.78	8.16	0.09	0.29	2.10	0.06	2.61	7.90	41.46	2.73	4.56
PRC	18.75	3.28	1.58	4.03	0.21	0.11	1.78	0.15	1.04	2.32	17.09	–	7.82
Hong Kong, China	10.77	1.52	1.19	2.67	0.04	0.07	0.89	0.06	0.46	1.76	9.92	52.32	4.05
Indonesia	10.09	2.92	0.63	1.62	0.08	0.04	1.56	0.06	1.19	0.85	8.09	11.27	16.57
Japan	11.62	1.23	0.97	2.86	0.04	0.11	0.65	0.06	0.38	1.99	15.28	19.68	–
Rep. of Korea	10.04	1.51	1.03	1.71	0.24	0.06	0.74	0.13	0.33	0.89	10.12	24.17	7.15
Lao PDR	9.47	1.08	0.57	2.41	0.00	0.08	0.66	0.09	0.25	3.21	1.85	24.64	2.98
Malaysia	10.36	0.99	1.16	2.65	0.04	0.08	0.52	0.07	0.28	1.03	8.29	13.14	11.51
Myanmar	2.29	0.50	0.03	0.81	0.00	0.00	0.08	0.00	0.42	0.61	0.00	16.34	5.77
Philippines	12.85	0.99	0.89	3.60	0.03	0.05	0.60	0.03	0.28	0.83	14.76	12.70	18.46
Singapore	9.35	0.68	1.49	1.64	0.23	0.09	0.24	0.03	0.11	1.62	5.37	10.42	4.49
Thailand	10.15	1.52	0.79	1.58	0.07	0.12	0.78	0.07	0.47	1.63	9.18	11.51	10.11
Viet Nam	16.90	3.62	1.75	4.37	0.12	0.06	1.68	0.13	1.63	2.26	17.63	10.61	11.07

Notes:
Brunei Dar. = Brunei Darussalam.
* Greece, Italy, Ireland, Portugal and Spain.

Sources: IMF-DOT database and national authorities.

Table 4.6   Foreign direct investment net inflow (US$ million)

	Intra-ASEAN			Extra-ASEAN		
	2008	2009	2010/p	2008	2009	2010/p
Brunei Dar.	0.9	3.2	89.6	238.3	366.5	539.9
Cambodia	240.9	174.0	349.0	574.3	365.1	433.6
Indonesia	3398.0	1380.1	5904.2	5920.1	3496.7	7400.1
Lao PDR	47.7	57.3	135.4	180.1	261.3	197.2
Malaysia	1645.5	(269.7)	525.6	5602.9	1650.7	8630.2
Myanmar	103.5	19.5	–	872.1	559.1	–
Philippines	139.9	(4.9)	(7.8)	1404.1	1967.9	1720.8
Singapore	659.5	2108.3	3377.0	7929.4	13170.7	32143.2
Thailand	508.4	1326.0	433.6	8031.0	3649.6	5886.1
Viet Nam	2705.0	428.7	1300.9	6874.0	7171.3	6699.1
Total	**9449.3**	**5222.5**	**12107.5**	**37626.3**	**32658.9**	**63650.2**

Notes: Brunei Dar. = Brunei Darussalam; p/ = preliminary number.

Source: ASEAN Secretariat Database.

Table 4.7   Top five sources of foreign direct investment inflow to ASEAN

	Value			Share to total inflow		
	2008	2009	2010/p	2008	2009	2010/p
EU	7010.1	9112.9	16984.1	14.9	22.4	20.6
ASEAN	9449.3	5222.5	12107.5	20.1	13.8	16.0
US	3517.5	4086.7	8578.1	7.5	10.8	11.3
Japan	4129.4	3762.6	8386.1	8.8	9.9	11.1
Rep. of Korea	1595.7	1471.5	3769.4	3.4	3.9	5.0

Note: p/ = preliminary number.

Source: The ASEAN Secretariat.

In equity markets, ASEAN investors, like their counterparts in the rest of the Asian region, have tended to invest and diversify their portfolios outside the region, and mainly in North American and European financial markets. In fact, only about 12 per cent of the flow of foreign portfolio investment of Asian investors in 2006 found its way into Asian financial markets, whereas about two-thirds of the foreign portfolio investment of EU investors was invested in the EU itself (Shanmugaratnam 2006). Eichengreen and Luengnaruemitchai (2006) found that this can in part be explained by the lower level of economic development, the lack of a common language, and fewer shared land borders in the region. However, intra-ASEAN portfolio investment has picked up pace in the post-2008 crisis period. Total portfolio investment from Malaysia to major ASEAN-4 economies (Indonesia, Philippines, Thailand and Singapore) for instance, was estimated to be around US$11.2 billion, or more than 17 times the 2001 level.

The interconnectedness of the ASEAN economies will be further strengthened by the globalization of the banking sector. A recent survey carried out by the SEACEN Centre identified a number of regional and global banks with a strong presence in major Asian economies (Siregar and Lim 2010). Table 4.8 lists those major banks ranked by asset size.

Table 4.8   Cross-border regional banks in ASEAN and other Asian economies

Economy	Top domestic FIs in the jurisdiction that have significant presence in the region	Top foreign FIs in the jurisdiction that originate from SEACEN member economies	Top other foreign FIs (apart from originating from SEACEN member economies) that have significant presence in that economy
Brunei Darussalam	The domestic banks have a presence only within the country	• Maybank (Malaysia) • UOB (Singapore) • RHB Bank Berhad (Malaysia)	• Citibank • HSBC • Standard Chartered Bank
Indonesia	• Bank Mandiri • Bank BRI • BCA	• CIMB Niaga (Malaysia) • Bank International Indonesia (Maybank Malaysia controls around 43%)	• Citibank • HSBC • Standard Chartered Bank
Rep. of Korea	• None	• DBS (Singapore) • UOB (Singapore) • OCBC (Singapore)	• Citibank • HSBC • Standard Chartered Bank
Malaysia	• Maybank • CIMB Group • Public Bank	• OCBC (Singapore) • UOB (Singapore) • Bangkok Bank (Thailand)	• Citibank • HSBC • Standard Chartered Bank

Table 4.8 (continued)

Economy	Top domestic FIs in the jurisdiction that have significant presence in the region	Top foreign FIs in the jurisdiction that originate from SEACEN member economies	Top other foreign FIs (apart from originating from SEACEN member economies) that have significant presence in that economy
Papua New Guinea	• Bank South Pacific	• Maybank (Malaysia)	• ANZ Bank (Australia) • Westpac Bank (Australia)
The Philippines	• Metropolitan Bank Corporation (Metrobank) • Philippine National Bank (PNB)	• China Trust (Taipei,China) • Maybank (Malaysia) • Korea Exchange Bank (Rep. of Korea)	• Citibank • HSBC • Standard Chartered Bank
Singapore	• DBS Bank Limited • OCBC • UOB	• Maybank (Malaysia) • Bangkok Bank (Thailand) • RHB Bank (Malaysia)	• Citibank • HSBC • Standard Chartered Bank
Taipei,China	• Bank of [Taipei,China] • [Taipei,China] Cooperative Bank • Mega International Commercial Bank	• DBS (Singapore) • OCBC (Singapore) • Bangkok Bank (Thailand)	• Citibank • HSBC • Standard and Chartered Bank
Thailand	• Bangkok Bank • Kasikorn Bank • Siam Commercial Bank	• UOB (Singapore) • CIMB Thai (Malaysia) • OCBC (Singapore)	• Citibank • HSBC • Standard Chartered Bank

Source: Siregar and Lim (2010).

The Hong Kong Shanghai Banking Corporation (HSBC), Citibank and Standard Chartered Bank are the three major international banks that have wide and extensive branch networks in the Asian region. In addition to these three international powerhouses, the region has also witnessed the emergence of its own multinational banks. Malaysian banks such as the Malayan Banking Berhad (Maybank), Commerce International Merchant Bankers Berhad (CIMB), and Rashid Hussain Berhad (RHB) have expanded their networks into the Southeast Asian economies and beyond. A number of Singaporean banks, namely the Development Bank of Singapore (DBS), the United Overseas Bank (UOB) and the Overseas Chinese Bank Corporation (OCBC), have achieved similar success in their efforts to become regional banks.

4.4.2 Capacity Building towards an Integrated Surveillance Office

Given the openness and interconnectedness of the trade sectors and the financial sectors of the ASEAN+3 economies, well-integrated surveillance work at AMRO must encompass two areas of coverage: (a) bilateral and multilateral surveillance; and (b) macroeconomic and financial sector surveillance. By a simple definition, bilateral surveillance focuses more on an individual economy, whereas multilateral surveillance takes more global and regional perspectives. The importance of such an integrative approach to surveillance has become more apparent especially following the recent 2007/2008 global financial crisis, where strong linkages between these areas of coverage were seen. The G20 Summit in November 2008, for instance, strongly urged the IMF to give "greater attention to ... the financial sector" and better integrate "the reviews with the joint IMF/World Bank financial sector assessment programs [with a view to strengthening] the role of the IMF in providing macro-financial policy advice".[10]

Given AMRO's relatively small size and budget compared with other multilateral surveillance offices, AMRO needs to carefully leverage upon the benefits and synergies of being a small office in close contact with regional policymakers. Under the present arrangement, whereby AMRO economists are involved in the production of all major reports of the institution, namely the AMRO Regional Economic Monitoring (AREM) report (covering cross-country economic outlook and multilateral surveillance), individual economic surveillance reports (often referred to as bilateral surveillance) and thematic research reports under each area study unit, an integrated surveillance process has naturally been established. Despite its small size, AMRO benefits from a collaborative working arrangement among economists with a free flow of knowledge across different areas of expertise and interaction between multilateral and bilateral surveillance.[11]

Another advantage of the present set-up derives from the direct access AMRO has to senior officials in member countries. While critics are quick to criticize the non-public nature of the current peer-review process, it yields several benefits when compared to a completely public process. Providing confidential advice and constructive criticism of policies at the highest official levels throughout the year, rather than making criticism publicly, avoids the creation of barriers to effective communication and cooperation with country authorities. This has benefited AMRO's surveillance work, with authorities being more receptive to its analysis and more frank in discussions.

Furthermore, AMRO's surveillance process has tried to address the shortcomings of policy dialogue processes of the past. First, AMRO's surveillance reports are submitted on a quarterly basis directly to senior officials of the ministries of finance and the central banks. Twice a year, in March and December, these reports are presented and discussed during the meetings of vice ministers of the Ministries of Finance and deputy governors of the central banks of the ASEAN+3 economies. The surveillance reports are submitted only a week ahead of these high-level official meetings. Such a practice allows a frank discussion of issues without the usual revision and pre-screening of controversial issues, which has been common in regional and international policy dialogue, and a hindrance to effective policy dialogue in the past. Second, AMRO surveillance reports and analysis are presented directly to the high-level policymakers in charge of relevant areas. Third, not publishing reports and surveillance results can foster an environment more conducive to an exchange of views and perspectives between the AMRO team and the members' policymakers in a setting where authorities are more receptive and open to frank discussions and criticism, an often overlooked particularity of Asian culture. Fourth, the non-publication process also facilitates timely dissemination of the reports to all member countries' officials, and prevents delays arising from requests for revision by the relevant country's authorities.

A number of improvements should be considered to further strengthen the vital surveillance work at AMRO. The most urgent one is to strengthen research capacities to support the surveillance team. As briefly discussed and shown in Figure 4.2, three teams of economists were established at AMRO in the first half of 2012. The focus of each team was largely on bilateral macroeconomic surveillance. Each economist is assigned to either one or two economies and his or her main day-to-day duty is to closely monitor developments in those economies, focusing especially on areas of potential risks and vulnerabilities. Each economist is also assigned an area study unit on fiscal matters, monetary and exchange rate matters, or financial markets. So there are two units of economists at AMRO: the

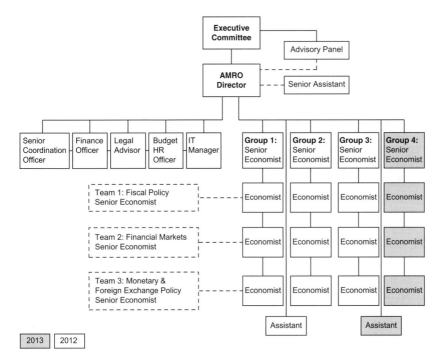

Source: AMRO.

Figure 4.2   AMRO's organizational structure as of July 2012

country surveillance unit (indicated as Groups 1–3 in Figure 4.2) and the area study unit. The area study unit in particular needs to be further developed and staffed strategically with experts and experienced professionals in each area.

A major weakness often highlighted in bilateral surveillance work is that analyses tend to focus too narrowly on the domestic economy and less on external factors, such as other regional economies and global financial markets. Hence, bringing on-board external and cross-country analyses into the country surveillance is critical and undoubtedly requires research support on the various pertinent and topical issues. The main responsibility of the economists in the area study unit is to carry out cross-country research on various thematic topics relevant to macroeconomic surveillance work on the ASEAN+3 economies[12] The high degree of interconnectedness of the banking sector of some of the ASEAN+3 economies, for instance, suggests a need to look into cross-border banking activities and carry out a comprehensive surveillance on the financial sectors of these economies. In this case, the primary responsibility of the area study unit would be to prepare an in-depth study of these globalized banking sectors to map, in particular, potential transmission channels of financial shocks from the banking sector arising from the activities of the global banks and regional ASEAN+3 banks. Recognizing the importance of financial stability risk, around 25 per cent of the content of AMRO Regional Economic Monitoring (AREM) reports has dealt with this issue. Moreover, the first thematic research carried out by the AMRO team was on the topic of a financial stress index. Acknowledging that the financial sectors of most ASEAN+3 economies are still dominated by banking, AMRO's second thematic study assessed the features, characteristics and implications of the globally interconnected banking sectors of these economies.

Given resource constraints, particularly in terms of personnel, as discussed earlier, it has been frequently suggested that AMRO should rely a lot more on the research and surveillance works carried out by global and national agencies, especially in the areas of multilateral surveillance (cross-country issues). Since the beginning of AMRO's surveillance work, there has been continuous engagement between AMRO's team of economists and their counterparts in multilateral agencies (e.g. IMF, ADB, World Bank, OECD), investment banks, universities and research institutions. During their consultation visits to the ASEAN+3 economies, AMRO's team visits representative offices of the global and regional multilaterals. AMRO economists have also hosted members of the IMF Article IV teams in their Singapore office and compared notes on the relevant economies. Such engagement, however, has been undertaken on a cooperative and unofficial basis; more official interaction which would entail joint-surveillance work, for instance, would need to be approved by the CMIM Executive Committee. Despite such interaction, AMRO must build its own research and expertise capacities. One challenge relates to the timeliness of information. Surveillance reports from other agencies tend to become available when they are already out of date for surveillance purposes. This has been especially true since the turbulent times the world economy has experienced from 2007–08, with the economic and financial landscape changing on a daily basis.

4.5   BRIEF CONCLUDING REMARKS

The 2007–08 global financial crisis has undoubtedly been a catalyst for the transformation of the CMI into the CMIM and the establishment of the ASEAN+3 Macroeconomic Research Office (AMRO). Considering that the CMIM was only established in 2010, the progress achieved within a period of only two years is testimony to the strong commitment of the

ASEAN+3 governments to strengthening regional financial cooperation. Alongside these accomplishments, however, significant questions on how to improve the effectiveness of the CMIM and AMRO remain, particularly on their capacities to become a regional financial safety net and credible surveillance unit for the ASEAN+3 economies.

Critics of the CMIM often dwell on the limited size of the available swap facility of only US$240 billion and other potential impediments to its effectiveness, such as limited resources for surveillance and limited experience with conditionalities. This chapter discussed some of these potential weaknesses and offers concrete solutions to overcome them. In particular the chapter underlines the need and the route to integrate the CMIM's multilateral swap facility with those of the bilateral facilities. The important issue of *ex-ante* and *ex-post* conditionalities has also been deliberated upon and lessons from the global experiences on designing conditionalities are considered for the disbursement of the CMIM facility. Regarding the surveillance work at AMRO, creating an integrated surveillance process takes center stage of discussion in the chapter.

In a nutshell, the CMIM has the strong support of ASEAN+3 governments and is the manifestation of these governments' pragmatic views on the need to build stronger regional financial cooperation, as much as possible to ring-fence their economies from shocks originating globally and from within the region. This commitment has provided a solid base for the early and future development of AMRO. While the resources at AMRO will not be as large as those of the regional and global multilateral surveillance offices such as the Asian Development Bank and the International Monetary Fund, this chapter touches on a number of advantages that AMRO can exploit to add value to the surveillance works on the economies of the region. Nevertheless, the CMIM and AMRO have to optimize the present momentum and opportunities to strengthen institutional capacities and thus to realize the visions of their founding fathers.

NOTES

1. Here ASEAN+3 includes the ASEAN economies (Brunei Darussalam, Cambodia, Indonesia, Lao PDR, Malaysia, Myanmar, Philippines, Thailand, Singapore, Viet Nam) and the Plus-3 (the PRC, Japan and the Republic of Korea), as well as Hong Kong, China.
2. The set of indicators is compiled to generate scorecards for each individual economy of the ASEAN+3.
3. The reports are submitted in March, June, September and November to early December every year.
4. Current members of AMRO's Advisory Panel include Dr Kang Jia, President, Research Institute for Fiscal Finance, People's Republic of China; Mr Shigeo Katsu, President, Nazarbayev University, Kazakhstan; Dr Junkyu Lee, senior international economic

advisor, Ministry of Strategy and Finance, Republic of Korea; Dato' Ooi Sang Kuang, special advisor, Bank Negara Malaysia; Dr Vincente B. Valdepenas Jr, consultant, Bangko Sentral ng Pilipinas; and Dr Chalongphob Sussangkarn, distinguished fellow, Thailand Development Research Institute (Advisory Panel chair).

5. There is a concern that a regional safety net mechanism such as the CMIM could potentially induce moral hazard within its own facility and also vis-à-vis global mechanisms such as the IMF (Sussangkarn 2011).
6. This was increased in May 2012, from a maturity and supporting period of 90 days and 1 year for the non-IMF-linked portion, and 90 days and 2 years for the IMF-linked portion, previously.
7. In fact, CMIM may be slightly stricter, as there are a number of *ex-ante* conditions and conditions precedents which need to be applied to all borrowers, while RFIs are emergency financing and thus condition-free.
8. The IMF's Precautionary and Liquidity Line (PLL), launched in November 2011, replaced the Precautionary Credit Line (PCL), and provided greater flexibility in its use than the PCL.
9. This average excludes Brunei Darussalam and Myanmar.
10. G-20 Summit Declaration on Financial Markets and the World Economy, Washington, DC, 15 November 2008.
11. As discussed in Takagi (2010), the area departments of the IMF work on individual country (bilateral) surveillance, whereas the research department focuses on multilateral surveillance.
12. Such an area study unit does not need to be large. At the early stage, three to four experienced economists should be the minimum size and as AMRO continues to grow the number should be increased.

REFERENCES

Bird, G. 2009. Reforming IMF conditionality: From 'streamlining' to 'major overhaul'. *World Economics*, **10**(3): July–September.
Eichengreen, B. and P. Luengnaruemitchai. 2006. Why doesn't Asia have bigger bond markets? BIS Papers chapters. In: *Asian Bond Markets: Issues and Prospects*. Vol. 30. Bank for International Settlements, pp. 40–77.
Independent Evaluation Office (IEO). 2007. Structural conditionality in IMF-supported programs. Evaluation Report. International Monetary Fund.
Jomo, K.S. 2011. Regional financial co-operation in East Asia. In: U. Volz and A. Caliari (eds) *Regional and Global Liquidity Arrangements*. Bonn, Germany: German Development Institute.
Shanmugaratnam, T. 2006. Asian monetary integration: Will it ever happen? Paper delivered for the Per Jacobsson Lecture.
Siregar, R.Y. and C.S.V. Lim. 2010. The role of central banks in sustaining economic recovery and in achieving financial stability. *Journal of Advanced Studies in Finance*, **1**: Summer.
Sussangkarn, C. 2011. Institutional building for macroeconomic and financial cooperation in East Asia. Mimeo.
Takagi, S. 2010. Regional surveillance for East Asia: How can it be designed to complement global surveillance? ADB Working Paper Series on Regional Economic Integration No. 50. Manila: Asian Development Bank.

5. Financial safety nets in Asia: genesis, evolution, adequacy and way forward*
Hal Hill and Jayant Menon

5.1 INTRODUCTION

The impetus for strengthening regional financial safety nets among Association of Southeast Asian Nations (ASEAN) countries came following the Asian Financial Crisis (AFC) of 1997–98, when the existing insurance mechanism in the form of the ASEAN Swap Arrangement (ASA) proved miserably inadequate. Forced to turn to the International Monetary Fund (IMF) for the massive bailouts required, and the resentment that ensued following the bitter medicine prescribed, a decision was taken to pursue a regional safety net that could provide a real alternative. The initial step was taken with the creation of the Chiang Mai Initiative (CMI) in 2000, which expanded the bilateral swaps of the ASA both in size and membership to include the People's Republic of China (PRC), Japan and the Republic of Korea. The CMI's first test came in September 2008 when, following the Lehman Brothers' collapse, short-term capital quickly exited emerging economies. However, members of the CMI that required liquidity support did not turn to it but instead rushed to secure bilateral swaps with the United States (US), the PRC, Japan, Australia and the multilaterals.

Once again, the regional financial safety net had failed its members. This brought about another significant change when in 2009, the CMI was multilateralized to become the Chiang Mai Initiative Multilateralization (CMIM), with the many swap lines now governed by a single agreement. This was soon followed by a number of other important changes, including the doubling in size to US$240 billion, increasing the share available without an IMF program to 30 per cent, and the setting up of its independent surveillance unit, the ASEAN+3 Macroeconomic Research Office (AMRO), in 2011. These are impressive developments, but are they enough to ensure that the CMIM will be called upon when the next crisis strikes? This is the key question that this chapter attempts to answer. And if it is not, what are the issues that still need to be addressed to make it viable, either as a co-financing facility with the IMF or as a stand-alone alternative?

The remainder of the chapter is in six sections. Section 5.2 looks at history, and traces the evolution of the ASA from its early beginnings to the CMI and its expansion. In section 5.3, we describe the basic structure and features of the CMIM and the AMRO. Some of the most significant developments to the CMIM have taken place recently, in the aftermath of the GFC, and these are discussed in section 5.4. Section 5.5 addresses the key question of the chapter as to whether these changes are sufficient to make the CMIM operationally viable. Since we find that it is still unlikely to be used, we canvass areas that need to be reformed, separating what is needed for it to work as a complement to the IMF from what more needs to be done for it to serve as a real alternative. Section 5.6 discusses the potential of CMIM as a complement to the IMF. Section 5.7 explores the viability of the CMIM as a stand-alone option and a final section concludes.

5.2 EARLY BEGINNINGS: FROM THE ASA TO THE CMI AND ITS EXPANSION

Although the impetus for strengthening regional financial safety nets among ASEAN countries came following the AFC, they have an even longer history than often recognized. Going back some three and a half decades to August 1977, the first step was taken when central banks and monetary authorities of the original five ASEAN5 – Indonesia, Malaysia, Philippines, Singapore and Thailand – agreed to establish reciprocal currency or swap arrangements. The ASEAN Swap Arrangement (ASA) was created primarily to provide liquidity support for those experiencing balance of payments difficulties. Originally intended to be in effect for just one year, the arrangement has been extended incrementally, while coverage and amounts involved have expanded significantly. The initial maximum total amount available for swap transactions under the ASA was initially a meager US$100 million, with the maximum total outstanding amount provided by each participant limited to US$20 million, but this was subsequently increased to US$200 million in 1978.

Nothing much happened with the ASA for about the next two decades and when the AFC struck, the amounts available were nowhere near adequate. The ASA was basically useless, but the AFC highlighted the need to revisit the issue to see what needed to be done in order to have an effective regional insurance scheme. This was driven in large part by the way in which the IMF managed the rescue programs. Three of the four crisis-affected countries, Indonesia, the Republic of Korea and Thailand, had to accept an IMF program, the quid pro quo for international support – the fourth, Malaysia, went it alone. The IMF grew extremely unpopular, not just for the prescribed bitter medicine, but because it had misdiagnosed the problems – a fact that it later acknowledged.

There was a resurgence of nationalist sentiment that quickly grew regional. The Japanese government proposed an alternative "Asian Monetary Fund" but, neglecting to consult the PRC first, there was insufficient regional support to counter predictable US opposition. Notwithstanding this, the first step was taken soon after in May 2000 with the launch of the CMI. Announced at the ASEAN+3 Finance Ministers' Meeting (AFMM+3) in the Thai city after which it is named, it initially expanded ASA to all ASEAN members. In November 2000, the total amount available for swap transactions was increased from US$200 million to US$1 billion. After expanding the ASA to include the new ASEAN economies, bilateral swap agreements (BSAs) were initiated in 2002 between the original ASEAN5 countries and the "plus 3" of the PRC, Japan and the Republic of Korea. The BSAs grew from US$17 billion in 2002 to US$31.5 billion in 2003 and US$36.4 billion in 2004. In May 2005, during the 8th AFMM+3, the amount of the ASA was doubled to US$2 billion.

But the action continued to center around the BSAs rather than the ASA, and the number of BSAs and the amounts involved continued to grow over time. By the time of the AFMM+3 in Madrid in May 2008, the size of the BSA had increased to US$84 billion (Table 5.1).

5.3 CMIM AND AMRO: BASIC STRUCTURE AND SALIENT FEATURES

If the AFC lit the fuse for the need to transform the ASA into the CMI, then the Global Financial Crisis (GFC) of 2008 highlighted the continued inefficacy of that transformation. As with the AFC, the regional safety net was inadequate when the GFC hit. Given the CMI's small size and absence of rapid-response mechanisms, affected countries resorted to bilateral swaps with the US, Japan, Australia and multilateral agencies. The meetings of the AFMM+3 that followed agreed to radically transform the CMI in other ways. First, the finance ministers decided to expedite the multilateralization of the CMI. They agreed that funds available under the multilateralized CMI (CMIM) should be a self-managed reserve pooling arrangement, governed by a single contract, reducing costly and

Table 5.1 *Swap arrangements under the Chiang Mai Initiative (as of December 2008)*

To/From	PRC	Japan	Rep. of Korea	Indonesia	Malaysia	Philippines	Singapore	Thailand	Total
PRC		3.0	4.0	4.0	1.5	2.0		2.0	16.5
Japan	3.0		13.0	6.0	1.0	6.0	3.0	6.0	38.0
Rep. of Korea	4.0	8.0		2.0	1.5	2.0		1.0	18.5
Indonesia			2.0						2.0
Malaysia			1.5						1.5
Philippines		0.5	2.0						2.5
Singapore		1.0							1.0
Thailand		3.0	1.0						4.0
Cambodia									0.0
Lao PDR									0.0
Myanmar									0.0
Viet Nam									0.0
Sub-total	**7.0**	**15.5**	**23.5**	**12.0**	**4.0**	**10.0**	**3.0**	**9.0**	**84.0**
ASEAN Swap Agreement (ASA; among the 10 ASEAN countries)									**2.0**
TOTAL									**86.0**

Source: Elaborations based on Japan's Ministry of Finance website. Available from: http://www.mof.go.jp/english/index.htm (accessed February 2009).

wasteful duplication. The finance ministers also confirmed that the proportion of the contribution between ASEAN and the plus three countries to the CMI would be 20 per cent for ASEAN, and 80 per cent for Japan, the PRC and the Republic of Korea (Japan and the PRC would contribute identical shares of the total reserve pool, 32 per cent, double the Republic of Korea's share). Second, they agreed to further expand the pool of foreign-currency reserves. The size of the fund thus grew from US$36.5 billion in 2001–05 to US$84 billion in 2008, and to US$120 billion in May 2009. The CMIM came into effect on 24 March 2010.

5.3.1 CMIM

The CMIM operates as a common US dollar liquidity pool: a member state can swap its local currency for US dollars from this pool in the event of a balance of payments (BOP) or liquidity crisis. As a self-managed reserve pooling system, contributions remain in the individual central banks of member countries and are not actually paid into a common or centralized fund. The availability of CMIM funds to a particular member country is limited by its borrowing quota (Table 5.2). The maximum amount that each country can borrow is based on its contribution multiplied by its respective borrowing multiplier. The multiplier coefficient of the CMIM's borrowing quotas is designed to favor the smaller ASEAN economies. The borrowing multiplier for Brunei Darussalam, Cambodia, Lao PDR, Myanmar and Viet Nam is therefore set at 5. For the rest, the borrowing multiplier is set at 2.5 for Hong Kong, China; Indonesia; Malaysia; Singapore; and Thailand; at 1 for the Republic of Korea; and at 0.5 for Japan and the PRC.

An economy which requests drawings has to meet conditions before voting for a swap request. These include a completed review of the economic and financial situation, compliance with covenants, such as submission of a periodic surveillance report, and participation in the ASEAN+3 Economic Review and Policy Dialogue (ERPD). These are hardly stringent conditions, and should not pose a problem for most, if not all, of the member countries. It is not the stringency of the requirements that is a problem, but rather the time involved. For instance, it is unclear how long a review of the economic and financial situation will take to complete, but it is unlikely to be quick, in terms of how time is measured when an emergency exists. In addition to these potentially time-consuming requirements, the actual activation procedures can add up to two weeks' delay.

To access the CMIM, a member must submit a request to the coordinating countries, that is, the two co-chairs of the ASEAN+3 Finance Minister Process (one from ASEAN and the other from +3 countries). The

Table 5.2 Contributions, borrowing multipliers and voting power under the CMIM

Economies	Financial contribution (billion US$)	Share (%)	Purchasing multiple	Maximum swap amount (billion US$)	Basic votes	Votes based on contribution	Voting power	
								%
Plus Three	**192.00**	**80.00**		**117.30**	**9.6**	**192.00**	**201.6**	**71.59**
PRC (excl. Hong Kong, China)	68.4	28.5	0.5	34.2	3.2	68.4	71.6	25.43
PRC Hong Kong, China	8.4	3.5	2.5	6.3	0.0	8.4	8.4	2.98
Japan	76.80	32.00	0.5	38.40	3.20	76.80	80.00	28.41
Rep. of Korea	38.40	16.00	1	38.40	3.20	38.40	41.60	14.77
ASEAN	**48.00**	**20.00**		**126.20**	**32.00**	**48.000**	**80.00**	**28.41**
Indonesia	9.104	3.793	2.5	22.76	3.20	9.104	12.304	4.369
Thailand	9.104	3.793	2.5	22.76	3.20	9.104	12.304	4.369
Malaysia	9.104	3.793	2.5	22.76	3.20	9.104	12.304	4.369
Singapore	9.104	3.793	2.5	22.76	3.20	9.104	12.304	4.369
Philippines	9.104	3.793	2.5	22.76	3.20	9.104	12.304	4.369
Viet Nam	2.00	0.833	5	10.00	3.20	2.00	5.20	1.847
Cambodia	0.24	0.100	5	1.20	3.20	0.24	3.44	1.222
Myanmar	0.12	0.050	5	0.60	3.20	0.12	3.32	1.179
Brunei Dar.	0.06	0.025	5	0.30	3.20	0.06	3.26	1.158
Lao PDR	0.06	0.025	5	0.30	3.20	0.06	3.26	1.158
Total	**240.00**	**100.00**		**243.50**	**41.60**	**240.00**	**281.60**	**100.00**

Note: Brunei Dar. = Brunei Darussalam.

Source: The Joint Statement of the 15th ASEAN+3 Finance Ministers and Central Bank Governors' Meeting (2012), 3 May, Manila.

coordinating countries deliver the swap request notice and other relevant information to the Executive Level Decision Making Body (ELDMB), a non-resident body. They then need to convene a meeting to decide on the swap request. The ELDMB must respond to the swap request within two weeks of receipt of the swap request notice. Decisions on drawings are made by a two-thirds majority (weighted voting system linked to contributions) of the ELDMB. Once the request is approved, the swap-providing countries transfer the funds to the account of the swap-requesting party, who in turn transfers the equivalent amount in local currencies to the accounts of swap-providing countries (AMRO 2012; BSP 2012; ASEAN Secretariat 2010).

In a comparison with other regional safety nets, Henning (2004, p. 61) concluded that "the Chiang Mai Initiative is more sensitive to preserving the central position of the IMF and not undercutting the IMF in negotiations with borrowing countries than these other arrangements". Although there have been changes since, the basic central relationship with the IMF remains. Up until recently, a country could draw up to 20 per cent of its quota without being subject to IMF conditionality. Should a country avail of its full quota, the remainder of the amount to be disbursed would be tied to an IMF program. This link was intended to address moral hazard issues, and to make up for the lack of an independent surveillance unit that could oversee the CMI's operations. The eventual establishment of AMRO in 2011 has led to a reconsideration of this link.

5.3.2   AMRO

During its May 2009 meeting in Bali, the AFMM+3 agreed to establish an ancillary institution in the form of an independent regional surveillance unit, AMRO. AMRO was incorporated on 20 April 2011 as a company limited by guarantee under the Companies Act, Cap. 50, of the Republic of Singapore. It commenced operations one month after, in May 2011.

The need for an independent surveillance unit was predicated on the multilateralization of the CMI. In a multilateralized setting, monitoring and surveillance had to be enhanced to detect emerging vulnerabilities. CMIM decision-making also had to be supported by an independent unit with a due diligence function, so that the borrowing countries' capacity to meet repayment conditions of lending countries could be assessed. Unconditional financing when there is a need for policy correction could create moral hazard, both for potential borrowers and for international investors, even when it does not adversely affect the prospect for timely repayment.

AMRO's activities are divided into functions during so-called peace time and crisis time. During peace or non-crisis periods, AMRO's main responsibility is to prepare quarterly consolidated reports on the overall macroeconomic assessment of the ASEAN+3 region as well as on individual ASEAN+3 countries. Should a crisis occur, however, its role and responsibilities multiply. During crisis time, AMRO is tasked to: (a) provide an analysis of the economic and financial situation of the CMIM swap-requesting country; (b) monitor the use and impact of the funds disbursed under the CMIM Agreement; and (c) monitor the compliance by the CMIM swap-requesting country with any lending covenants to the CMIM Agreement.

AMRO is governed by an Executive Committee (EC) comprised of deputy finance ministers and deputy central bank governors of member countries. The EC oversees AMRO and is responsible for providing guidance, setting broad policy direction for the management of AMRO, and appointing the AMRO director and advisory panel members. An advisory panel consisting of six members provides strategic, technical and professional guidance to AMRO. The panel is independent from the director and staff of AMRO, and is accountable to the EC.

At present, AMRO is being run by a small complement of 12 professional staff, led by the AMRO director. There are plans to expand the complement of professional staff initially to 16 in the near future. Since its establishment in 2011, AMRO has initiated a secondment scheme, and created linkages with international financial institutions and various authorities in CMIM member countries. AMRO has also conducted a number of surveillance visits in the region, and presented economic review and policy dialogue reports at recent meetings of ASEAN+3 Finance and Central Bank Deputies.

5.4 POST-CMIM DEVELOPMENTS

The ongoing uncertainty over the recovery in the US and the crisis in the euro area have highlighted the need to further strengthen the CMIM's capacity to act as a regional financial safety net (Azis 2012). To address this need, the 15th Meeting of ASEAN+3, held on the sidelines of the Asian Development Bank (ADB)'s Annual Meeting in Manila in May 2012, agreed to do the following: (a) double the total size of the CMIM from US$120 billion to US$240 billion; (b) increase the IMF de-linked portion to 30 per cent in 2012 with a view to increasing it to 40 per cent in 2014, subject to review should conditions warrant; and (c) introduce a crisis prevention facility.

These three outcomes were the key decisions announced at this meeting. Another change of an institutional nature that occurred there was the upgrading of the AFMM+3 to the ASEAN+3 Finance Ministers and

Central Bank Governors' Meeting (AFMGM+3). For the first time, the central bank governors of the 13 member countries and the head of the Monetary Authority of Hong Kong, China were invited to participate in this forum. This was an important development in that it brought together officials responsible for tax and expenditure programs with those handling monetary and exchange rate policies. The crisis prevention facility was introduced in response to calls for *ex-ante* liquidity support similar to those of the IMF – the Flexible Credit Line (FCL) and the Precautionary Credit Line (PCL) – introduced in the wake of the global financial crisis.[1]

As such, the CMIM will now have two separate instruments: a short-term liquidity support facility to address sudden but temporary liquidity shortages, and a crisis resolution facility to address more medium-term liquidity and structural problems. The crisis prevention mechanism will be called the CMIM Precautionary Line (CMIM-PL), while the crisis resolution mechanism will be called the CMIM Stability Facility (CMIM-SF). To be able to access the CMIM-PL, the requesting country must meet the following criteria as *ex-ante* qualifications and *ex-post* conditionality: (i) external position and market access; (ii) fiscal policy; (iii) monetary policy; (iv) financial sector soundness and supervision; and (v) data adequacy.[2]

The total amount that can be drawn by each member country, either for prevention or resolution purposes, shall be within the maximum swap amount set aside for that country. Dual-drawing from both CMIM-SF and CMIM-PL shall be restricted, with the CMIM-SF replacing the CMIM-PL if the recipient party is hit by a crisis and needs additional support. For the CMIM-PL, the duration of access is six months with three renewals, totaling two years in arrangement period. Maturity is at six months for the IMF-de-linked portion and one year for the IMF-linked portion. Monitoring will be conducted on a biannual basis. For the CMIM-SF, the maturity of the IMF de-linked portion is set at six months with three renewals allowed, totaling up to two years in supporting period. Maturity of the IMF-linked portion is set at one year with two renewals possible, totaling up to three years in supporting period. As with the CMIM-PL, monitoring is also to be conducted on a biannual basis.[3]

5.5 THE WAY FORWARD: FILLING IN THE REMAINING GAPS IN THE REGIONAL SAFETY NET

The agreements reached at the recently concluded 15th Meeting of ASEAN+3 Finance Ministers and Central Bank Governors represent a significant step towards transforming the CMIM into a more formidable regional financial safety net. This notwithstanding, the key question remains as to whether these changes, however significant, are actually sufficient to make the CMIM an option that members are likely to turn to in the event of a liquidity crisis. And as of now, it only makes sense to think of the CMIM as catering for a liquidity crisis, and not a fiscal one requiring a structural adjustment program. So, the question is, have these changes made the CMIM useable to counter a liquidity crisis? And if so, useable in what way? There are two options. At the moment, the CMIM is set up to act as a co-financing mechanism with the IMF. This is not to downplay its role but rather to recognize that the bulk of its resources are tied to an IMF program. From Table 5.3, which describes and compares the salient features of the other regional financial mechanisms that exist around the world, we can see that most also operate in a somewhat similar fashion. This is the first and current prospect. The other option is for it to operate as an independent mechanism, serving as an alternative to the IMF. It is worth noting that "alternative" in this context does not necessarily mean excluding any role for the IMF, but rather one where the CMIM plays the lead or dominant role.

Despite the significant changes made, it appears that the CMIM, as it currently stands, can do neither. In its current configuration, it is unlikely that the regional safety net will be called upon at all, as evidenced by the fact that it has never been used despite the need for liquidity by several members during the GFC. At the moment, it is neither a complement nor an alternative to the IMF. We now examine what is required in terms of operationalizing each of these two options.

For the CMIM to serve its immediate function as a complement to the IMF, a number of issues relating to operating procedures need to be resolved. Fixing these procedural problems is also necessary for making it viable as an alternative to the IMF, but not sufficient. For it to evolve into an alternative to the IMF some longer-term issues relating to size, membership and surveillance capacity need consideration as well.

5.6   CMIM AS A COMPLEMENT TO THE IMF

Irrespective of whether the CMIM is to be a complement or an alternative to the IMF, it needs to urgently address the speed and efficiency with which requests for assistance can be activated. As noted earlier, a request for emergency support could take up to two weeks to process. There is also some uncertainty over the steps involved, precise information to be provided and the like (Azis 2012). Part of the problem lies with the fact that the CMIM is not a fund, but rather a reserve pooling system whereby country contributions remain with the respective central banks or monetary authority. The fact that the decision also rests with a high-level, non-resident body further increases the risk of delay. The EC as the decision-making body is after all comprised of deputy finance ministers and deputy central bank governors of member countries.

The real competitor to the CMIM-IMF option is bilateral swaps, and other similar standby arrangements. These are not only fast-disbursing but also come without explicit conditionalities as they are adequately collateralized, in most cases. Although the introduction of the CMIM-PL was supposed to help improve the flexibility and timeliness of liquidity support to address short-term liquidity problems, the procedural issues mentioned earlier combined with its continued linkage to an IMF program may very well undermine its actual usefulness. As noted earlier, countries have been reluctant to apply for financing under the IMF's own crisis prevention facilities for fear of adverse signaling effects (Pickford 2011).

It has been suggested that linkage to a standard IMF program should not be required in the case of temporary, short-term liquidity problems. Sussangkarn (2011) argues that an IMF program should only be invoked if a country needs to roll over the swap more than a certain predetermined number of times, with the IMF joining the battle only if the problem becomes a more medium-term structural problem. Under the CMIM's current arrangements, this would mean that the linkage would only apply to financing under the CMIM-SF. By not invoking an IMF link immediately, countries with temporary liquidity problems will be more willing to use the CMIM if they feel that the funds would be available without delay. At the same time, knowing that an IMF link will be required after a certain period will encourage the country to take appropriate corrective actions to avoid having to be under an IMF program. This could go a long way towards making the CMIM-IMF option viable as a liquidity support mechanism. But the largest contributors, Japan and the PRC, who are in essence "creditors" because they can withdraw less than the amount they have put in (multiplier of 0.5) must feel that their contributions are secure under such an arrangement. With AMRO still in its infancy, it is likely that they will continue to seek "cover" from IMF involvement to ensure that their funds are safeguarded, even when used for short-term liquidity support.

5.7   CMIM AS AN ALTERNATIVE TO THE IMF

Next we turn to the viability of the CMIM as a stand-alone option, or one without IMF involvement. At present, this applies only if a country avails itself of up to 30 per cent of its quota. There are basically three outstanding issues that need to be addressed in order to further strengthen the viability

Table 5.3   Regional safety nets and financing mechanisms: salient features

	Year established	Purpose	Resources	Members
Multilateralized Chiang Mai Initiative	2000	Address short-term liquidity and balance of payments difficulties in the region and supplement the existing multilateral financial arrangements.	US$240 billion. Members commit to provide financial support within the agreed amount of contribution. Funds are transferred from the central banks/monetary authorities only when a request for drawing is made.	ASEAN + PRC, Japan and Rep. of Korea.
Arab Monetary Fund	1976	Broad, including correct balance-of-payments disequilibria, support structural reforms in private financing and banking, and promote exchange rate stability.	US$2.7 billion. The Arab Monetary Fund may borrow from member countries, Arab and foreign monetary and financial institutions and markets, and can issue securities.	22 Arab countries in North Africa and Middle East.
Latin American Reserve Fund	1991, as successor to the Andean Reserve Fund	Support member countries' balance of payments through credit and guarantees.	US$2.34 billion. FLAR has an AA Composite credit rating.	Bolivia, Colombia, Ecuador, Costa Rica, Peru, Uruguay and Venezuela.

Functions	Instruments	Decision-making/ governance	Link to IMF	Recent Activity
Lending and surveillance (through AMRO)	Members swap their local currencies with US dollars up to a multiple of their contributions to the scheme. The 90-day swaps can be renewed up to seven times.	Decisions on drawings made by 2/3 majority at the Executive Level Decision-Making Body consisting of deputy level representatives of the ASEAN+3 Finance Ministries and Central Banks and the Monetary Authority of Hong Kong, China. Voting power is distributed to members according to the amount of contribution, supplemented by basic votes allocated equally.	Initially, a country could draw up to 20% of its quota without being subject to IMF conditionality. This amount was increased to 30% in 2012 and potentially 40% in 2014. Drawing of the remaining amount is conditional on the existence of an IMF-supported program.	None.
Lending	Mix of six lending facilities to address both short-term liquidity problems and medium-term structural problems, including an unconditional automatic loan facility, and an ordinary loan facility tied to an IMF program.	Executive Board composed of the chairman and eight members elected by the Board of Governors. 2/3 majority required for a quorum.	Access to ordinary loan facility must be accompanied by an IMF program.	Four new loans in 2010 amounting to $548 million, the highest level of lending in the past two decades.
Lending and surveillance	Five types of lending instruments: balance of payments credit, foreign debt	Each member country has the same voting power (one vote) irrespective of their paid-in capital.	No official links, although FLAR shares information with IMF unofficially.	Balance of payments loan to Ecuador in 2009. Historically, FLAR has been

Table 5.3   (continued)

	Year established	Purpose	Resources	Members
North American Framework Agreement	1994	Provide short-term liquidity support.	US$9 billion.	United States, Canada and Mexico.
European Financial Stabilization Mechanism	2010	Provide external financial assistance to a member state experiencing, or seriously threatened with, a severe economic and financial disturbance caused by exceptional circumstances beyond such member states' control.	€60 billion. Funding is obtained by issuing own instruments in euros. The maximum financing capacity of the EFSM is €60 billion and is backed by a European Union (EU) budget guarantee.	All EU members.
European Financial Stability Facility	2010	Preserve financial stability of Europe's monetary union by providing temporary assistance to euro-area member states in difficulties, i.e. unable to borrow on markets at acceptable rates,	€440 billion. Funding is obtained by issuing own debt instruments or by entering into other financing arrangements with financial and monetary institutions.	All members of euro area.

Functions	Instruments	Decision-making/ governance	Link to IMF	Recent Activity
	restructuring of central banks, liquidity credit, contingent credit and treasury credit.	Decisions are made by a 3/4 majority.	No official links, although FLAR shares information with IMF unofficially.	relevant particularly for the smaller member countries.
Lending	Two-way bilateral central bank swaps for 90-days, renewable up to one year	Disbursal only requires bilateral agreement between two participating countries.	US Treasury requires letter from IMF Managing Director.	None.
Lending	Loans and credit lines. Amount, average duration (normally about five years), and disbursement terms of a loan or credit line are decided by the Council, based on funding conditions.	Financial assistance is granted by a decision by the Council, acting by a qualified majority on a proposal from the Commission. Policy conditionality is defined by the Commission in consultation with the European Central Bank (ECB) and spelled out in a MoU. The Commission is delegated the authority to monitor the program and approve disbursements. ECB is involved in program design and monitoring, and as paying agent.	While legally the EFSM allows financing solely by the EU, the ECOFIN Council has explicitly stated that activation would only be in the context of a joint EU/ IMF program.	Activated for Ireland (2010) and Portugal (2011).
Lending	Loans and bond purchases through the primary market. Funding instruments under the EFSF are expected to have the same financial profile as the related loans but	Key decisions under the EFSF Framework agreement are reserved to euro area member states and generally require unanimity, including the decision to approve loan facility agreements and disbursements under	The framework agreement establishes that financial support by the EFSF is to be provided in conjunction with the Fund and subject to	Activated for Ireland (2010), Portugal (2011), and Greece (2011).

Table 5.3　　(continued)

	Year established	Purpose	Resources	Members
		caused by exceptional circumstances beyond such member states' control.	Guarantees by euro-area member states to the EFSF are on a pro rata basis, in accordance with their share in the paid-up capital of the European Central Bank (ECB).	All members of euro area
European Stability Mechanism	Entry into force on July 2012	Permanent crisis management mechanism to safeguard financial stability in the euro area as a whole, replacing temporary solutions such as the EFSM and the EFSF.	€500 billion	All members of euro area.

Sources:　Authors' compilation drawing upon information from IMF (2010a); Arab Monetary Fund (2011); ECB (2011); Lamberte and Morgan (2012); Park (2011).

of this option. These relate to: size, membership and surveillance capacity. Although these reforms are desirable, they are not equally important. Some are complementary, such as size of the fund and country membership, while building up surveillance capacity and credibility of AMRO could make the small size or membership of the CMIM less binding a constraint.

Functions	Instruments	Decision-making/ governance	Link to IMF	Recent Activity
Lending	the guarantors may permit EFSF to use a degree of funding flexibility as regards the currency, timing, interest rate base and maturity of the funding instruments.	such agreements. ECB is involved in program design and monitoring, and as paying agent.	conditionality set out in a MoU negotiated in liaison with the IMF and the ECB. IMF provided co-financing for Ireland, Portugal and Greece programs.	
Lending	Assistance will predominantly take the form of loans, known as ESM stability support (ESS). ESS will be conditional on agreement to and compliance with a strict macroeconomic adjustment program. The maturity of the ESS loans will depend on the nature of the imbalances and the beneficiary country's prospects of regaining access to financial markets.	Key decisions in relation to the ESM will be taken by its Board of Governors. A second decision-making body, the Board of Directors, will be responsible for specific tasks delegated by the Board of Governors. ECB involved in conducting debt sustainability analysis, program design and monitoring, and as paying agent.	ESM financial assistance will only be activated upon receipt by the Eurogroup and ECOFIN Presidents, and the Managing Director of the IMF, of a request from a euro area country. Following this request, the IMF will be involved in assessing whether there is a risk to the financial stability of the euro area as a whole, conducting debt sustainability analysis, program design, negotiation and monitoring.	None

5.7.1 Further Increasing the Size of the CMIM

The crisis in the euro area is a potent reminder of the massive amounts of financing required to stem a systemic liquidity crisis. Although the euro area crisis had its roots in fiscal insolvency, the point remains that the sums involved in a bailout for any kind of crisis that spreads across regional countries is likely to be massive. Although the CMIM's size has been increased substantially since 2008 to currently stand at US$240 billion, it is unlikely to be sufficient if there is a full-blown systemic crisis in East Asia, especially if it spreads across several members. During the AFC, Thailand received over US$17 billion in emergency liquidity. Yet Thailand (and the other original ASEAN members) can access only a fraction of this amount, about US$7 billion in today's dollars, from the CMIM without an IMF program. Indonesia received almost six times (US$40 billion) of what is its de-linked portion of the CMIM, or an even greater multiple if converted into today's dollars. The Republic of Korea was the other crisis-hit country that availed itself of an IMF-led program that totaled US$57 billion, when today its full quota with the CMIM is about US$38 billion.

For the CMIM to be a viable stand-alone option, either the size of the overall fund or the percentage of the de-linked portion needs to be increased substantially before it is attractive to the original ASEAN5 members. These countries have bilateral swaps that they are more likely to call upon should a crisis hit, as recent experience has shown. From Table 5.4, we can see that the Philippines has bilateral swaps with the PRC, Japan and the Republic of Korea; Indonesia has them with the PRC and Japan; while Singapore, Thailand and Malaysia each have swaps with the PRC. These are the ones that are currently in force, but others are up for renegotiation, as listed in Table 5.5. If national reserves are the first line of defense in the event of a liquidity crisis, bilateral swaps are designed to supplement them. But these bilateral swaps themselves might be insurance against a regional insurance scheme like the CMIM when it is perceived to be unusable.

It is apparent that the CMIM was never intended for use by the Republic of Korea or its two other biggest contributors, the PRC and Japan. This point has been reinforced by the bilateral swaps between these three countries announced virtually in tandem with the doubling of the Initiative. The Plus Three countries have also agreed to promote investment by the foreign reserve authorities in one another's government bonds.

So if the CMIM was never intended for use by its largest contributors, and if country quotas of the original five ASEAN countries are insufficient when judged by the experience of the AFC, could the CMIM be used by ASEAN's newer, smaller members? After all, for these countries, their full quotas are a quite substantial share of their individual reserves (Table 5.6). Nevertheless, they may still be insufficient for a bailout. For example, Cambodia's contribution of US$240 million enables it to borrow up to five times that amount but only US$360 million if it wants to avoid signing

Table 5.4   Bilateral swap agreements, ASEAN+3 economies, in force

Country	Partner	Amount	Effectivity
Japan	Rep. of Korea	US$30 billion Won-to Yen-swap Additional US$30 billion Dollar-to-local currency swap	Oct 2011–Oct 2012 (one year)
	Philippines	Philippines: US$6 billion from Japan Japan: US$500 million from the Philippines	May 2012–May 2015 (3 years)
Rep. of Korea	Japan	US$30 billion Won-to-Yen-swap Additional US$30 billion Dollar-to-local currency swap	Oct 2011–Oct 2012 (one year)
	PRC	US$56 billion	Oct 2011–Oct 2014 (3 years)
PRC	Rep. of Korea	US$56 billion	Oct 2011–Oct 2014 (3 years)
	Hong Kong, China	US$63 billion	Nov 2011–Nov 2014 (3 years)
	Malaysia	US$28.6 billion	Feb 2012–Feb 2015 (3 years)
	Singapore	US$22.12 billion	July 2010–July 2013 (3 years)
	Thailand	US$11 billion	Dec 2011–Dec 2014 (3 years)

Sources:
Bank of Japan website. Available at: http://www.boj.or.jp/en/intl_finance/cooperate/index.htm/.
ROK Ministry of Foreign Affairs and Trade. ROK expands currency swap with Japan and China. Available at: http://news.mofat.go.kr/enewspaper/articleview.php?master=&aid=3974&ssid=24&mvid=1219.
Reuters. Philippines renews $6 billion swap deal with Japan, gets Korean loan. 4 May 2012. Available at: http://af.reuters.com/article/worldNews/idAFBRE8430M520120504.
Centralbanking.com. Malaysia and China extend currency swap arrangement. 8 Feb 2012. Available at: http://www.centralbanking.com/central-banking/news/2144895/malaysia-china-extend-currency-swap-arrangement.
Bloomberg News. China, Hong Kong Expand Currency-Swap Pact to $63 Billion. 22 Nov 2011. Available at: http://www.businessweek.com/news/2011-11-22/china-hong-kong-expand-currency-swap-pact-to-63-billion.html.
Bangkok Post. China, govt sign currency swap deal. 23 Dec 2011. Available at: http://www.bangkokpost.com/news/asia/272071/china-govt-sign-currency-swap-deal.
China Daily. China signs currency swap pact with Singapore. 23 July 2010. Available at: http://www.chinadaily.com.cn/china/2010-07/23/content_11043563.htm.
MNI Deutsche Boerse Group. China Data Table: PBOC Currency Swap Agreements. 26 June 2012. Available at: https://mninews.deutsche-boerse.com/content/china-data-table-pboc-currency-swap-agreements-2.

Table 5.5   Bilateral swap agreements, ASEAN+3 countries, up for renegotiation

Country	Partner country	Amount	Last BSA signed (Year)
Japan	Indonesia	US$12 billion	2009, but under the CMI
Rep. of Korea	Philippines	US$2 billion	2008
PRC	Indonesia	US$16 billion	2009
	Philippines	US$2 billion	2007

Sources:
Bank of Japan website. Available at: http://www.boj.or.jp/en/intl_finance/cooperate/index.
htm/.
MNI Deutsche Boerse Group. China Data Table: PBOC Currency Swap Agreements.
26 June 2012. Available at: https://mninews.deutsche-boerse.com/content/
china-data-table-pboc-currency-swap-agreements-2.
The Standard. Swap pool to hit US$120b. 23 Feb 2009.
Available at: http://www.thestandard.com.hk/news_detail.
asp?pp_cat=5&art_id=78611&con_type=1&d_str=20090223.
Manila Bulletin. BSP Reviews Bilateral Swap Arrangements. 28 May 2012. Available at:
http://mb.com.ph/node/360671/b.

Table 5.6   Total reserves minus gold (current US$ million), CMIM economies, latest available data

Economy	Total reserves	As of
Brunei Darussalam	1693	2011 Aug.
Cambodia	3640	2012 Feb.
Hong Kong, China	294493	2012 Mar.
PRC	3326602	2012 Mar.
Indonesia	106611	2012 Mar.
Japan	1248875	2012 Apr.
Rep. of Korea	313801	2012 Mar.
Lao PDR	703	2010 Dec.
Malaysia	133991	2012 Apr.
Myanmar	6732	2011 Sep.
Philippines	65685	2012 Mar.
Singapore	243582	2012 Mar.
Thailand	170729	2012 Apr.
Viet Nam	14815	2011 Oct.
Total	**5931952**	

Source: IMF International Financial Statistics.

on to an IMF program. As of February 2012, Cambodia's total reserves (less gold) stood at US$3.64 billion, which is just more than three times its borrowing limit with the CMIM. Should a crisis strike, and given the small size of Cambodia's country quota as a share of its reserves, Cambodia could either rely on its own reserves or would need to go beyond the CMIM, depending on the severity of the crisis. The same is likely to be true of the other new members of ASEAN.

But the smaller, poorer economies of ASEAN+3 – Cambodia, Lao PDR, Myanmar and Viet Nam (CLMV) – face another potential risk by being part of the CMIM. To illustrate, consider a situation where some other country faces a liquidity crisis and decides that it will call upon the CMIM for at least part of its emergency funding needs. If this happens, the CLMV, like other members except the requesting country, will be called upon to contribute to their share (the "contribution" column in Table 5.2) of the rescue. As noted above, the contributions of the CLMV as a share of their respective national reserves are significant, and we could have a situation where the poorest economies are assisting in bailing out a much richer economy. If the requesting economy is afflicted by a crisis that is not purely domestic or of its own making, the possibility of contagion raises the level of vulnerability of other economies, and further increases the cost of having to contribute to its bailout. We have seen this happen during the euro area crisis when Slovakia, a much poorer country, contributed to Greece's bailout package. The CMIM Agreement does provide for an opt-out or escape clause, but this requires either the approval of the EC or the existence of highly extenuating circumstances.[4] If one or more countries start opting out, and if this leads to a domino or snowballing effect, the CMIM will simply fail to deliver. The associated loss of credibility may be irreversible.

It has been suggested that member economies may have to move away from self-insurance in the form of holding large foreign reserves, and start shifting funds towards the CMIM. Apart from further increasing member economies' contributions to the CMIM, Sussangkarn (2011) also proposes attaching additional bilateral swaps from willing member economies to a CMIM swap. Although this is an interesting proposal, the question as to why bilateral swaps are being pursued in tandem with the CMIM needs to be answered first. If it is to circumvent the procedural difficulties and associated delays, these issues need to be addressed before any such linkage is likely to be possible. As noted earlier, it may well be the case that these bilateral swaps are being pursued as an alternative defense mechanism to the CMIM and therefore attaching them to the CMIM is either unlikely to be favored, if CMIM procedures apply, or purely cosmetic, if they do not.

If this is indeed the case with the CMIM, even the seemingly innocuous statement by Takehiko Nakao, Japan's Vice Finance Minister for International Affairs, that "having this kind of mechanism is better than having nothing", may have been more than just generous, but also possibly wrong.[5] If the CMIM is unusable for one or more members, it can actually reduce the capacity of these members to stave off a liquidity crisis by reducing their uncommitted national reserves – an economy's first line of defense. How can an unusable CMIM increase the vulnerability of members to crisis? Consider what happened during the GFC – Indonesia, the Republic of Korea and Singapore were forced to pursue bilateral swaps when capital started rapidly exiting their economies. The fact that they had to pursue this option itself suggests that national reserves were considered "insufficient": "insufficient" in the sense that a country would not want to completely or even severely deplete its reserves in times of a crisis whose full magnitude is still unknown. In times of potential or impending crisis, perceptions matter even more – a view underlined by the fact that bilateral swaps are often negotiated before, rather than during or after, a liquidity shortfall. At the margin, however, it could be that the commitment that a country without plentiful reserves such as Indonesia, for instance, had made to the CMIM could have made the difference in terms of such perceptions of sufficiency. The problem only grows in magnitude as the CMIM is expanded in size but continues to be unusable, for whatever reason. But the effects will vary by economy, depending on how abundant their reserves are to begin with; again, the smaller, poorer economies will be most at risk, while the bigger, richer ones will be least affected.

Members also cannot operate by ignoring the amount of their reserves committed or promised to the CMIM, or the system will break down. For instance, consider again the case of the CLMV. Since these are economies without the ability to secure a bilateral swap given the low collateral value of their domestically-issued currencies, they may have to resort to the CMIM (and/or IMF) in times of crisis. If other members are also fearing or fighting their own liquidity crises, and therefore ignore their commitment, there is a real possibility that the CMIM may not be able to deliver on one or more requests from the CLMV. As with a domino effect with opt-out requests, this too would mark the end of the CMIM, both in theory and in practice.

It also remains to be seen whether the recent increase in bilateral currency swap arrangements among the Plus Three countries will be extended to other CMIM members to bolster existing swap lines with these countries. And even if they did, it is unclear if the Plus Three countries would be amenable to managing these bilateral swaps under the same conditions as the CMIM swap, unless of course they did not want them to be used.

The IMF has already raised the possibility of establishing a Multi-Country Swap Line (MSL) mechanism that would enable it to offer liquidity lines to a limited set of countries with sound policies and track records (IMF 2010b). This would form part of a broader Global Stabilization Mechanism (GSM), a framework that would allow proactive provision of financing during a systemic crisis to stem contagion. The GSM also envisions a multipolar liquidity safety network, involving national monetary authorities and regional RFMs, with the IMF at the center. The establishment of such a mechanism, and its involvement with the CMIM, would provide more avenues for increasing the size of liquidity support available to the region beyond the CMIM pool. Even this option for expansion, however, is contingent on the CMIM cleaning up and streamlining its operational procedures.

5.7.2 Expanding Membership of the CMIM

If the CMIM is to become a stand-alone option, or if it is to evolve into an Asian Monetary Fund type institution someday, then the issue of membership needs to be considered. Expanding the membership of the CMIM has less to do with potentially increasing the size of the fund than it does with diversifying it. More than just increasing membership, there is a need to broaden it to include economies that are less directly or immediately connected to East Asian business cycles. This would increase the ability of the fund to cater for the liquidity needs of a clutch of countries requiring support in the event of a contagious crisis if a sufficient number of contributors are unaffected by it. There is no denying that the process of trying to expand membership is likely to be a complicated and sensitive one. But, however difficult, the discussion needs to be started if the CMIM is to survive and prosper as a viable financial safety net, let alone evolve into a de facto Asian Monetary Fund.

The obvious candidates for the first enlargement would be those originally joining ASEAN+3 in the East Asian Summit: Australia, New Zealand and India. India already has a bilateral swap with Japan, while Australia is a contributor to the recent standby arrangement with Indonesia, managed by ADB. Although this expansion makes sense regionally, it is unlikely to diversify the fund to any significant extent given that Australia's economic fortunes are very closely linked to the PRC's, and India's are increasingly becoming so. Even New Zealand's economic fortunes are indirectly linked through its strong ties to Australia and growing ties with the PRC. But the larger the number of contributing members, the greater the likelihood that some will be largely immune from a contagious regional crisis. This is perhaps best illustrated by the fact that Australia was the only advanced country that did not undergo a recession when the GFC hit. Like any risk diversification exercise, the number usually matters.

Candidates for any subsequent enlargement are less obvious, although it is quite unlikely that either the US or the Russian Federation, the newest members of the ASEAN+8 grouping, are likely to want to participate. Should Timor-Leste accede to ASEAN, this small island state will almost certainly also sign up for most of ASEAN's protocols, including presumably the CMIM. Should India join the CMIM, the possibility of other South Asian nations joining will also be significantly enhanced. There could be a snowballing effect following initial enlargement of membership of the CMIM.

5.7.3 Strengthening AMRO's Credibility

Although these reforms are desirable, they are not equally important. If AMRO could gain credibility as an independent surveillance unit, the small size or membership of the CMIM would be less binding constraints. After all, even the IMF relied upon other partners to fund the bail-out in Asia in 1997–98 and now Europe. But the IMF led the rescue and set the terms in Asia, and this is what matters. AMRO needs to be able to do the same. In short, the amount of funds available need not be a constraint if the capacity to lead a rescue exists; in fact, even if the funds were sufficient, they may be of merit in a joint rescue program involving collaboration amongst other regional and/or non-regional partners. In this respect, it is also worth emphasizing that leading a rescue does not entail excluding the IMF, for instance, from participating in setting the terms either; it means having the final say, but not the only say.

Ultimately, the CMIM must rely more on its own independent assessment to make lending decisions – including both in the amount of loans and any conditionality. At present, AMRO still lacks the research capacity, human resources, experience and the institutional set-up to serve effectively as a professional secretariat to the CMIM. Although AMRO has come a long way as a relatively new institution, it still functions mostly as a research office for the CMIM, and undertakes a basic surveillance function producing macroeconomic and financial monitoring assessments. The current ERPD process[6] at which these assessments are presented is still largely a venue for information-sharing at best, and a beauty contest at worst, with weak peer review or policy coordination (Menon 2012). Unless there is a commitment from member countries to significantly increase the resourcing of AMRO so that it may strengthen and expand its functions, it is unlikely that it will be able to perform its role as an independent and credible surveillance unit, let alone a full functioning secretariat for the CMIM.

Although the Joint Statement of the 15th AFMM re-emphasized the importance of strengthening AMRO's role as an "independent regional surveillance unit in contributing to effective monitoring and analysis of regional economies, early detection of risks, swift implementation of remedial actions, and effective decision-making of the CMIM", they could propose little more than further collaboration and cooperation with the IMF, ADB and World Bank. Although they asked the deputies to find out how AMRO's organizational capacity could be strengthened by the November 2012 deputies' meeting, the fact that they never even alluded to the possibility of any increase in funding is telling.

If these are the things that the CMIM and AMRO need to do in order to become effective, there is also at least one thing that it should not do in order to achieve the same. It should avoid the temptation to give in to mission creep and focus on core functions, particularly surveillance activities. For instance, recent suggestions that AMRO should introduce a Regional Monetary Unit (Kawai 2010; Rana et al. 2012) are premature and could derail the building of core competencies. There is room for specialization and collaboration, and more specialized functions such as these should be left to other institutions.

Although the CMIM was established with the aim of supplementing existing international financial arrangements, ultimately its goal should be to be able to lead any rescue package in the region. As Henning (2011) and ADB (2011) correctly note, the IMF is still unique among crisis-fighting facilities in the universality and diversity of its membership, its resources and its experience with designing rescue packages, and remains the final resort in efforts to combat regional contagion. In its current incarnation, it also seems unlikely that the CMIM alone will be adequate to address region-wide systemic financial crises. An optimistic scenario would see the CMIM evolve towards a regime in which the roles are reversed over time, with the CMIM defining conditionality and the IMF being a complementary source of funds. If this optimism is to be justified, then ASEAN+3 must commit to AMRO's development through a substantial increase in its resources. So far, there is little evidence of any such real commitment.

5.8 CONCLUSIONS

Financial safety nets in Asia take four forms. The first line of defense has always been national holdings of foreign exchange reserves. The second, and most popular of late, is bilateral foreign currency swap arrangements. The third is regional safety nets, and the one most discussed in this chapter is the expanded CMIM. Finally, we have the global lender of last resort, the International Monetary Fund (IMF). The importance of strengthening regional financial safety nets grew from the Asian Financial Crisis (AFC) of 1997–98. When the AFC struck, the ASEAN Swap Arrangement (ASA) was basically too small (US$200 million) to be of any use. There was no alternative but to turn to the IMF for the massive bailouts required. The IMF grew extremely unpopular, however, not just for the prescribed bitter medicine, but because it misdiagnosed the problems – a fact that it later acknowledged. There was a resurgence of nationalist sentiment that quickly grew regional.

This led to the birth of the Chiang Mai Initiative (CMI) in 2000, which expanded the bilateral swaps of the ASA both in size and membership to include the PRC, Japan and the Republic of Korea. The CMI's first test came in September 2008 when, following the Lehman Brothers' collapse, short-term capital quickly exited emerging economies. But when the Global Financial Crisis (GFC) hit, members of the CMI that required liquidity support did not turn to it but instead rushed to secure bilateral swaps with the US, the PRC, Japan, Australia and the multilaterals. Once again, the regional financial safety net had failed its members. This brought about another significant change when in 2009 the CMI was multilateralized to become the CMIM, with the many swap lines now governed by a single agreement.

More recently, the CMIM has been doubled to US$240 billion, the share available without an IMF program increased to 30 per cent (and maybe 40 per cent in 2014), and the introduction of a precautionary line of credit similar to that of the IMF. Its surveillance unit, the ASEAN+3 Macroeconomic Research Office (AMRO), has also been up and running in Singapore since 2011. All of this is impressive, and does reflect how far financial safety nets in Asia have come, but is it enough? Is it likely that the CMIM will be called upon when the next crisis strikes? Unfortunately, the CMIM still appears unusable, either as a co-financing facility with the IMF or as a stand-alone alternative. There are a number of reasons, and therefore an equal number of issues, that need to be addressed to make it viable.

First, as a reserve-pooling arrangement, there is no fund but a series of promises; this is not a problem per se but it is when there are no rapid-response procedures to handle a fast-developing financial emergency. Unless these procedures are streamlined, the CMIM is unlikely to be called upon even as a co-financing facility when bilateral swaps or even the IMF may be able to deliver the needed liquidity in the required time.

If the CMIM is to be a real substitute for the IMF and serve its role as a true regional alternative, then the size of the fund, or the portion de-linked from an IMF program, also needs to be increased substantially. Membership would also need to increase beyond ASEAN+3, not just to bolster the size of the fund, but to diversify it. But if AMRO could gain sufficient credibility, then the small size or membership of the CMIM would be less binding constraints. After all, even the IMF relied upon other partners to fund the bailout in Asia in 1997–98. But the IMF led the rescue and set the terms, and this is what matters. AMRO needs to be able to do the same.

Without these changes, and still wary of the IMF stigma, ASEAN+3 is unlikely to turn to the CMIM as a co-financier or a substitute – which explains why countries continue to take the high-cost mercantilist route of self-insurance through excessive holdings of foreign exchange reserves, or why they continue to pursue bilateral swaps separately, often with other CMIM members. In fact, bilateral swaps are quickly becoming the main instrument in Asia's financial safety net. Furthermore, shifting national reserves to a regional fund that is unlikely to be used could actually be counter-productive as it weakens a country's first line of defense. Although ASEAN+3 may appear to have a co-financing facility with the IMF in the CMIM, it is not a useable one. If it wants its own regional safety net, it has a long way to go. How long is still unclear, but hopefully it can be made workable before, rather than because of, the next crisis.

NOTES

* We are grateful to Charles Adams and Chia Wai Mun for written comments, and to Anna Cassandra Melendez for excellent research assistance. Parts of this paper draw upon Hill and Menon (2014). Any remaining errors are our own.
1. The ASEAN+3 Finance Ministers had commented on the desirability of such a facility even at their 2011 Hanoi meeting, noting that "we instructed the Deputies to initiate a study on the design of a possible crisis prevention function for CMIM, including the size, further collaboration with the IMF, and the role of AMRO".
2. The Joint Statement of the 15th ASEAN+3 Finance Ministers and Central Bank Governors' Meeting (2012).
3. Ibid.
4. The escape clause states: "In principle, each of the CMIM parties may only escape from contributing to a swap request by obtaining an approval of the Executive Level Decision Making Body. In exceptional cases such as an extraordinary event or instance of *force majeure* and domestic legal limitations, escape is possible without obtaining ELDMB approval."
5. Quoted in Anthony Rowley, Sid Verma and Mark Townsend (2012), "New fund seen as Asia's own IMF", *Emerging Markets*, 4 May. Available at: http://www.emerg

ingmarkets.org/Article/3023530/New-fund-seen-as-Asias-own-IMF.html?LS=EMS64
8101.
6. The ERPD is carried out in two stages. The first stage is an unofficial forum where
surveillance reports (from AMRO, ADB and IMF) are presented to the AFDM+3 held
biannually in March or April and November. The second stage focuses more on issues
related to policy involving the AFMM+3, and is conducted once a year on the sidelines
of the ADB Annual Meeting.

REFERENCES

Arab Monetary Fund. 2011. Arab Monetary Fund Annual Report, 2010. Available
at: http://www.amf.org.ae/annualrep.
ASEAN Secretariat. 2010. Financial Integration Factsheet.
ASEAN+3 Macroeconomic Research Office (AMRO). 2012. Key points of
CMI Multilateralization Agreement. Available at: http://www.amro-asia.org/
wp-content/uploads/2011/12/Key-Points-of-CMIM.pdf.
Asian Development Bank (ADB). 2011. *Reshaping Global Economic Governance
and the Role of Asia in the Group of Twenty (G20)*. Manila: ADB.
Azis, I. 2012. Asian regional financial safety nets? Don't hold your breath. *Public
Policy Review* **8**(330) (July): 357–76. Policy Research Institute. Ministry of
Finance. Japan.
Bangko Sentral ng Pilipinas (BSP). 2012. Chiang Mai Initiative Multilateralization
FAQ.
ECB. 2011. The European Stability Mechanism. *ECB Monthly Bulletin*. July.
Available at: http://www.ecb.int/pub/pdf/other/art2_mb201107en_pp71–84en.
pdf.
Henning, R.C. 2004. *East Asian Financial Cooperation*. Washington, DC: Institute
for International Economics.
Henning, R.C. 2011. Coordinating regional and multilateral financial institu-
tions. Working Paper No. WP11–9. Washington, DC: Peterson Institute for
International Economics. Paper commissioned by ADB through Research and
Development Technical Assistance Project 7501, Asia's Strategic Participation
in the Group of Twenty for Global Economic Governance Reform, Available
at: http://www.www.piie.com/publications/wp/wp11–9.pdf
Hill, H. and J. Menon. 2014. Does East Asia have a working financial safety net?
Asian Economic Journal **28**(1): 1–17.
International Monetary Fund (IMF). 2010a. Seminar on Regional Financial
Safety Nets: Background Information on Participating RFAs. 8 October.
International Monetary Fund. 2010b. The fund's mandate: Future financing role.
Public Information Notice (PIN) No. 10/51. 22 April. Available at: http://www.
imf.org/external/np/sec/pn/2010/pn1051.htm.
Kawai, M. 2010. Reform of the international financial architecture: An Asian
perspective. *Singapore Economic Review* **53**: 207–92.
Lamberte, M. and P. Morgan. 2012. Regional and global monetary cooperation.
ADBI Working Paper No. 346. Tokyo: ADBI.
Menon, J. 2012. Regional and global financial safety nets. Presentation to the
Conference on The Evolving Global Architecture: From a Centralized to a
Decentralized System, Nanyang Technological University and ADB Institute,
Singapore, 26–27 March.

Park, S. 2011. Global financial safety net and regional financial arrangement: IMF cooperation. *Korea Institute of Finance Weekly Economic Review* **20**: 30.

Pickford, S. 2011. Global financial safety nets. Chatham House International Economics Briefing Paper. October 2011. Available at: http://www.chathamhouse.org/sites/default/files/public/Research/International%20Economics/1011bp_pickford.pdf.

Rana, P.B., W.M. Chia and Y. Jinjarak. 2012. ASEAN+3 monetary integration: Perception survey of opinion leaders. *Journal of Asian Economics* **23**: 1–12.

Sussangkarn, C. 2011. Institution building for macroeconomic and financial cooperation in East Asia. Available at: http://www.amro-asia.org/wp-content/uploads/2011/11/CS-CMIM-AMRO.pdf.

The Joint Statement of the 15th ASEAN+3 Finance Ministers and Central Bank Governors' Meeting. 2012. 3 May. Manila, Philippines.

6. Regional financial regulation in Asia

Masahiro Kawai and Peter J. Morgan

6.1 INTRODUCTION

This chapter examines the potential roles and institutional implementation of regional financial regulation in Asia. National-level financial surveillance and regulation continue to be the workhorse and the first line of action for preserving financial stability. Under the auspices of the Group of Twenty (G20) following the global financial crisis of 2007–09, there has been an attempt to forge a global consensus on financial reform measures based on proposals made by the Financial Stability Board (FSB) and to strengthen the role of the International Monetary Fund (IMF) both as a surveillance unit and as a global financial safety net. In this chapter we argue that there is a mediating role for regional-level institutions of financial regulation in Asia. This role includes: (i) monitoring financial markets and capital flows to identify regional systemic risks such as capital flows; (ii) coordinating financial sector surveillance and regulation to promote regional financial stability; and (iii) cooperating with global-level institutions in rule formulation, surveillance and crisis management.

The Asian Financial Crisis of 1997–98 highlighted the potential value of financial regionalism, that is, regional-level cooperation in economic and financial policy. Many economies in the region found themselves subject to similar shocks and contagion, leading to volatile capital movements and the risk of "sudden stops" and reversals of capital flows. The move of the Association of Southeast Asian Nations (ASEAN) member states toward economic and financial integration, known as the ASEAN Economic Community (AEC) is one manifestation of this.[1] Another important development was the creation of the Chiang Mai Initiative (CMI) in 2000 as a regional financial safety net based on bilateral currency swap arrangements, which was eventually transformed into a multilateralized form: the Chiang Mai Initiative Multilateralization (CMIM). The Economic Review and Policy Dialogue (ERPD), established in 1999 under the auspices of the ASEAN+3 Finance Ministers' Meeting,[2] provided a forum for discussing regional economic and financial policy issues.

The global financial crisis of 2007–09 and the subsequent eurozone sovereign debt and banking sector crisis of 2011–12 added to the urgency for greater financial cooperation by providing reminders of the vulnerability of Asian economies to shocks emanating from the global financial market. Moreover, one of the key lessons of the eurozone crisis is that greater financial market integration requires greater integration of financial regulation and supervision as well. These developments led to the creation of the ASEAN+3 Macroeconomic Research Office (AMRO) under the process of the ASEAN+3 finance ministers and central bank governors monitoring economic and financial risks in the region.

Other factors contributed as well. First, the rising regional economic and financial interdependence in Asia, including ASEAN, the People's Republic of China (PRC), Japan and the Republic of Korea, as a result of the establishment of supply chain networks and financial liberalization, raised synchronization of economic and financial activity in the region. Second, the presence of large global or regional financial firms in the region increases the risk of spillovers and contagion, and calls for a more coordinated approach to supervision, including the establishment of supervisory colleges.[3] Third, although the global financial crisis stimulated a wave of new financial regulation under the auspices of the G20, the agenda was still very much driven by issues in developed economies. A global regulatory approach of "one size fits all" may not be appropriate for Asia, which increases the need for Asian economies to articulate their viewpoints in global forums such as the FSB and the G20. Finally, a large body of literature suggests that financial development and integration can benefit economic growth,[4] and increased regional regulatory harmonization and mutual recognition can both support this process and reduce systemic risks associated with it.

Financial regulation encompasses three broad aspects: ensuring that all market participants understand the risks they face and take on only those they are capable of coping with in order to promote efficient allocation of credit; protecting consumers from unfair and fraudulent practices; and maintaining systemic stability by monitoring common risk exposures, the solvency of individual financial firms, the proper functioning of markets, the operation of the payment and settlement structures, and the levels of a variety of buffers that provide comfort to participants (Fullenkamp and Sharma 2012). The experience of the global financial crisis showed that maintaining systemic stability requires both microprudential and macroprudential regulatory approaches. This chapter focuses mostly on the systemic stability aspects, since this is arguably where regional cooperation can probably make the largest contribution.

Although financial integration efforts in Asia, even in ASEAN, are much more modest than those in Europe, the basic goal of increased integration has been well established, especially among ASEAN countries under the AEC. This points fundamentally to the need for greater regional regulatory cooperation between ASEAN and ASEAN+3 economies to reduce risks associated with greater integration.[5] Since regional financial integration is most advanced in Europe, its experience should provide valuable lessons (both positive and negative) for Asia. Nonetheless, the levels of economic and financial development and financial integration in Europe and Asia are very different. Asian economies encompass much greater diversity in terms of economic development, institutional capacity, and financial market depth and openness than do European economies. This suggests that the European experience represents an important reference point, but not a template or a benchmark, and that the appropriate level of financial regulatory cooperation and kinds of regional institutions will differ substantially from those that have developed in Europe.

This chapter is organized as follows. Section 6.2 compares and contrasts economic and financial development and financial integration in Europe and Asia. Section 6.3 examines the experience of regional financial regulation, focusing on that of Europe, the region where economic and financial integration has progressed most. Section 6.4 discusses the experience of regional financial cooperation and regulation in Asia. Section 6.5 identifies various challenges of regional financial regulation and provides recommendations for strengthening institutions of regional financial regulation. Section 6.6 concludes.

6.2   COMPARISON OF ECONOMIC AND FINANCIAL DEVELOPMENT IN EUROPE AND ASIA

This section compares the levels of economic and financial development, financial integration and institutional quality in Europe and Asia. The aim is to provide perspectives about the relevance of Europe's experience to that of Asia, and to identify where different approaches may be desirable. The trend to financial integration in Europe accelerated around 1990, including the deregulation of capital movements within the European Monetary System (EMS) economies in 1988 and the adoption of the Maastricht Treaty and the decision in 1992 to establish the Economic and Monetary Union (EMU). Therefore, we believe it is appropriate to compare conditions in Europe at that time with conditions in Asia currently, to gauge the potential for regional financial integration and regulatory cooperation.

6.2.1 Economic Development

Table 6.1 compares levels of per capita real gross domestic product (GDP) in the European Union 15 (EU15), that is, EU member countries in 1990 plus Austria, Finland and Sweden, versus those in the ASEAN+3 economies in 2012. The data are shown in 1990 Geary–Khamis dollars

Table 6.1   Real per capita GDP in Europe and Asia

EU15 countries (1990)		ASEAN+6 (2012)	
Country	GDP per capita (1990 Geary–Khamis dollars)	Country	GDP per capita (1990 Geary–Khamis dollars)
Austria	16 895	Australia	26 356
Belgium	17 197	Brunei Darussalam	27 273
Denmark	18 452	Cambodia	2702
Finland	16 866	PRC	8631
France	17 647	India	3690
Germany	16 306	Indonesia	5207
Greece	10 015	Japan	22 002
Ireland	11 818	Rep. of Korea	22 879
Italy	16 313	Lao PDR	3127
Luxembourg	23 028	Malaysia	10 733
Netherlands	17 262	Myanmar	4248
Portugal	10 826	New Zealand	18 915
Spain	12 055	Philippines	3178
Sweden	17 069	Singapore	29 851
United Kingdom	16 430	Thailand	9677
		Viet Nam	3504
Simple average	15 879	**Simple average**	12 623
Population-weighted average	15 850	**Population-weighted average**	7131
Standard Deviation	3377	**Standard Deviation**	10 089

Notes:
GDP = gross domestic product; EU15 = The 15 Member States of the European Union (EU) as of 31 December 2003, before the new Member States joined the EU (the 15 Member States are Austria, Belgium, Denmark, Finland, France, Germany, Greece, Ireland, Italy, Luxembourg, Netherlands, Portugal, Spain, Sweden, and the United Kingdom); ASEAN+6 = Association of Southeast Asian Nations (ASEAN = Brunei Darussalam, Cambodia, Indonesia, Lao PDR, Malaysia, Myanmar, Philippines, Singapore, Thailand and Viet Nam) plus PRC, Japan, Republic of Korea, Australia, India and New Zealand; PRC = People's Republic of China.
Figures for Brunei Darussalam and Lao PDR estimated using Geary–Khamis conversion factors for Singapore and Cambodia, respectively.

Source: The Conference Board Total Economy Database™, January 2013, http://www.conference-board.org/data/economydatabase/ and Key Indicators for Asia and the Pacific 2013 (http://www.adb.org/publications/key-indicators-asia-and-pacific-2013?ref=publications/series/key-indicators-for-asia-and-the-pacific).

to make them comparable.[6] Clearly, economic conditions were much more uniform in Europe in 1990 than in Asia in 2012. Interestingly, the unweighted average real income levels were not that different – US$15 900 for Europe versus US$12 600 for Asia – but the population-weighted average is less than half in Asia, reflecting the large population weights of the PRC and India. Also, the dispersion in Europe was much less, with a standard deviation of US$3400 versus US$10 100 for the Asian economies. The minimum income level in Europe was US$10 000 versus only US$2700 for Asia.

6.2.2   Financial Development

Financial development is frequently measured by the ratio of total financial assets to GDP, since capital deepening generally accompanies economic development. Table 6.2 shows the levels and standard deviations of the ratios of private bank credit to GDP for the two regions. The average ratio for Europe in 1990 was actually lower than in Asia in 2011 – 69 per cent versus 75 per cent – and the gap in the GDP-weighted averages was even larger. However, the standard deviation was much lower – 25 per cent versus 45 per cent – indicating a smaller diversity of development.

Table 6.3 shows total bond issues outstanding as ratios of GDP for the two regions, including both domestic and international issues. The simple average level was somewhat higher in Europe – 69 per cent versus 59 per cent – but the GDP-weighted average was much lower. Again, the standard deviation was only about half of that in Asia. Viet Nam and Myanmar in particular stand out with a ratio of only 2–3 per cent.

Table 6.4 shows the ratio of stock market capitalization to GDP. The average ratio for the European countries in 1990 was only about half of the Asian level in 2011 in both unweighted and weighted terms, but the standard deviation was also much lower. Interestingly, Greece, Austria, Portugal and Italy had lower stock market levels in 1990 than did Viet Nam in 2011.

Overall, the average level of financial development of Asia currently compares favorably with that of Europe in 1990. Nonetheless, the much higher variance of financial development in Asia does indicate obstacles to financial integration, although they do not appear to be as great as those for income levels.

6.2.3   Financial Integration

Financial openness and financial integration are not quite the same thing, but clearly an economy must be financially open to make integration possible, especially on the capital account. Capital account openness has been

Table 6.2   Ratio of bank private credit to GDP in Europe and Asia

EU15 countries (1990)		ASEAN+6 (2011)	
Country	Bank private credit/GDP (%)	Country	Bank private credit/GDP (%)
Austria	85.7	Australia	121.2
Belgium	35.8	Brunei Darussalam	32.6
Denmark	50.2	Cambodia	26.8
Finland	82.3	PRC	121.5
France	89.6	India	47.2
Germany	88.1	Indonesia	25.4
Greece	34.1	Japan	105.7
Ireland	45.3	Rep. of Korea	98.4
Italy	52.8	Lao PDR	22.0
Luxembourg	110.4	Malaysia	106.4
Netherlands	77.2	Myanmar	8.2
Portugal	48.0	New Zealand	143.9
Spain	76.7	Philippines	29.8
Sweden	53.8	Singapore	104.2
United Kingdom	108.5	Thailand	101.9
		Viet Nam	107.7
Simple average	69.2	**Simple average**	75.2
GDP-weighted average	79.2	**GDP-weighted average**	102.3
Standard Deviation	25.1	**Standard Deviation**	45.3

Notes:
GDP = gross domestic product; EU15 = The 15 Member States of the EU as of 31 December 2003, before the new Member States joined the EU (the 15 Member States are Austria, Belgium, Denmark, Finland, France, Germany, Greece, Ireland, Italy, Luxembourg, Netherlands, Portugal, Spain, Sweden and the United Kingdom); ASEAN+6 = Association of Southeast Asian Nations (ASEAN = Brunei Darussalam, Cambodia, Indonesia, Lao PDR, Malaysia, Myanmar, Philippines, Singapore, Thailand and Viet Nam) plus PRC, Japan, Republic of Korea, Australia, India and New Zealand; PRC = People's Republic of China.

Source: World Bank Global Financial Development database. http://data.worldbank.org/ data-catalog/global-financial-development; for Lao PDR, CEIC Database https://ceicdata. com; for Myanmar, IMF (2013).

measured empirically both in de jure (based on laws and regulations) and de facto terms. De jure openness is perhaps more important for financial integration. One popular measure of de jure openness is the Chinn–Ito Index (Chinn and Ito 2006), which is an index compiled based on the IMF's Annual Report on Exchange Rate Arrangements and Exchange Restrictions (IMF 2012). The index values range between 2.5 (fully open) and –1.8 (fully closed).

Table 6.3   Ratio of total bonds outstanding to GDP in Europe and Asia

EU15 countries (1990)		ASEAN+6 (2011)	
Country	Outstanding bonds/GDP (%)	Country	Outstanding bonds/GDP (%)
Austria	52.7	Australia	126.5
Belgium	141.5	Brunei Darussalam	N/A
Denmark	151.5	Cambodia	N/A
Finland	38.8	PRC	47.0
France	72.8	India	34.5
Germany	59.6	Indonesia	16.8
Greece	41.5	Japan	263.5
Ireland	54.7	Rep. of Korea	118.2
Italy	102.5	Lao PDR	N/A
Luxembourg	62.9	Malaysia	127.4
Netherlands	62.0	Myanmar	3.3
Portugal	40.6	New Zealand	36.2
Spain	39.3	Philippines	48.7
Sweden	77.9	Singapore	55.4
United Kingdom	37.5	Thailand	65.8
		Viet Nam	2.3
Simple average	69.1	**Simple average**	59.1
GDP-weighted average	68.1	**GDP-weighted average**	119.1
Standard Deviation	36.1	**Standard Deviation**	70.5

Notes:
EU15 = The 15 Member States of the EU as of 31 December 2003, before the new Member States joined the EU (the 15 Member States are Austria, Belgium, Denmark, Finland, France, Germany, Greece, Ireland, Italy, Luxembourg, Netherlands, Portugal, Spain, Sweden and the United Kingdom); ASEAN+6 = Association of Southeast Asian Nations (ASEAN = Brunei Darussalam, Cambodia, Indonesia, Lao PDR, Malaysia, Myanmar, Philippines, Singapore, Thailand and Viet Nam) plus PRC, Japan, Republic of Korea, Australia, India and New Zealand; GDP = gross domestic product; PRC = People's Republic of China; N/A = not available.
Since values for countries with data not available are likely to be small, the averages and standard deviation were calculated assuming zero values for those countries.

Source: World Bank Global Financial Development Data database. http://data.worldbank.org/data-catalog/global-financial-development; CEIC Database https://ceicdata.com.

Figure 6.1 shows the comparative values for European countries in 1990 and Asian countries in 2011 (the latest year available). Interestingly, both regions showed a considerable divergence of capital market openness with the standard deviations being very similar, but the average index value of openness in Europe in 1990 was much higher: 1.01 versus 0.18 for Asia in

Table 6.4   *Ratio of stock market capitalization to GDP in Europe and Asia*

EU15 countries (1990)		ASEAN+6 (2011)	
Country	Stock market capitalization/GDP (%)	Country	Stock market capitalization/ GDP (%)
Austria	11.6	Australia	103.5
Belgium	38.0	Brunei Darussalam	0
Denmark	31.9	Cambodia	0.3
Finland	20.9	PRC	58.8
France	30.0	India	69.7
Germany	18.7	Indonesia	45.1
Greece	11.3	Japan	68.8
Ireland	38.1	Rep. of Korea	96.2
Italy	15.2	Lao PDR	7.4
Luxembourg	89.6	Malaysia	144.1
Netherlands	51.7	Myanmar	0
Portugal	13.8	New Zealand	40.1
Spain	24.6	Philippines	73.9
Sweden	48.0	Singapore	148.1
United Kingdom	87.1	Thailand	81.7
		Viet Nam	15.4
Simple average	35.4	**Simple average**	59.6
GDP-weighted average	34.1	**GDP-weighted average**	69.8
Standard Deviation	25.0	**Standard Deviation**	48.3

Notes:
EU15 = The 15 Member States of the EU as of 31 December 2003, before the new Member States joined the EU. The 15 Member States are Austria, Belgium, Denmark, Finland, France, Germany, Greece, Ireland, Italy, Luxembourg, Netherlands, Portugal, Spain, Sweden and the United Kingdom; ASEAN+6 = Association of Southeast Asian Nations (ASEAN = Brunei Darussalam, Cambodia, Indonesia, Lao PDR, Malaysia, Myanmar, Philippines, Singapore, Thailand and Viet Nam) plus PRC, Japan, Republic of Korea, Australia, India and New Zealand; GDP = gross domestic product; PRC = People's Republic of China.
Ireland data is for 1995, Cambodia data is for April 2012 (initial public offering), and Lao PDR data is for January 2012. Brunei Darussalam and Myanmar do not have stock markets.

Source: World Bank Global Financial Development Data database. http://data. worldbank.org/data-catalog/global-financial-development; Lanexang Securities Public Co. (2013) and Cambodia Securities Exchange http://www.csx.com.kh/main.do.

2011. In Europe, only Greece was relatively closed, while seven countries in Asia have high negative scores against only three being completely open. Moreover, as a result of the Maastricht Treaty of 1992, Denmark, France, Ireland and Italy had moved to complete financial market openness by 1996.

New global economic architecture

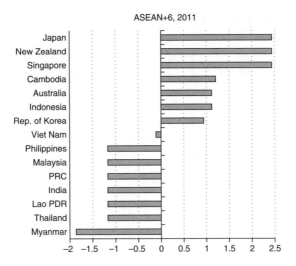

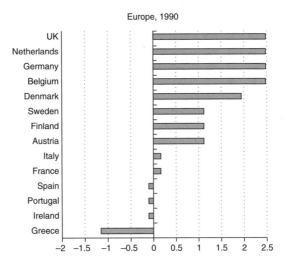

Notes:
ASEAN+6 = Association of Southeast Asian Nations (ASEAN = Brunei Darussalam, Cambodia, Indonesia, Lao PDR, Malaysia, Myanmar, Philippines, Singapore, Thailand and Viet Nam) plus PRC, Japan, Republic of Korea, Australia, India and New Zealand; PRC = People's Republic of China; UK = United Kingdom.
Indexes are not available for Luxembourg or Brunei Darussalam.

Source: Chinn and Ito (2006). The latest data can be found at http://web.pdx.edu/~ito/ Chinn-Ito_website.htm.

Figure 6.1   De jure capital market openness in Europe and Asia

Table 6.5   Intra-regional portfolio investment in Asia rising but still lags behind Europe

	Share of total portfolio investments, %			
	2001		2012	
Region	Assets	Liabilities	Assets	Liabilities
ASEAN	10.5	11.9	10.2	13.4
ASEAN+3	5.3	9.1	13.2	12.4
ASEAN+6	8.6	13.2	18.2	17.2
EU15	60.0	57.1	60.4	60.4
EU27	60.0	57.2	60.5	60.5

Notes:
ASEAN = Brunei Darussalam, Cambodia, Indonesia, Lao PDR, Malaysia, Myanmar, Philippines, Singapore, Thailand and Viet Nam.
ASEAN+3 = ASEAN plus PRC, Japan and Republic of Korea.
ASEAN+6 = ASEAN+3 plus Australia, India and New Zealand.
EU15 = Austria, Belgium, Denmark, Finland, France, Germany, Greece, Ireland, Italy, Luxembourg, Netherlands, Portugal, Spain, Sweden and United Kingdom.
EU27 = EU15 plus Bulgaria, Cyprus, Czech Republic, Estonia, Hungary, Latvia, Lithuania, Malta, Poland, Romania, Slovak Republic and Slovenia.

Source: IMF Coordinated Portfolio Investment Survey database. http://cpis.imf.org/ (accessed 26 November 2013).

Other data also suggest that financial integration in Asia is much less advanced than in the EU. For example, Table 6.5 shows the share of intra-regional cross-border portfolio investment in total cross-border investment for a number of regions for the year 2001 (the earliest year data are available) and 2012. Intra-regional cross-border portfolio investment in Asia represents a much smaller share of total cross-border investment in Asia than in Europe, although it has increased over the past decade, especially in the ASEAN+3 and ASEAN+6 countries.[7] Foreign entry into banking is still heavily restricted in many Asian economies as well.

6.2.4   Institutional Quality

Finally, there are considerable differences between the EU in 1996 (the earliest year data are available) and Asia in 2012 in terms of institutional quality. Table 6.6 focuses on regulatory quality, based on the World Bank World Governance Indicators database. Not only is the average percentile ranking in Asia considerably lower than in the EU, the variance is also greater. Greece had the lowest ranking in the EU (71 per cent) while Asia has seven countries below the 50th percentile, including an astonishingly

Table 6.6   Regulatory quality considerably lower in Asia than in the EU

EU15 countries (1996)		ASEAN+6 (2012)	
Country	Percentile ranking	Country	Percentile ranking
Austria	95.1	Australia	97.1
Belgium	86.3	Brunei Darussalam	84.7
Denmark	98.5	Cambodia	39.2
Finland	93.1	PRC	43.5
France	78.9	India	34.0
Germany	91.2	Indonesia	43.1
Greece	71.1	Japan	83.7
Ireland	96.6	Rep. of Korea	77.0
Italy	76.0	Lao PDR	22.0
Luxembourg	97.1	Malaysia	69.9
Netherlands	98.0	Myanmar	1.9
Portugal	89.7	New Zealand	96.2
Spain	84.8	Philippines	51.7
Sweden	90.2	Singapore	100.0
United Kingdom	99.5	Thailand	57.9
		Viet Nam	27.3
Simple average	89.7	**Simple average**	58.1
GDP-weighted average	87.4	**GDP-weighted average**	62.0
Standard Deviation	8.8	**Standard Deviation**	29.9

Note: PRC = People's Republic of China.

Source: World Bank World Governance Indicators database. http://info.worldbank.org/governance/wgi/index.aspx#home.

low level for Myanmar at 1.9 per cent. This suggests the presence of a relatively greater potential for systemic risks in Asia, and hence a preference for less integrated financial markets.

6.2.5   Summary

Surprisingly, average measures of economic and financial development for the EU in 1990 (or the earliest year when data are available) versus the ASEAN+6 economies in recent years are similar. However, this masks a much greater degree of diversity in the latter group, both in terms of income levels and financial development. Moreover, capital markets in Asia are still relatively closed compared with the level that prevailed in the EU in 1990, not to mention the fully open capital markets there today.

This may partly reflect the substantially lower level of regulatory quality in developing countries in Asia today than in Europe in the mid-1990s. Thus Asia needs a more modest and measured approach to regional financial surveillance and regulation compared with what has been seen in the EU over the past two decades.

Although the EU experience provides many valuable lessons for Asian financial integration, it should only be regarded as a comparison point, not a benchmark or a template. Nonetheless, Asia will inevitably experience progressive, but most likely gradual, capital account liberalization and consequent financial integration. Greater financial integration entails risks as well as benefits, particularly the easier transmission of financial shocks. This highlights the need over time for regional regulatory cooperation to help reduce such risks in Asia.

6.3 EXPERIENCE OF REGIONAL FINANCIAL SECTOR POLICY IN THE EUROPEAN UNION

This section describes and analyzes lessons from existing experiences of regional financial sector policy, focusing on the EU.

The EU provides by far the richest source of information and experience about regional financial sector policy. The EU has the tightest regional political, economic and financial structure with the longest history, and also has faced some of the most difficult challenges as a result of the eurozone sovereign debt and banking sector crisis in recent years. Although financial integration in Asia is far less advanced than in Europe, Asian economies can still learn valuable lessons from the European experience. This section examines four aspects of European financial regulation: microprudential supervision; macroprudential supervision; resolution capacity and deposit insurance; and financial safety net for liquidity support.

Legislation in the EU has evolved substantially since the creation of the three European Supervisory Authorities (ESAs) – the European Banking Authority (EBA), the European Securities and Markets Authority (ESMA) and the European Insurance and Occupational Pensions Authority (EIOPA). Since then, the main divide has been between EU legislation and delegated acts. Most delegated acts are adopted by the European Commission on the basis of proposals by the ESAs, though this is still largely a work in progress. Not surprisingly, it has been found difficult to implement in practice such a complex and cumbersome process.

The main challenge seems to be substance, because there is no agreed benchmark to guide regulatory and supervisory convergence (Winkler 2012). These difficulties are compounded by two asymmetries within the

EU: the presence of some countries (such as Ireland, Luxembourg and the United Kingdom) operating international financial centers that often have a vested interest in light regulation; and the integration process between home and host country member states, as regards regulation and supervision of cross-border financial institutions. Finally, even if principles are the same, actual implementation may still vary by country depending on local laws, institutions, practices and specific exceptions, so inconsistencies are bound to occur. Wymeersch (2010, p. 205) concluded that "the European financial regulatory system is far from effectively harmonized and not fully conducive to the creation of an internal financial market." For example, implicit and explicit national guarantees were a major distorting factor of the single market, as widely evidenced in the crisis.

Recent reforms strengthened the abilities of the EU institutions to adopt legislation that is binding on member countries, a shift generally signaled by reference to a "single rulebook" (De Larosière Report, European Commission 2009). However, member nations can introduce their own legislation as well, sometimes before relevant EU directives emerge. A notable example is financial regulation in the United Kingdom, which follows recommendations made by the Vickers Report (ICB 2011). As will be discussed below, special resolution regimes have been developed in an uncoordinated manner at the national level, for example, Germany, United Kingdom, Ireland, Belgium and Sweden, although the resolution issue is now being addressed in a coordinated way.

6.3.1 Microprudential Supervision

The area of microprudential supervision – the monitoring of individual financial firms – has seen (and continues to see) major changes in response to the eurozone sovereign debt and banking sector crisis, which has highlighted the weaknesses of the previous system of essentially national-level supervision of cross-border banks. First, in January 2011, legislative changes created the three ESAs and granted them a coordinating role over microprudential supervision. Increased powers of the ESAs related to microprudential supervision included: (i) resolving cases of disagreement between national supervisors, where legislation requires them to cooperate or to agree; (ii) promoting coherent functioning of supervisory colleges;[8] and (iii) coordinating policies in emergency situations (EU 2011). Nevertheless, the extent and effectiveness of these new powers is still unclear. Supervision is still primarily at the national level.

As a result, the EU has committed itself to creating a banking union – comprising EU-wide bank supervision, resolution and deposit insurance – under the supervision of the European Central Bank (ECB). This was crystallized by the decision taken at the European Summit in June 2012 to create a Single Supervisory Mechanism (SSM). In addition to the single rulebook, an integrated financial framework for the EU is seen to require three central elements: single European banking supervision; a common deposit insurance; and a common resolution framework (van Rompuy 2012). Also, introducing the SSM is directly related to the decision to allow the possibility of direct recapitalization of banks by the European Stability Mechanism (ESM). To this end, the summit leaders called for the Council to develop proposals for the SSM by the end of 2012, and the European Council meeting later in the year called for the "legislative framework" to be completed by that time (European Council 2012b). The leaders specifically referred to the need to "break the vicious circle between banks and sovereigns" (European Council 2012a, p. 1).

The European Commission's draft proposal of September 2012 calls for the ECB to take responsibility for supervision of all credit institutions in the euro member countries, "with the objective to promote the safety and soundness of credit institutions and the stability of the financial system" (European Commission 2012, p. 3). The ECB is charged to carry out its tasks within the framework of the European System of Financial Supervision (ESFS) and to cooperate closely with national supervisors and the EBA.[9] Specific proposed supervisory tasks for the ECB include:

> authority for licensing and authorizing credit institutions, assessing qualifying holdings, ensuring compliance with the minimum capital requirements, ensuring the adequacy of internal capital in relation to the risk profile of a credit institution (Pillar 2 measures), conducting supervision on a consolidated basis, and supervisory tasks in relation to financial conglomerates. Furthermore, the ECB will also ensure compliance with provisions on leverage and liquidity, apply capital buffers and carry out, in coordination with resolution authorities, early intervention measures when a bank is in breach of, or is about to breach, regulatory capital requirements. (European Commission 2012, p. 4)

Also, the ECB will have all necessary investigatory powers to be able to carry out its tasks. However, it is expected that most day-to-day verifications and other supervisory activities would be exercised by national supervisors operating as an integral part of the SSM. The precise allocation of responsibilities between the ECB and national supervisors remains a controversial issue.

An innovation of this magnitude has major implications for the regulatory structure in the EU, including the relationships of the ECB with the EBA and non-euro-member states, but these have not yet been resolved. The proposal states that "the ECB should therefore be required to cooperate closely with the EBA, the [ESMA] and the [EIOPA], within the framework of the EFSF" (European Commission 2012, p. 13). Regarding the EBA, the Commission proposal notes that "the EBA will keep its powers and tasks to further develop the single rulebook and ensure convergence and consistency of supervisory practice" (European Commission 2012, p. 4). Most of the ECB's increased responsibilities will be shifted from national supervisors, not the EBA. However, it seems likely that the EBA's role will need to be modified gradually over time (Véron 2012b).

Regarding the non-euro-member states wishing to enter the banking union, the Commission proposal notes that they "will be able to enter into a close supervisory cooperation with the ECB subject to meeting specific conditions" (European Commission 2012, p. 6). One of these conditions is that those member states abide by and implement relevant ECB acts. This area also remains controversial.

The proposal notes that the new ECB role does not affect in any way the position of non-euro-member states in existing colleges of supervisors for EU financial firms. Until now, the primary vehicles for cross-border supervisory cooperation are memorandums of understanding (MOUs) among national supervisors. However, these are not legally binding and can be fragile. As noted above, the ESAs supposedly have powers to resolve disputes within colleges of supervisors, but these have not been tested much yet. Moreover, the proliferation of MOUs creates a complex environment in which to operate. Finally, such MOUs have tended to be supplanted in times of crisis by ad hoc measures, for example, the case of the Fortis financial group in 2008 (Véron 2012a). However, this issue should be largely resolved, at least for financial firms within the region, with the transfer of supervisory authority to the ECB.

6.3.2 Macroprudential Supervision

As mentioned above, EU-wide macroprudential regulation was introduced in 2011 with the creation of the European Systemic Risk Board (ESRB). The ESRB has a mandate to study macroprudential, or systemwide, risks to stability. It is chaired by the President of the ECB, and members include the ECB, national central banks, the three ESAs, one high-level representative per Member State of the competent national supervisory authorities, the European Council, and the Economic and Financial Committee (EFC) – 61 members in all (ESRB 2012a). Notably, however, the national supervisory authorities do not have voting rights, which leaves the voting membership very much dominated by the ECB and national central banks. It does not appear that the change in the ECB's supervisory role described in the previous section will affect its role in macroprudential supervision, since that role is already quite large.

The ESRB has a surveillance function but no binding powers. It can issue risk warnings that should prompt early responses to avoid a build-up of systemic problems and the risk of a future crisis, and it may also recommend specific actions to address any identified risks. The ESRB cannot impose measures on member states or national authorities, but can expect replies to its assessments. It also has the ability, along with the ESAs, to identify emergency situations, and has responsibility for coordinating its actions with those of international financial organizations, particularly the IMF and the FSB, as well as the relevant bodies in third countries on matters related to macroprudential oversight (ESRB 2012b).

The Commission report on the proposed expansion of the ECB's supervisory role calls for strict separation from the ECB's monetary policy tasks to eliminate potential conflicts of interest between the objectives of monetary policy and prudential supervision. However, it remains to be seen whether or not such a strict separation is practical. Experience suggests that its monetary and macroprudential policy tools cannot be operated totally independently. For example, if monetary conditions are easy, borrowers will find ways to evade various macroprudential restrictions on lending.

6.3.3 Resolution Capacity and Deposit Insurance

A weak link in the EU's region-wide financial regulatory capacity is the lack of an EU-wide framework for resolution of cross-border banks and other financial firms and for deposit insurance. The approach to cross-border bank resolution is still based on MOUs – which may prove fragile – and insolvency laws are not harmonized. Moreover, national fiscal authorities are not included in such MOUs, even though they must make the critical decision of whether or not to inject public funds into an institution. To be sure, the EU has also created crisis resolution groups, in which treasuries are members, precisely to address this weakness.

Deposit insurance in the EU is currently implemented only at the national level. While there have been waves of harmonization – for instance in 2009 a uniform minimum coverage of 100 000 euros was introduced – they still display significant national differences across the EU. As such, they are not well equipped to deal with the failure of cross-border banks within the EU. Moreover, deposit guarantee schemes are unfunded in many countries, which means that their fiscal position could be affected significantly by the failure of a large bank. Although they have been recently strengthened by various measures, they do not substitute for an EU-wide scheme.

This situation will change dramatically following the commitment to create a banking union, including EU-wide supervision, resolution arrangements and a deposit insurance scheme. The latter two are needed together, and van Rompuy (2012, p. 5) has noted that "the deposit insurance scheme and the resolution fund could be set up under the control of a common resolution authority." Constâncio (2012) has suggested that the US Federal Deposit Insurance Corporation could be a model. The European Commission was charged with developing such a resolution and deposit insurance framework.

Progress is being made on the establishment of an EU-wide resolution mechanism. European Commission (2013b) proposed a legislative framework for a new Single Resolution Mechanism (SRM). The SRM will apply a single rulebook on bank resolution for ailing banks from the participating member states in this mechanism. The SRM will consist of uniform rules and procedures to be applied by the Single Resolution Board (SRB), together with the Commission and the resolution authorities of the participating member states. The SRB, made up of representatives from the ECB, the European Commission and the relevant national authorities, would prepare the resolution of a bank. It would have broad powers to analyze and define the approach for resolving a bank: which tools to use, and how the European Resolution Fund should be involved. A Single Bank Resolution Fund would be set up under the control of the SRB to ensure the availability of medium-term funding support during the restructuring process. It would be funded by contributions from the banking sector, replacing the national resolution funds of the euro area member states and those non-euro states participating in the banking union. The law was approved by the European Parliament in 2014.

However, not much progress has been observed on the deposit insurance scheme even in 2013. If this is implemented successfully, it will represent a marked improvement over the current system, which is carried out mostly at the national level, and augmented only by relatively weak MOUs and ad hoc responses. Van Rompuy (2012) has argued that a European deposit insurance scheme would strengthen the credibility of the existing arrangements and serve as an important assurance that eligible deposits of all credit institutions are sufficiently insured.

6.3.4   Financial Safety Net

The European financial safety net also evolved over time in response to the sovereign debt and banking crisis. In June 2010, the European Council created the European Financial Stability Facility (EFSF) by which euro member states provided a mainly credit-funded facility to lend to small countries that had lost access to capital markets. However, when the financial crisis contagion spilled over into large member states, especially Italy, the original EFSF bailout fund was insufficient and the European Council increased the fund's resources from the initial amount of 440 billion euros to 780 billion euros in July 2011. However, when Italy had to refinance approximately 350 billion euros in 2012 and there were large liquidity risks for lenders, the European Council in October 2011 agreed to leverage the EFSF up to 1 trillion euros, but even this measure failed to calm the markets. In October 2012, this temporary facility was transformed into a permanent European Stability Mechanism (ESM).

A more lasting solution to the crisis was found through the development of the "troika" financial safety net, comprising the EFSF (afterward the ESM), the ECB and the IMF. The troika's first project was the bailout for Ireland in November 2011, followed by that for Portugal in May 2012, and the second Greek bailout in September 2012 (European Commission 2013a). These measures finally stabilized markets and allowed sovereign bond yields to decline substantially in the crisis countries. Nevertheless, the earlier lack of a regional financial safety net led to virtual shut-off of intraregional capital flows, which in turn hampered the transmission of monetary policy throughout the region.

6.3.5 Summary

The EU has created by far the most highly developed regional institutions for financial supervision, regulation and resolution, and has achieved by far the highest regional financial integration and harmonization of rules, standards, procedures and so on. Nonetheless, it is still very much a work in progress. Significant differences in national practices and institutions remain, and have proven a substantial barrier to fully harmonizing financial regulations, tax systems, corporate law and other systemic aspects. The role of regional supervisory agencies has been strengthened, but microprudential supervision is still carried out mainly at the national level, while regional macroprudential institutions appear cumbersome and lack enforcement powers. Information-sharing by national supervisors remains inadequate, and MOUs underlying supervisory colleges and deposit insurance schemes are still fragile.

The eurozone crisis has revealed a number of shortcomings in the previous architecture, as essentially national-level regulation could not cope with the high degree of financial integration in the region, and the "doom loop" mechanism could not be avoided. The decision to create a full-fledged banking union in coming years will dramatically alter this situation, and should mark a major improvement. The imminent establishment of the SSM marks the first step in this process, and the agreement on an

EU-wide resolution mechanism is another step forward, but a full union will also require establishing a unified deposit insurance scheme with EU-wide fiscal backing.

6.4 EXPERIENCE FROM REGIONAL FINANCIAL COOPERATION AND REGULATION IN ASIA

Regional financial cooperation and regulation in Asia is much less developed than in the EU, but some significant developments have emerged, including economic and financial surveillance; financial regulatory harmonization; and a regional financial safety net. This section describes these developments.

6.4.1 Economic and Financial Surveillance

A number of regional forums have emerged for the purposes of information exchange, economic monitoring, policy dialogue and peer pressure for better policies. The ASEAN finance ministers established the ASEAN Surveillance Process in 1998. Its objective is to strengthen cooperation by: (i) exchanging information and discussing economic and financial development of member states in the region; (ii) providing an early warning system and a peer review process to enhance macroeconomic and financial stability in the region; (iii) highlighting possible policy options and encouraging early unilateral or collective actions to prevent a crisis; and (iv) monitoring and discussing global economic and financial developments which could have implications for the region and propose possible regional and national level actions. The ASEAN Surveillance Process includes the ASEAN Finance Ministers' Meeting and the ASEAN Select Committee, comprising the members of the ASEAN Senior Finance Officials' Meeting and the ASEAN Central Bank Forum (IIMA 2005).

The ASEAN+3 Finance Ministers' Meeting process has the Economic Review and Policy Dialogue (ERPD), which meets once a year mainly to discuss macroeconomic and financial issues in East Asia. Starting in 2012, the members' central bank governors joined this forum, which consequently has been renamed the ASEAN+3 Finance Ministers and Central Bank Governors' Meeting. The ERPD receives inputs from the Asian Development Bank (ADB). In addition, the ASEAN+3 finance deputies meet twice a year. Other meetings of Asian finance ministers include Asia-Pacific Economic Cooperation (APEC) and the Asia-Europe Meeting (ASEM). The policy dialogue and surveillance process among ASEAN+3 members is in transition from the "information sharing" stage to the "peer review and peer pressure" stage, while the "due diligence" process has yet to start in a serious manner (Kawai and Houser 2008).

Another key forum is the Executives' Meeting of East Asia-Pacific Central Banks (EMEAP), a cooperative group of central banks and monetary authorities in the East Asia and Pacific region.[10] Its primary objective is to strengthen the cooperative relationship among its members. The EMEAP has activities at three levels: Governors' Meetings, Deputies' Meetings, and working groups. Another organization is the South East Asian Central Banks (SEACEN) Research and Training Centre in Kuala Lumpur, Malaysia, which now has 19 member central banks.[11] As part of it, the SEACEN Expert Group (SEG) on Capital Flows was established by the SEACEN Centre in May 2000, in response to the need to manage capital flows to ensure stability in regional financial markets. In addition to the 19 SEACEN central bank members, it includes as observers the Reserve Bank of Australia, Hong Kong Monetary Authority, and Bank of Japan (IIMA 2005).

Finally, the ASEAN+3 Macroeconomic Research Office (AMRO) was established in 2011 in Singapore as the surveillance arm of the Chiang Mai Initiative Multilateralization (CMIM). Its staff resources are still quite small – about twenty economists currently – but it has been tasked with conducting full-fledged surveillance of the ASEAN+3 member countries. This distinguishes it from the other forums described above, which do not have their own full-time staff. It is expected that the AMRO will grow over time in terms of staff numbers and will become an international organization, although it will be a long time before it can achieve a size and depth commensurate with that of the IMF.

6.4.2 Financial Regulatory Harmonization

The ASEAN Economic Community (AEC) offers the most advanced regional framework for financial regulatory harmonization in Asia. The AEC project is summarized in the AEC blueprint, ratified by ASEAN leaders in 2007 (ASEAN Secretariat 2007). The ambitious target of the AEC is to create its Economic Community by 2015 as a region with free movement of goods, services, investment, skilled labor and "freer" flow of capital. The broad aims of the project are both to enjoy the scale economies of a unified market and to reduce the development gap among its member countries. To be sure, the blueprint recognizes in practice that some countries will progress faster than others, and liberalization will be done on a voluntary basis, which it characterizes as the "ASEAN minus X" formula. This is a necessary aspect of the voluntary nature of ASEAN cooperation. Regarding the financial services sector, the blueprint aims for a first round of liberalization by 2015, with other subsectors or modes being liberalized by 2020 (ASEAN Secretariat 2007).

Important components of the AEC include the ASEAN Framework Agreement on Services (AFAS) and ASEAN capital market integration. The aims of the AFAS are to: (i) enhance cooperation in services amongst member states in order to improve the efficiency and competitiveness, and to diversify production capacity and services supply and distribution by their service providers within and outside ASEAN; (ii) eliminate substantially restrictions to trade in services amongst member states; and (iii) liberalize trade in services by expanding the depth and scope of liberalization beyond those undertaken by member states under the GATS with the aim of realizing a free trade area in services (ASEAN Secretariat, 1995, p. 1).

The ASEAN capital market integration program aims at developing a unified pan-ASEAN market for financial services and capital flows under the ASEAN Capital Markets Forum (ACMF).[12] In order to strengthen ASEAN capital market development and integration, the blueprint calls for the following actions (ASEAN Secretariat 2007, p. 17):

- achieve greater harmonization in capital market standards in ASEAN in the areas of offering rules for debt securities, disclosure requirements and distribution rules;
- facilitate mutual recognition arrangement or agreement for the cross-border recognition of qualification and education and experience of market professionals;
- achieve greater flexibility in language and governing law requirements for securities issuance;
- enhance withholding tax structure, where possible, to promote the broadening of investor base in ASEAN debt issuance; and
- facilitate market-driven efforts to establish exchange and debt market linkages, including cross-border capital-raising activities.

It further notes that the liberalization of capital movements is to be guided by the following principles: (i) promoting an orderly capital account liberalization consistent with member countries' national agenda and readiness of the economy; (ii) allowing adequate safeguard against potential macroeconomic instability and systemic risk that may arise from the liberalization process, including the right to adopt necessary measures to ensure macroeconomic stability; and (iii) ensuring the benefits of liberalization are to be shared by all ASEAN countries (ASEAN Secretariat 2007, p. 17).

An overall assessment of the achievements of the AEC is difficult to make, as many country scorecards have not yet been released publicly. Clearly, progress has been slower than desired. One recent development is that the ACMF devised the ASEAN and Plus Standards Scheme, a framework for information disclosure standards that apply to regional cross-border securities issuance (equities and bonds). ASEAN Standards are common to all ASEAN member countries and conform to the International Organization of Securities Commissions (IOSCO) international standards, and the associated accounting and auditing standards are identical to international standards. On the other hand, the Plus Standards are an additional set of standards necessitated by the accepted practices, laws and regulations of individual countries. In June 2009, securities market regulators in Malaysia, Singapore and Thailand announced their decision to adopt this framework. Other countries are planning to join the framework, but have not yet specified any dates (The 21st Century Public Policy Institute 2011). Harmonization in the EU was driven to a large extent by market liberalization and adoption of international standards (see, for example, Posner and Véron 2010), but, in the current environment and taking into account the diverse levels of economic and financial development within the region, this force is weaker in ASEAN. Nonetheless, given the essentially voluntary nature of ASEAN cooperation, strong peer pressure is needed to produce more effective results.

6.4.3 Financial Safety Net

Following dissatisfaction with the role played by the IMF during the Asian Financial Crisis of 1997–98, a regional cooperative financing arrangement to supplement IMF resources was agreed in May 2000 at the ASEAN+3 Finance Ministers' Meeting in Chiang Mai, which was referred to as the "Chiang Mai Initiative". It initially took the form of a network of bilateral currency swap agreements, but in May 2007 the member countries agreed to convert the bilateral schemes of the CMI into a multilateralized self-managed reserve pooling scheme governed by a single contractual agreement, or the Chiang Mai Initiative Multilateralization (CMIM). The size of the agreement was set at US$120 billion, and the amount of the allocation that would be withdrawn without triggering an IMF program was raised from 10 per cent to 20 per cent (so-called "IMF conditionality" or "IMF linkage") (Sussangkarn 2010). As mentioned above, the AMRO was established in May 2011 to provide surveillance capability within the region.

However, the CMI (later CMIM) was never used, even during the global financial crisis of 2007–09. The link to IMF conditionality was one problem,[13] due to the "IMF stigma" in the region, but the process for releasing funds was also considered cumbersome and untested. The CMI (or CMIM) needed various other improvements to make it more effective as well. First, the CMI (or CMIM) borrowing quota was not likely to be enough if more than one economy got into serious problems. Second, instead of just borrowing from the CMI (or CMIM), economies could arrange bilateral currency swap facilities with CMI (or CMIM) members or other authorities – such as Australia and New Zealand. Finally, the AMRO needed to have sufficient resources and staffing to support the capabilities of an Asian monetary fund (AMF) (Sussangkarn 2010).

To address these issues, the ASEAN+3 Finance Ministers and Central Bank Governors announced a number of reforms in May 2012, including: doubling the CMIM resources to US$240 billion; increasing the IMF-delinked portion to 30 per cent with a view to increasing it to 40 per cent in 2014; lengthening the maturity and supporting period for the IMF-linked portion from 90 days to 1 year and from 2 years to 3 years, respectively; lengthening the maturity and supporting period of the IMF-de-linked portion from 90 days to 6 months and from 1 year to 2 years, respectively; and introducing a crisis prevention facility called CMIM Precautionary Line (CMIM-PL) (ASEAN Secretariat 2012). The last would correspond to the Flexible Credit Line and Precautionary Credit Line facilities of the IMF. These improvements should enable the CMIM to move closer to becoming a full-fledged AMF.

6.5 CHALLENGES FOR REGULATORY COOPERATION AND POLICY RECOMMENDATIONS

This section discusses challenges for cooperation in financial regulation in the EU and Asia, highlights the differences between regional regulatory approaches in the EU and ASEAN, and describes some of the challenges in extending the ASEAN model to the rest of Asia. It then describes policy recommendations for strengthening regional financial regulation in Asia.

6.5.1 Cooperation Challenges in the EU

As discussed in sections 6.2 and 6.3, even with elaborate regional legal and political structures and integrated economic and financial systems, the EU still faces many obstacles to effective regional regulation, including: continued diversity of financial systems, laws and regulatory structures and practices; a complex system, with a large number of players with overlapping responsibilities and potential conflicts of interest; continued evolution of EU-wide supervisory agencies with largely untested powers; large size, potential cumbersomeness, and lack of strong authority of the ESRB; national resistance to an expanded EU-wide authority and a tendency to protect domestic financial industries; inadequate information sharing; weak cross-border supervisory cooperation based on MOUs lacking legal force and tending to be overridden in crisis; and lack of a legal framework for resolution and deposit insurance of cross-border financial firms.[14]

These shortcomings demonstrate that the institutional frameworks for the single financial market in the single currency area are seriously inadequate, and they indeed directly contributed to the severity of the eurozone sovereign debt and banking sector crisis. First, the lack of a regional financial safety net allowed the development of the "doom loop" between sovereigns and banks at the national and regional levels. Second, regulation at the national level substantially lagged monetary and financial integration in the region. In the presence of such a lag, the close interconnectedness of European banks led to the easy transmission of financial shocks across borders, tended to create negative externalities for other countries, and contributed to the build-up of macroeconomic imbalances within Europe. Third, the lack of a region-wide financial safety net led to a fragmentation of European financial markets via a virtual shut-off of intraregional capital flows, which in turn hampered the transmission of monetary policy easing throughout the region. These developments partly reflected the inadequacies of national-level home-host supervisor arrangements in the presence of high financial integration.

The direction of the solution is clear: financial regulatory functions – including supervision, resolution and deposit insurance – need to be elevated to the regional level. First, regulation needs to be consistent with the cross-border activities of European financial firms, especially those within the euro member countries. Second, introducing the SSM is directly related to the decision to allow the possibility of direct recapitalization of banks by the ESM, the European financial safety net. Third, it is necessary to promote financial integration in Europe to enhance the transmission of monetary policy.

The commitment of the EU to create a banking union – including supervision, resolution and deposit insurance – means that implementation now represents the major challenge for the EU. Issues include how to deal with the non-euro-member countries, how to enforce a sufficient degree of regulatory harmonization, and how to establish the EU-wide resolution and deposit insurance scheme. The latter also requires a commitment to a fiscal union, which in turn implies success in establishing a political union, since otherwise the fiscal union will lack political legitimacy. As noted above, the establishment of the SSM is only the first step in a lengthy process, and many difficult political decisions remain to be made.

6.5.2 Cooperation Challenges in Asia

Asia has no over-arching political structure comparable to the EU, and there is little willingness in the region to concede national sovereignty in these areas. The AEC provides a possible model for wider Asian cooperation, but progress even within ASEAN has been slow, and institutions weak. Barriers to stronger regionalization of political and economic institutions in Asia include: the lack of an overall agreement on the definition of "Asian" membership; great diversity in terms of economic and financial development, financial and economic systems, institutional quality, capital account openness and regulatory regimes; weak and under-developed regional institutions, with no legal authority; and the voluntary nature of cooperation even within ASEAN.

The weaker structure of regional institutions and greater diversity in financial development and capital market openness in ASEAN (and even more so in ASEAN+6 as a whole) require a different approach than in the EU. The EU approach in principle has been to fully harmonize laws and regulations, mainly in accordance with international standards, while only small, unharmonized parts are addressed through mutual recognition, and it has completely liberalized controls on cross-border capital transactions. In contrast, ASEAN is aiming for general harmonization, coupled with mutual recognition given for complementary purposes. It aims to attain increased levels of capital flows within the region, but stops well short of calling for complete deregulation of capital flows. This difference points to a key role for mutual recognition in the financial integration process in ASEAN, as discussed in greater detail above.

Within ASEAN, perhaps the first challenge is to promote financial development in those countries that are lagging behind, mainly the "CLMV" countries (Cambodia, Lao PDR, Myanmar and Viet Nam). Only stronger convergence within the region can set the stage for achieving the targets of financial integration and regulatory harmonization laid out in the AEC as described in section 6.4. Until such convergence is achieved, ASEAN member countries will need to pursue a multi-track approach, with those countries that have achieved the relevant milestones of financial development committing to further steps of financial opening. Along with this, ASEAN economies need to strengthen institutions for regional cooperation to promote regional harmonization of regulations, taxation and so on, using the ASEAN finance ministers' surveillance process as the starting point. This is particularly important in view of the great divergence of regulatory performance and capacity within the region. One beneficial step would be to include financial regulators and deposit insurance corporations in at least some deliberations so that the monitoring of regional financial stability could be strengthened.

Institutions for regulatory cooperation need to be strengthened at the level of the ASEAN+3 countries as well. One challenge is to strengthen the CMIM and the AMRO to fulfill their functions as a regional financial safety net and surveillance unit, respectively. Monitoring and exchanging information about potential economic imbalances and volatile capital flows can reduce the threat to economic and financial stability presented by them.

6.5.3 Recommendations for Regional Financial Regulation in Asia: Improving the ASEAN Economic Community Process

The AEC process can be improved through promoting mutual recognition, increasing regulatory harmonization and enhancing cross-border supervisory cooperation via MOUs. Recommended steps to promote mutual recognition include:

- ensuring conformity to IOSCO principles to the extent possible, including expanding the scope of the ASEAN and Plus Standards Scheme;
- expanding mutual recognition to the maximum extent possible by preserving domestic market soundness while securing investor protection and ensuring proper management of systemic risk; and
- strengthening cooperation and information exchange among different regulatory authorities.

Mutual fund passporting is one example of an area that could benefit substantially from mutual recognition.

Major ways to increase regulatory harmonization include:

- standardizing and integrating direct market infrastructures (trading platforms, clearing/settlement systems);
- harmonizing indirect infrastructures (laws and regulations, credit rating agencies, accounting/auditing standards, tax systems); and
- harmonizing foreign exchange regulations.

Studies have identified tax withholding rules as a major hurdle to participation in regional bond markets by international investors (The 21st Century Public Policy Institute 2011).

Enhancing cross-border supervisory cooperation via MOUs has the potential to improve the effectiveness of monitoring globally or regionally systemically important financial institutions (SIFIs), although experience shows that MOUs can be relatively ineffective, especially in a crisis. The AMRO has already begun regional monitoring, but this effort needs to involve national supervisory bodies as well. One key problem is dealing with global SIFIs whose headquarters are outside the region. In this case, supervisory colleges with a global reach are the appropriate institution, but they could still prove problematic if home country authorities are distant from Asia – such as in the US and Europe – and not knowledgeable about conditions there. In that case, requiring Asian branches of these global SIFIs to become subsidiaries may be a desirable option. However, the pros and cons of requiring Asian branches of global SIFIs to become subsidiaries would need to be carefully assessed, both in terms of financial stability and the costs and impacts such ring-fencing would entail for cross-border capital allocation.

Next steps for ERPD, CMIM and AMRO
The ERPD so far has been mostly a beauty contest. The policy dialogue among the finance ministers and central bank governors needs to be strengthened. The inclusion of the central bank governors in the ASEAN+3 finance ministers' process in 2012 was a positive first step. Important further steps include: developing a "peer review" methodology and practice; and regularly monitoring capital flows and exchange rate movements.

As mentioned above, a number of steps were taken over the past several years to significantly strengthen the CMIM, including doubling the size of its resources, increasing the portion of the quota that can be tapped without an IMF program, and introducing precautionary lending instruments. The size of the facility that each member can borrow should be further enlarged either through an additional increase in the total resources or through a change in the formula to define the maximum amount each member economy can borrow. The ASEAN+3 authorities should also consider extending CMIM membership to Australia, New Zealand and India, and should encourage the development of a financial safety net in South Asia as well. In the future, the CMIM should aim to reduce its link with the IMF over time, ultimately to zero, by providing sufficient resources for the AMRO and improving its surveillance capacity. It also needs to operationalize its financial safety net functions, which have not yet been tested. At the same time, it needs to develop a framework for cooperation with the IMF in the event that a widespread systemic shock occurs involving multiple countries. With these, a de facto AMF will have emerged.

Creating an Asian financial stability dialogue
To make substantial progress in improving regional financial stability, there needs to be a suitable driving force. Kawai (2011), Plummer (2012),

and others support the idea of an Asian financial stability dialogue (AFSD), which was first suggested by Kuroda (2008). The AFSD would provide a forum for broader information sharing in the areas of macroeconomic and financial stability, including financial regulators and deposit insurance corporations, as well as finance ministries and central banks. The AFSD could discuss regional financial vulnerabilities, regional capital flows, common issues for financial sector supervision and regulation, and common efforts at financial integration.

There is currently an Asian regional forum led by the Bank for International Settlements (BIS), but such a forum should be led by Asian countries (in the form of an AFSD), and they may invite the BIS to participate. This entity could build on existing institutions in the region, including the ERPD and the EMEAP. The body should include the participation of finance ministries, central banks, financial market regulators and supervisors, and deposit insurance corporations, that is, a wider scope than that of the ERPD, which focuses on macroeconomic policy issues. Its objective would be to monitor factors affecting regional financial stability, including national financial market conditions and capital flows, and to induce appropriate policy actions including macroprudential policy and coordination of capital flow management.

For example, policy spillovers (e.g. cross-border impacts of blanket guarantees of deposit insurance, capital control measures, or adoption of macroprudential policies) are likely to have side-effects on capital flows that could be destabilizing for other economies in the region, and call for concerted action at the regional level. Table 6.7 summarizes recent measures affecting capital inflows introduced in Asian economies. The AFSD could identify regional SIFIs and discuss how the national authorities in the region can improve cross-border supervision over them. It could also provide a regional counterpart to the FSB, an element of regional institutional architecture that is currently missing. In particular, the AFSD could liaise with the FSB for Asia's non-FSB member countries.[15]

In the early stages, such an arrangement could focus on issues that would help advance the areas of common interest that have already been identified and that are largely being dealt with under separate initiatives, such as the management of volatile short-term capital flows. Plummer (2012) sees it initially focusing on improving early warning systems, being able to assist in negotiations on common exchange rate changes, and, perhaps, helping in crisis management. The principal question is how far an AFSD might proceed beyond simply monitoring, diagnosing potential threats and suggesting remedies. One of the problems revealed in the run-up to the global financial crisis was that some organizations, particularly the BIS, did diagnose various sources of fragility, but they had no powers to act upon them.

Table 6.7   Recent measures affecting capital inflows in Asia

Outright prohibitions on funds transfer and payments	
Taipei,China	2009: Prohibited use of time deposits by foreign funds.
	2010: One-week deadline for money to be invested or repatriated.
	2010: Measures to curb trading in foreign currency.

Explicit quantitative limits or approval procedures	
PRC	2002: QFII introduced.
	2006: QDII limits introduced.
	2011: Limits on Hong Kong, China's banks' net open positions and ability to access Yuan through mainland foreign exchange market; also RQFII limits introduced.
India	2013: Cut maximum outward direct investment by companies and individuals to 100% of net worth.
Rep. of Korea	2010: Limits on FX derivative contracts on domestic banks (50% of capital) and foreign banks (250%).
	2011: Limits on FX derivative contracts on domestic banks (40% of capital) and foreign banks (200%).
	2012: Limits on FX derivative contracts on domestic banks (30% of capital) and foreign banks (150%).

Explicit taxes on cross-border flows (Tobin tax)	
Indonesia	2010: One-month holding period on SBIs (central bank notes).
Rep. of Korea	2011: Withholding tax on treasury and monetary stabilization bonds.
Thailand	2010: 15% withholding tax on capital gains and interest income on foreign bonds.

Compulsory reserve or deposit requirements (URR)	
Thailand	2006: Unremunerated reserve requirements (30%) on loans, bonds, mutual funds, swaps and non-resident Baht accounts (abolished 2008).

Notes: PRC = People's Republic of China (PRC); QFII = qualified foreign institutional investors; QDII = qualified domestic institutional investors; RQFII = PRC renminbi QFII; FX = foreign exchange; SBIs = central bank notes of Bank Indonesia; URR = unremunerated reserve requirement.

Sources: Central bank reports and other reports.

To maximize its effectiveness, the AFSD should complement and coordinate with existing regional entities, including the ERPD, EMEAP and AMRO. For example, the AMRO and ERPD could focus mainly on macroeconomic policies and surveillance, so the AFSD could focus more on financial stability issues. Since not all Asian economies are members of the FSB or the Basel Committee on Banking Supervision, the AFSD could help to consolidate the viewpoints of Asian economies so they could be delivered in global forums such as the FSB and the BIS. One question is whether the AFSD would have its own secretariat or whether it would be dependent on other institutions such as the AMRO for macroeconomic and financial sector surveillance.

6.6 CONCLUSIONS

An increasingly financially integrated Asia will need more intensive financial cooperation, including greater efforts to harmonize and coordinate financial supervision and regulation. In particular, greater financial openness increases the potential vulnerability of Asian economies to the vicissitudes of volatile capital flows, underlining the needs for regional efforts to improve financial stability. Increased economic integration as a result of trade liberalization and the development of supply chain networks has also increased the value of policy coordination, including stabilizing intraregional exchange rates. Finally, a gap has opened up between national regulation efforts and global regulatory cooperation centered on the G20, the IMF and the FSB, especially for non-G20 economies. Establishing a regional regulatory architecture can help to fill that gap.

The EU represents the most advanced stage of regional financial integration and regulation in the world today, and can provide valuable lessons for Asia, although it is by no means a benchmark or a template. The eurozone sovereign debt and banking sector crisis has highlighted many weaknesses in the EU regional architecture that need to be addressed. Fundamentally, the largely national-level regulatory structure was ill-equipped to deal with the high level of financial integration in the EU. Supervisory colleges based on voluntary MOUs have proved to be weak reeds, and have tended to be supplanted by ad hoc arrangements in an emergency. EU-wide supervisory institutions have been strengthened recently, but their new powers are largely untested, and most power still rests with national-level supervisors. Regulatory harmonization has made great progress, but continued national variations make full harmonization elusive. Regimes for resolution and deposit insurance in particular remain unharmonized.

In response to these perceived inadequacies, the EU has committed itself to shifting financial regulation from the national to the regional level by establishing a banking union. This regionwide regulatory framework will include the Single Supervisory Mechanism headed by the ECB (launched in 2013) and regionwide resolution and deposit insurance structures. These measures will have to be supported by fiscal union and greater political union as well. This means that the implications of the single market and the single currency are at last being followed to their necessary conclusions. Without these developments, there can be no lasting solution to the eurozone sovereign debt and banking sector crisis.

Asia has not reached the EU's stage of having regional political and legal institutions and integrated financial markets, let alone a single currency, so it is not feasible or necessary to emulate EU-wide policy arrangements at this stage. Despite rather high average levels of economic and financial development, financial openness and institutional regulatory capacity vary much more widely in Asia than in the EU. Moreover, while harmonization in the EU was driven to a large extent by market liberalization and adoption of international standards, this force is weaker in ASEAN, reflecting both the current economic environment and varying levels of economic and financial development within the region.

Despite its shortcomings and slow pace, the ASEAN Economic Community process probably provides the most feasible and relevant model for regulatory cooperation on a voluntary basis. It would be desirable to extend this framework further within Asia, say to the ASEAN+3 countries for a start. This approach will require a greater tolerance for different timetables of liberalization and harmonization. Only those member countries that have achieved the requisite development milestones should move on to higher stages of integration and regulatory harmonization. The AEC can be strengthened further by taking steps to implement best practice regulation, promote mutual recognition in areas such as fund management, harmonize market infrastructure and promote cross-border supervisory MOUs. Use and publication of country "scorecards" should be increased to incentivize harmonization efforts.

Even within this less ambitious framework, Asian economies can strengthen regional financial cooperation in various ways. They can strengthen the ERPD by giving greater teeth to the surveillance process. They can enhance and diversify the resources, functions and membership of the CMIM and AMRO for surveillance and provision of a financial safety net which may eventually develop into an Asian monetary fund. They can create an AFSD to monitor regional financial markets, facilitate policy dialogue and cooperation, and secure regional financial stability.

These regional regulatory institutions can also strengthen ties with their respective global institutions, primarily the IMF and the FSB.

NOTES

1. ASEAN includes: Brunei Darussalam, Cambodia, Indonesia, Lao People's Democratic Republic, Malaysia, Myanmar, Philippines, Singapore, Thailand and Viet Nam.
2. ASEAN+3 includes the 10 ASEAN member countries plus the People's Republic of China (PRC), Japan and the Republic of Korea.
3. The eurozone sovereign debt and banking sector crisis has led to increased calls for EU-wide supervision of major financial institutions, e.g. Barroso (2012).
4. See, for example, King and Levine (1993); Cecchetti and Kharroubi (2012); Levine (2005); Beck et al. (2000); and Rajan and Zingales (1998). Whether this effect is causal or not remains controversial, especially in light of the role of financial innovation (Rodrik 2008; Schularick and Steger 2010).
5. Such efforts could eventually be extended to other parts of Asia as well.
6. The Geary–Khamis dollar is a hypothetical unit of currency that has the same purchasing power parity that the United States (US) dollar has in the US at a given point in time. The data are obtained from The Conference Board Total Economy Database™, January 2013, http://www.conference-board.org/data/economydatabase/.
7. ASEAN+6 includes ASEAN+3 plus Australia, India and New Zealand.
8. "Supervisory colleges" refer to multilateral working groups of relevant supervisors that are formed for the purpose of enhancing effective coordinated supervision of an international banking group on an ongoing basis. EU authorities have developed a framework of cooperation which is legally binding for all supervisory authorities from the European Economic Area (in particular the Capital Requirement Directive-CRD no. 2006/48/EC7) (Basel Committee on Banking Supervision 2010).
9. The ESFS includes the three ESAs and national financial supervisors in the EU.
10. It comprises the central banks of eleven economies: Reserve Bank of Australia, People's Bank of China, Hong Kong Monetary Authority, Bank Indonesia, Bank of Japan, the Bank of Korea, Bank Negara Malaysia, Reserve Bank of New Zealand, Bangko Sentral ng Pilipinas, Monetary Authority of Singapore and Bank of Thailand (IIMA 2005).
11. These include: Autoriti Monetari Brunei Darussalam; National Bank of Cambodia; People's Bank of China; Reserve Bank of Fiji; Reserve Bank of India; Bank Indonesia; Bank of Korea; Bank of the Lao PDR; Bank Negara Malaysia; Bank of Mongolia; Central Bank of Myanmar; Nepal Rastra Bank; Bank of Papua New Guinea; Bangko Sentral ng Pilipinas; Monetary Authority of Singapore; Central Bank of Sri Lanka; central bank of Taipei,China; Bank of Thailand; and State Bank of Vietnam.
12. Established in 2004 under the auspices of the ASEAN Finance Ministers, the ACMF focuses on strategic issues to achieve greater integration of the region's capital markets under the AEC Blueprint 2015. Members include the relevant capital market supervisory agencies in ASEAN member countries.
13. Previously, members needed to have an IMF program to be able to tap more than 20 per cent of their borrowing quota. This was raised to 30 per cent in May 2012. In view of the negative perception of the IMF that developed during and after the Asian Financial Crisis, going to the IMF has become anathema in much of Asia since then.
14. As mentioned above, the Single Resolution Mechanism was approved in 2014.
15. To be sure, the FSB established in 2011 the Regional Consultative Group for Asia (and similar groups in other regions) with the specific intention of communicating with non-FSB-member countries in Asia (FSB 2012). However, it still seems likely that an AFSD

would have greater ownership by Asian members and could speak for them with more authority.

REFERENCES

ASEAN Secretariat. 1995. ASEAN Framework Agreement on Services. Jakarta: ASEAN Secretariat. Available at: http://www.aseansec.org/6628.htm (accessed 11 June 2012).
ASEAN Secretariat. 2007. ASEAN Economic Community Blueprint. Jakarta: ASEAN Secretariat. Available at: http://www.aseansec.org/21083.pdf (accessed 18 April 2012).
ASEAN Secretariat. 2008. Joint Statement of the 11th ASEAN Plus Three Finance Ministers' Meeting. Madrid, 4 May. Available at: http://www.mof.go.jp/english/if/as3_080504.htm (accessed 12 April 2012).
ASEAN Secretariat. 2012. Joint Statement of the 15th ASEAN+3 Finance Ministers and Central Bank Governors' Meeting. Manila, 3 May. Available at: http://www.aseansec.org/Joint%20Media%20Statement%20of%20the%20 15th%20ASEAN+3%20Finance%20Ministers%20and%20Central%20Bank% 20Governors'%20Meeting.pdf (accessed 16 May 2012).
Barroso, J.M. 2012. State of the Union 2012 Address. Brussels: European Commission. 12 September. Available at: http://europa.eu/rapid/press-release_ SPEECH-12-596_en.htm?locale=en (accessed 8 December 2013).
Basel Committee on Banking Supervision. 2010. Good practice principles on supervisory colleges. Basel, Switzerland: Bank for International Settlements. Available at: http://www.bis.org/publ/bcbs177.pdf (accessed 18 April 2012).
Beck, T., R. Levine and N.V. Loayza. 2000. Finance and the sources of growth. *Journal of Financial Economics* **58**(1–2): 261–300.
Cecchetti, S. and E. Kharroubi. 2012. Reassessing the impact of finance on growth. BIS Working Papers No. 381. Basel, Switzerland: Bank for International Settlements. Available at: http://www.bis.org/publ/work381.pdf (accessed 30 July 2012).
Chinn, M. and H. Ito. 2006. What matters for financial development? Capital controls, institutions, and interactions. *Journal of Development Economics* **81**(1): 163–92.
Constâncio, V. 2012. Towards a European Banking Union. Lecture held at the start of the academic year of the Duisenberg School of Finance, Amsterdam, 7 September. Available at: http://www.ecb.int/press/key/date/2012/html/ sp120907.en.html (accessed 3 December 2012).
European Commission. 2009. *The High-Level Group of Financial Supervision in the EU*. Brussels: European Commission.
European Commission. 2012. Proposal for a Council Regulation conferring specific tasks on the European Central Bank concerning policies relating to the prudential supervision of credit institutions. Brussels: European Commission. 12 September.
European Commission. 2013a. *EFSF Lending Operations*. Brussels: European Commission. Available at: http://www.efsf.europa.eu/about/operations/index. htm (accessed 8 January 2013).

European Commission. 2013b. Proposal for a Regulation of the European Parliament and of the Council establishing uniform rules and a uniform procedure for the resolution of credit institutions and certain investment firms in the framework of a Single Resolution Mechanism and a Single Bank Resolution Fund and amending Regulation (EU) No. 1093/2010 of the European Parliament and of the Council. Brussels: European Commission. Available at: http://eur-lex.europa.eu/LexUriServ/LexUriServ.do?uri=COM:2013:0520:FIN:EN:PDF (accessed 10 January 2014).

European Council. 2012a. *Euro Area Summit Statement*. Brussels: European Council. 29 June. Available at: http://www.european-council.europa.eu/council-meetings.aspx (accessed 4 July 2012).

European Council. 2012b. *European Council Conclusions on Completing EMU*. Brussels: European Council. 18 October.

European Systemic Risk Board. 2012a. *Organisation and Structure*. Available at: http://www.esrb.europa.eu/about/orga/board/html/index.en.html (accessed 18 April 2012).

European Systemic Risk Board. 2012b. *Mission, Objectives and Tasks*. Brussels: European Commission. Available at: http://www.esrb.europa.eu/about/tasks/html/index.en.html (accessed 18 April 2012).

European Union. 2011. Financial services: Additional legislative proposal to complete the framework for financial supervision in Europe. Press release. 19 January. Available at: http://europa.eu/rapid/pressReleasesAction.do?reference=IP/11/49&format=HTML&aged=0&language=EN&guiLanguage=en (accessed 17 April 2012).

Financial Stability Board (FSB). 2012. Press release: Second Meeting of the Financial Stability Board Regional Consultative Group for Asia. Basel, Switzerland: Bank for International Settlements. 14 May. Available at: http://www.financialstabilityboard.org/press/pr_120514.pdf (accessed 4 July 2012).

Fullenkamp, C. and S. Sharma. 2012. *Good Financial Regulation: Changing the Process is Crucial*. London: International Centre for Financial Regulation and Financial Times. Available at: http://www.icffr.org/assets/pdfs/February-2012/ICFR---Financial-Times-Research-Prize-2011/C-Fullenkamp-and-S-Sharma---Good-Financial-Regulat.aspx (accessed 13 June 2012).

Independent Commission on Banking (ICB). 2011. *Final Report Recommendations*. London: Independent Commission on Banking.

Institute for International Monetary Affairs. 2005. *Economic Surveillance and Policy Dialogue in East Asia*. Jakarta, Indonesia: ASEAN Secretariat. Available at: http://www.aseansec.org/17890.pdf (accessed 20 April 2012).

International Monetary Fund (IMF). 2012. *Annual Report on Exchange Arrangements and Exchange Restrictions*. Washington, DC: International Monetary Fund.

International Monetary Fund (IMF). 2013. Myanmar 2013 Article IV Consultation and First Review Under the Staff-Monitored Program. IMF Country Report No. 13/240. Washington, DC: International Monetary Fund.

Kawai, M. 2011. G-20 financial reforms and emerging Asia's challenges. In K. Dervis, M. Kawai and D. Lombardi (eds) *Asia and Policymaking for the Global Economy*. Washington, DC: The Brookings Institution.

Kawai, M. and C. Houser. 2008. Evolving ASEAN+3 ERPD: Toward peer reviews or due diligence? In OECD (eds) *Shaping Policy Reform and Peer Review in Southeast Asia: Integrating Economies amid Diversity*. Paris: Organisation for Economic Co-operation and Development.

King, R.G. and R. Levine. 1993. Finance and growth: Schumpeter might be right. Policy Research Working Paper Series No. 1083. Washington, DC: The World Bank.

Kuroda, H. 2008. Asia's contribution to global development and stability. Closing remarks presented at the ADBI Annual Conference. Tokyo, 5 December. Available at: http://www.adbi.org/speeches/2008/12/05/2760.closing.remarks.kuroda.asia.global.financial.crisis.conference/

Lanexang Securities Public Company. 2013. *Lao Investment Guide*. Vientiane: Lanexang Securities Public Company. Available at: http://www.lxs.com.la/files/Lao%20Investment%20Guide/Lao%20Investment%20Guide%20%5BEnglish-Version%5D%20-%20October%202013.pdf (accessed 9 January 2014).

Levine, R. 2005. Finance and growth: Theory and evidence. In P. Aghion and S. Durlauf (eds) *Handbook of Economic Growth*. Amsterdam: Elsevier Science.

Plummer, M. 2012. Regional monitoring of capital flows and coordination of financial regulation: Stakes and options for Asia. In M. Kawai, D. Mayes and P. Morgan (eds) *Implications of the Global Financial Crisis for Financial Reform and Regulation in Asia*. Cheltenham, UK and Northampton, MA, USA: Edward Elgar Publishing.

Posner, E. and N. Véron. 2010. The EU and financial regulation: Power without purpose? *Journal of European Public Policy* **17**(3): 400–15.

Rajan, R. and L. Zingales. 1998. Financial dependence and growth. *American Economic Review* **88**(3): 559–86.

Rodrik, D. 2008. A practical approach to formulating growth strategies. In J. Stiglitz and N. Serra (eds) *The Washington Consensus Reconsidered: Towards a New Global Governance*. New York: Oxford University Press.

Rompuy, H. van. 2012. Towards a genuine economic and monetary union. Report by President of the European Council. Brussels: European Council. 26 June.

Schularick, M. and T. Steger. 2010. Financial integration, investment, and economic growth: Evidence from two eras of financial globalization. *Review of Economics and Statistics* **92**(4): 756–68.

Sussangkarn, C. 2010. The Chiang Mai Initiative Multilateralization: Origin, Development and Outlook. ADBI Working Paper No. 230. Tokyo: Asian Development Bank Institute. Available at: http://www.adbi.org/files/2010.07.13.wp230.chiang.mai.initiative.multilateralisation.pdf (accessed 13 March 2012).

The 21st Century Public Policy Institute. 2011. *Asian Bond Markets Development and Regional Financial Cooperation*. Tokyo: The 21st Century Public Policy Institute. Available at: http://asianbondsonline.adb.org/publications/external/2011/Asian_Bond_Markets_Development_and_Regional_Financial_Cooperation.pdf (accessed 2 March 2012).

Véron, N. 2012a. Financial reform after the crisis: An early assessment. PIIE Working Paper WP 2–12. Washington, DC: Peterson Institute for International Economics. Available at: http://www.piie.com/publications/wp/wp12–2.pdf (accessed 15 May 2012).

Véron, N. 2012b. *Europe's Single Supervisory Mechanism and the Long Journey towards a Banking Union*. Brussels: Directorate General for Internal Policies, European Parliament.

Winkler, A. 2012. The financial crisis: A wake-up call for strengthening regional monitoring of financial markets and regional coordination of financial sector policies? In M. Kawai, D. Mayes and P. Morgan (eds) *Implications of the Global Financial Crisis for Financial Reform and Regulation in Asia.* Cheltenham, UK and Northampton, MA, USA: Edward Elgar Publishing.

Wymeersch, E. 2010. Global and regional financial regulation: The viewpoint of a European securities regulator. *Global Policy* 1(2): 201–08.

7. Evolving trade policy architecture and FTAs in Asia

Masahiro Kawai and Ganeshan Wignaraja*

7.1 INTRODUCTION

Asia's trade policy architecture is witnessing a proliferation of free trade agreements (FTAs) with significant implications for economies and firms alike. This marks a break with past trade policy in the region. Asia's famous economic rise as the "global factory" over several decades was facilitated by outward-oriented development strategies and a multilateral approach based initially on the General Agreement on Tariffs and Trade (GATT) and then its successor, the World Trade Organization (WTO). Free trade agreements (FTAs), as trade-policy instruments in Asia, were largely absent in the region's trade policy architecture during Asia's economic rise.[1]

Today, the region is a leader in global FTA activity with about 76 concluded FTAs in 2013 (up from only 3 in 2000). Its largest economies (People's Republic of China [PRC], India and Japan) as well as a few advanced ASEAN economies (e.g. Singapore and Thailand) have become key players in FTA activity (see Appendix Table 7A.1). Reflecting the growth of FTAs, the importance of FTAs to Asia's trade has also increased. Several reasons seem to underlie the spread in Asian FTAs, including market access for goods trade, the need to remove impediments to deepening regional production networks and supply chains, the intensification of FTA activity in Europe and the Americas, and slow progress in WTO Doha Round trade talks.

Various concerns over Asia's evolving FTA-centric trade policy architecture have been raised in a growing body of literature on Asian FTAs (e.g. Banda and Whalley 2005; Manchin and Pelkmans-Balaoing 2007; Bhagwati 2008; Drysdale and Armstrong 2010). Issues highlighted in this literature include: shallow coverage of agricultural trade, limited services trade liberalization, insufficient WTO-plus elements, low use of FTA preferences, and an Asian noodle bowl of multiple rules of origin (ROO). This chapter examines these concerns on the role of FTAs in Asia's trade policy architecture from a pragmatic perspective, with a view to providing better informed policy decisions. These topics are the front line of contemporary Asian trade negotiations and of interest to policy-makers. This chapter scrutinizes these concerns using new data on the contents of existing FTAs and business impacts of FTAs. It also explores policy implications from the growth of Asian FTAs including competition among the Asia-led Regional Comprehensive Economic Partnership (RCEP) and the US-led Trans-Pacific Strategic Economic Partnership (TPP) as the future basis for a region-wide FTA as well as the role of the WTO.

The remainder of the chapter is structured as follows. Sections 7.2–7.6 discuss the concerns; section 7.7 explores policy implications at national, regional and multilateral levels. Section 7.8 concludes.

7.2   SHALLOW COVERAGE OF AGRICULTURAL TRADE

A major concern about Asian FTAs may be the extent of coverage of agricultural goods trade. The literature shows that the coverage of agricultural trade differs markedly among current Asian FTAs (Feridhanusetyawan 2005). Agricultural trade tended to be excluded from most of the early agreements due to pressure from powerful farm lobbies or social concerns regarding poverty in rural areas.

Two problems have hampered empirical research on the coverage of agricultural goods trade in Asian FTAs. First, little systematic data and analysis have been available on the treatment of agricultural products across Asian FTAs. Second, clear criteria for the "substantially all trade" rule do not seem to exist. With the development of new databases on Asian FTAs – for example, the Asian Development Bank's (ADB) Asia Regional Integration Center database – new sources of FTA data are now available. Furthermore, tariff lines for agricultural products can be used as a basis to gauge the criteria of the majority of all trade.

A simple three-fold classification system was used to categorize Asian FTAs according to tariff line coverage of agricultural products. Given the complexity of provisions for agriculture in many agreements, and the availability of tariff schedules and exclusion lists at the product level, a combination of coverage of product lines and exclusions was used to assess each agreement. The classifications are as follows:

1. Comprehensive coverage: at least 85 per cent of all agricultural product lines in a given agreement are covered, or not more than 150

product lines are excluded. FTAs with these features for agricultural products are taken as covering the majority of all trade.
2. No, or limited, coverage: agricultural products are completely excluded in the agreement, or less than 100 product lines are included.
3. Some coverage: more agricultural products are included in FTAs than "no or limited coverage", but fewer products are covered than "comprehensive coverage". Agreements with such coverage typically include more than 100 agricultural product lines, but less than 85 per cent of agricultural product lines. These agreements may also exclude over 150 agricultural product lines.

It was possible to apply this classification system to examine the agricultural coverage of concluded Asian FTAs during 2000–13 and the results are provided in Table 7.1. The first part of the table suggests Asian FTAs have become more comprehensive in their coverage of agricultural products over time. AFTA, for instance, was originally proposed for only 10 manufacturing sectors, and included agriculture at a later stage. The three concluded FTAs in 2000 had no or limited coverage of agriculture. Concluded FTA numbers grew to 22 in 2005. Of these 8 (36 per cent) were regarded as comprehensive in coverage of agriculture, 5 (23 per cent) had some coverage and 9 (41 per cent) had no or limited coverage. Further expansion of FTAs occurred thereafter. Of the 77 agreements for which texts[2] were available in December 2013, 40 (52 per cent) have comprehensive coverage of agriculture while another 19 (25 per cent) have some coverage of these items. The remaining 18 (23 per cent) have limited or no coverage.

The Republic of Korea has comprehensive coverage of agriculture in its FTAs. For instance, under the Republic of Korea–United States FTA (KORUS), the Republic of Korea will eliminate tariffs on almost two-thirds of current US agricultural exports upon entry into force, including wheat, corn and cotton. Tariffs and import quotas on most other agricultural goods will be phased out within 10 years. The Republic of Korea even agreed to eliminate its 40 per cent tariff on beef muscle meats over a 15-year period.[3]

7.3 LIMITED SERVICES TRADE LIBERALIZATION

A second concern is limited services trade liberalization in Asian FTAs. Services account for more than half the GDP of most Asian countries and trade in services has grown rapidly (Hoekman and Mattoo 2011). Studies suggest that impediments to trade in services, particularly regulatory restrictions on foreign services and service providers, exist across Asia

Table 7.1   The architecture of FTAs in Asia

Year	Total concluded FTAs in Asia[a]	Agriculture coverage[b]			Services coverage[c]			% of FTAs covering goods and/or services	WTO plus rules[d]	
		% of FTAs with no or/limited coverage	% of FTAs with some coverage	% of FTAs with comprehensive coverage	% of FTAs with no or/limited coverage	% of FTAs with some coverage	% of FTAs with comprehensive coverage		% of FTAs covering partial WTO plus elements	% of FTAs covering comprehensive WTO plus elements
2000	3	100.0	0.0	0.0	66.7	0.0	33.3	66.7	33.3	0.0
2005	22	40.9	22.7	36.4	31.8	22.7	45.5	36.4	27.3	36.4
2010	59	28.8	27.1	44.1	23.7	37.3	39.0	27.1	49.2	23.7
2013	77	23.4	24.7	51.9	22.1	32.5	45.5	23.4	50.6	26.0

Notes:

a   Concluded FTAs include those that are in effect and those that have been signed but are not yet in effect. Asia includes the 10 ASEAN countries; PRC; Hong Kong, China; Japan; Republic of Korea; Taipei,China; and India.

b   Agricultural products and chapters are classified according to World Trade Organization (WTO) classification. "Comprehensive" means agriculture is substantially covered (at least 85% of agricultural product lines) or not more than 150 product lines are excluded. "Excluded or Limited" means agriculture is completely excluded or less than 100 product lines or 5% of the total tariff lines. "Some coverage" refers to those in between excluded/limited and comprehensive.

c   "Comprehensive" means coverage of the five key sectors of the General Agreement on Trade in Services (GATS): business and professional services, communications services, financial services, transport services, and labor mobility/entry of business persons. "Excluded/limited" means FTA either excludes services trade liberalization or provides only general provisions thereof, or covers only one of the five key sectors in addition to some other sectors. Coverage of other sectors may also be included. "Some coverage" refers to those in between excluded/limited and comprehensive.

d   (i) narrow agreements that deal with goods and/or services; (ii) somewhat broader agreements covering goods, services and some Singapore issues (partial WTO plus); (iii) comprehensive agreements covering goods, services and all four Singapore issues (comprehensive WTO plus). (ii) and (iii) can be considered WTO plus FTAs.

Sources: Legal annexes of FTAs (www.aric.adb.org) and WTO reports; data as of December 2013.

(Findlay et al. 2009). Such impediments may occur in ownership rules, technical regulations, licensing and qualification requirements.

A lack of data on trade in services makes it hard to estimate the value of the services trade covered by an FTA. There also seems to be limited consensus on the meaning of "substantial sectoral coverage" in the services trade and an assessment of "national treatment" requires detailed subsectoral analysis. Furthermore, varying liberalization approaches to services (e.g. positive, negative or hybrid approaches to negotiations on the General Agreement on Trade in Services, or GATS) and an absence of disaggregated data on trade in services makes it difficult to quantify substantial sector coverage.

A practical way forward is to focus on requirement (i) of the GATS and to interpret "substantial sectoral coverage" to mean that a high-quality FTA should cover key service sectors.[4] The GATS classification list of 12 service sectors is a useful input for creating a simple three-fold classification of Asian FTAs as follows:

1. Comprehensive coverage of services: FTA covers the five key sectors of the GATS: business and professional services, communications services, financial services, transport services, and labor mobility/ entry of business persons. Coverage of other sectors may also be included. The five sectors were chosen as the yardstick because they are the main sectors in terms of the value of services trade in Asia and also subject to multiple regulatory barriers on foreign services and service providers.
2. Excluded or limited coverage of services: FTA either excludes services trade liberalization or provides only general provisions thereof, or covers only one of the five key sectors in addition to some other sectors.
3. Some coverage of services: FTA is not otherwise classified as comprehensive, excluded or limited. Such an FTA would typically cover between two and four key sectors of the GATS and some minor sectors.

A sector is considered as covered if at least one party includes its GATS and GATS-plus commitments, regardless of the number of sub-sectors, volume of trade affected, or the four modes of supply.[5] This classification system was applied to Asian FTAs during 2000–13 (see the second part of Table 7.1). The evidence indicates a trend in Asian FTAs towards progressively liberalizing the service sectors of participants and providing for deeper regulatory cooperation in services over time. In the early 2000s, the majority of FTAs had limited or some coverage of services. By 2005, 10

FTAs[6] (45 per cent) were deemed to be comprehensive in covering at least five key services, 5 (23 per cent) provided coverage of between two and four key sectors, and 7 (32 per cent) had little or no coverage. Thereafter, most new FTAs typically incorporated either comprehensive or some coverage of services. Of the 77 FTAs in 2013, 35 (45 per cent) were comprehensive and another 25 (33 per cent) had some coverage. Only 17 (22 per cent) had no or limited coverage.

Many Asian FTAs adhere to key GATS principles such as market access (quota elimination); national treatment (equal treatment of local and foreign service providers); MFN treatment (service suppliers of an FTA member will automatically receive benefits given to other future FTA parties); reasonable, impartial and objective domestic regulations; transparency; and mutual recognition agreements (MRAs). MRAs enable the qualifications of professional services suppliers to be mutually recognized by signatory member states, thereby facilitating the easier movement of professional service providers among the member countries.

Several Asian FTAs also provide for GATS-plus commitments, meaning that the FTA liberalization goes beyond WTO commitments in relation to subsectors or regulations. The Japan–Singapore agreement is particularly comprehensive, with each side expanding its commitments in more than 130 sectors focusing on national treatment (i.e. treating service suppliers from the FTA partner country as nationals). Additional comprehensive disciplines for financial and telecommunications services are imposed through two separate annexes. In the EU–Republic of Korea FTA, the Republic of Korea commits to liberalize more than 100 sectors, including telecommunications, environmental, transport, construction, financial, postal and express delivery, professional services such as legal, accounting, engineering and architectural services. Finally, in the ASEAN–Australia–New Zealand FTA (AANZFTA), the six original ASEAN members expanded the liberalization of their telecommunication services to additional subsectors, while four others (Indonesia, Malaysia, Philippines and Singapore) went even further with their commitments in financial services. Australia and New Zealand have also made GATS-plus commitments covering modes 1–3 (refer to note 5) in a number of sectors, including business and financial services.

Although there is variation across Asian FTAs in terms of coverage of services, more emphasis is being placed on services trade liberalization than before. Newer agreements, particularly those between developed and developing countries, typically encompass the five key sectors of the GATS (business and professional services, communications services, financial services, transport services, and labor mobility/entry of business persons).

New global economic architecture

7.4 INSUFFICIENT WTO-PLUS ELEMENTS

A third concern relates to insufficient coverage of Asian FTAs regarding new issues which go beyond the WTO framework. The WTO system that emerged from the Uruguay Round in the mid-1990s consisted of substantive agreements on goods and services. The subsequent WTO Doha Development Round initiated in 2001 has focused on liberalization in agricultural and non-agricultural market access. The four Singapore issues (competition policy, investment, trade facilitation and government procurement) were conditionally included in the work program for the Doha Round, but were dropped at the WTO Ministerial Conference in Cancun in 2004. WTO-plus agreements and "new age" FTAs, which are comprehensive and address the Singapore issues, are becoming more common globally (Fiorentino et al. 2009; Freund and Ornelas 2010). An increase in WTO-plus elements in the landscape of Asian FTAs has been identified as a pressing challenge for economies. Studies suggest that Asian FTAs vary considerably in their scope, with some sophisticated agreements alongside limited FTAs (Banda and Whalley 2005; Plummer 2007).[7] Yet systematic cross-country evidence on the scope of Asian FTAs is lacking, particularly with regard to more recent agreements.

The last part of Table 7.1 also shows the scope of all concluded Asian FTAs between 2000 and 2013 and Figure 7.1 by economy for 2013 accord-

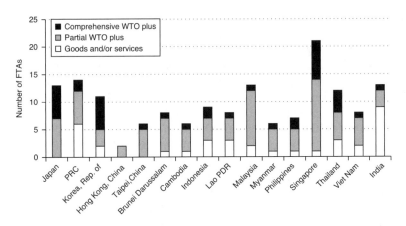

Note: The data covers 77 FTAs in Asia.

Source: ADB ARIC FTA Database (www.aric.adb.org); data as of December 2013.

Figure 7.1 *Scope of concluded FTAs in Asia (number of FTAs with narrow and WTO-plus coverage by economy)*

ing to (i) narrow agreements that deal with goods and/or services; (ii) somewhat broader agreements covering goods, services and some Singapore issues (partial WTO-plus); (iii) comprehensive agreements covering goods, services and all four Singapore issues (comprehensive WTO-plus). Agreements (ii) and (iii) can be considered WTO-plus FTAs. The scope of concluded agreements reflects a combination of economic interests, economic strength and negotiation capacity. The pattern is striking. The early Asian FTAs seemed to be concerned largely with goods and services. From the mid-2000s onwards, however, significantly more emphasis was given to broad agreements with many WTO-plus elements. By 2013, 20 (26 per cent) were goods and/or services only FTAs, 39 (51 per cent) were partial WTO-plus FTAs, and 18 (23 per cent) were comprehensive WTO-plus FTAs.

Three leading participants in Asian FTAs – Japan, Singapore and Republic of Korea – strongly favor a WTO-plus approach to FTAs and are increasingly emphasizing comprehensive agreements. All of Japan's agreements and most of Singapore's and the Republic of Korea's are WTO-plus. Likewise, Thailand, Malaysia, Brunei Darussalam, Indonesia, Philippines and Viet Nam largely follow a WTO-plus format.

7.5   LOW USE OF FTA PREFERENCES

Low preference use at the firm level is a fourth concern associated with Asian FTAs. Well designed and comprehensive FTAs provide numerous benefits, including preferential tariffs, market access and new business opportunities. One might assume that firms would desire to avail themselves of such benefits once a given FTA is in effect. Previous studies at the country and industry levels, however, suggest that FTA preference utilization rates – based on shares of export value enjoying preferences – are low in Asian countries and that FTAs are underutilized (Baldwin 2006; World Bank 2007; Drysdale and Armstrong 2010; Ravenhill 2010). This is mainly due to the increasing number of zero MFN tariff lines. Accordingly, Asian FTAs are often viewed as discriminatory and a drain on scarce trade negotiation capacity in developing countries (Bhagwati 2008).

Information on certificates of origin, based on databases of customs authorities or business associations, covers all the users of FTA preferences in a given country. One of the difficulties in investigating the evolution of FTA preferences is that most Asian countries do not publish official information. Fortunately, Thailand is an exception and publishes official FTA use information in the Thai language which was obtained from secondary sources (JETRO 2010, 2012). Data for the Republic of Korea, Malaysia and Viet Nam are not published but were obtained from

Table 7.2   Share of export value with FTA preferences (%), 2008–11

	2008	2009	2010	2011
Rep. of Korea	48.3	53.2	51.1	49.4
Thailand	26.8	37.5	37.2	42.2
Malaysia	10.3	28.3	22.7	23.5
Viet Nam	11.3	35.0	24.3	32.7
4-country average	24.2	38.5	33.8	37.0

Sources: Republic of Korea (Korea Customs Services), Malaysia and Thailand (JETRO 2010, 2012) and Viet Nam (Tran Ba Cuong 2012).

secondary or official sources. Table 7.2 shows annual FTA use data for 2008–11 for the four countries and a four-country average.

Several findings are worth highlighting. First, Average FTA use in the four countries is higher than expected from previous studies. Strikingly the four-country average FTA use rose markedly from 24 per cent in 2008 to 39 per cent in 2009. After a modest decline between 2009 and 2010, this figure reached a respectable 37 per cent in 2011.

Second, all countries show notable levels of FTA use since 2008 but the pattern varies by country. The Republic of Korea is an outlier for having achieved particularly high FTA use of 48 per cent in 2008 which increased slightly to 49 per cent in 2011. Other countries show significant increases in FTA use over the same period: Thailand's FTA use rates rose from 27 per cent to 42 per cent, Malaysia's more than doubled from 10 per cent to 24 per cent, and Viet Nam's trebled from 11 per cent to 33 per cent.

Third, country-level FTA use varies by trading partner.[8] Some examples are useful. In the case of the Republic of Korea, the most used were the US–Republic of Korea FTA (69 per cent), the EU–Republic of Korea FTA (79 per cent) and the Republic of Korea–Chile FTA (99 per cent). Meanwhile, other agreements such as the Republic of Korea–India FTA (16 per cent) and the ASEAN–Republic of Korea FTA (33 per cent) were used less. In Thailand's case, the agreements with high use include the ASEAN–Republic of Korea FTA (49 per cent), the Thailand–Australia FTA (59 per cent) and the ASEAN–India FTA (80 per cent), while the less used ones were the ASEAN–PRC FTA (35 per cent), AFTA (28 per cent) and the Japan–Thailand FTA (25 per cent). In Viet Nam, the ASEAN–Republic of Korea FTA had the highest use (91 per cent) while the ASEAN–India FTA had the lowest use (7 per cent). In Malaysia, the ASEAN–Republic of Korea FTA (51 per cent) had highest use, the ASEAN–Japan FTA reasonable use (31 per cent), and the ASEAN–Australia and New Zealand FTA the lowest use (14 per cent). Underlining the role of FTAs in facilitating market access, some agreements with major markets appear to have higher FTA use (e.g. the US–Republic of Korea FTA and EU–Republic of Korea FTA) than others. More attractive tariff preferences for key products and more simplified rules of origin may help explain why some FTAs are often more attractive to firms than other agreements.

While certificate of origin data comprehensively cover FTA users, they do not highlight the characteristics of FTA users nor impediments to using FTAs. Accordingly, more micro-level analysis using firm surveys in several countries are required to highlight these issues. Six comprehensive surveys of manufacturing exporting firms conducted in 2007–08 by ADB, the Asian Development Bank Institute (ADBI) and several partner researchers in Japan, PRC, Republic of Korea, Singapore, Thailand and Philippines shed light on the use of FTA preferences (see Kawai and Wignaraja 2011b; Wignaraja 2010). In addition, surveys of Indonesia and Malaysia were conducted by ADB and ADBI in 2011 and 2012 respectively (see Wignaraja 2013). The surveys yielded 1281 Asian sample firms and the details of the firm survey methodology are provided in Kawai and Wignaraja (2011b).[9]

The reasons that the majority of Asian sample firms do not currently use FTA preferences are not widely known. The ADB/ADBI surveys generated responses on the reasons for non-use of FTA preferences and some of these results are shown in Table 7.3. Surprisingly, a lack of information on FTAs was the most significant reason for non-use of preferences as reported by 56 per cent of firms surveyed in the Philippines, 51 per cent in Malaysia, 45 per cent in PRC, 40 per cent in Indonesia and 34 per cent in the Republic of Korea. Low margins of preference and delays and administrative costs associated with rules of origin were the second and third most common reasons cited. Other reasons for non-use included: not interested in trading with FTA partners; use of other schemes such as export processing zones and the Information Technology Agreement for exporters, which also provide incentives for exporters; and non-tariff measures in partner countries that inhibit exports and, hence, use of FTA preferences.

7.6   AN ASIAN "NOODLE BOWL" OF MULTIPLE RULES OF ORIGIN (ROOS)

ROOs are another potential concern for Asian FTAs. These are devices to determine which goods will enjoy preferential tariffs in order to prevent trade deflection among FTA members. An influential strand of literature argues that Asian FTAs have complicated ROOs, sparking concerns about

Table 7.3　Impediments to using FTAs (% of respondents)

Impediments	PRC	Rep. of Korea	Philippines[a]	Indonesia	Malaysia
Lack of information	45.1	34.2	55.5	39.8	50.9
Use of EPZ schemes of ITA	8.8	–	20.0	14.6	15.0
Delays and administrative costs[b]	10.6	10.8	21.9	11.7	20.9
Small preference margins	14.2	35.8	5.8	3.9	26.1
Too many exclusions	4.4	–	9.0	–	–
Rent seeking	5.3	–	12.9	10.7	23.1
NTMs in FTA partners	6.2	4.2	3.9	3.9	3.4
Confidentiality of information required[b]	10.6	–	7.1	–	–
Not interested in trading with FTA partners	–	–	–	9.7	30.3
Number of respondents[c]	226	120	155	206	234

Notes:
FTA = free trade agreement; EPZ = export processing zone; NTM = non-tariff measures; ITA = Information Technology Agreement; PRC= People's Republic of China.
[a]　AFTA only.
[b]　Rules of origin requirement.
[c]　Multiple responses were allowed.
–　Indicates the category was not included in the survey for the country under consideration.

Sources:　Author's calculations based data reprinted in Kawai and Wignaraja (2011a) and Wignaraja (2013).

what the attendant rules and administrative procedures would imply for the cost of doing business (Manchin and Pelkmans-Balaoing 2007; Tumbarello 2007). With the rapid spread of FTAs throughout Asia, this literature further suggests that multiple ROOs in overlapping FTAs place a severe burden on SMEs, which have less ability to meet such costs. Originally termed a "spaghetti bowl" of trade deals (Bhagwati 1995), this phenomenon has become widely known as the "noodle bowl" effect in Asia.[10]

　　To what extent are multiple ROOs perceived as a problem by businesses in Asia? The ADB/ADBI firm surveys provide interesting insights into this issue.[11] The evidence suggests that multiple ROOs impose a limited burden on firms in Asia. Of the 1281 firms that responded to the question on this issue, 362 firms (28 per cent) said that multiple ROOs do significantly add to business costs. Meanwhile, the bulk of the sample firms did not think that they were a problem at present. However, the aggregate figure masks interesting country-level variations in perceptions (see Figure 7.2). Malaysian firms had the most negative perceptions of multiple ROOs (46

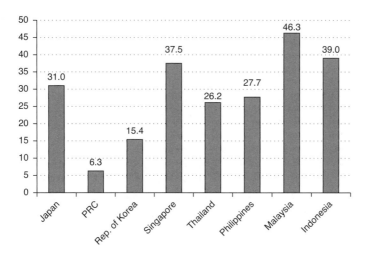

Figure 7.2   Burden imposed by multiple ROOs in FTAs (% of respondents)

per cent), while PRC firms had the least negative perceptions (6 per cent). Between these two extremes were Singaporean, Japanese, Philippine, Thai and Korean firms. National FTA strategies, industrial structures and the quality of institutional support may underlie differences in perceptions of ROOs across Asian countries.

The surveys also suggest that larger firms in Asia have more negative perceptions of multiple ROOs than SMEs, which was an unexpected finding. The relationship between firm size and concerns about multiple ROOs presents an interesting puzzle for research. Econometric analysis to resolve the puzzle shows that large established firms tend to export to multiple markets and change their business plans in response to FTAs. Therefore, they are more likely to complain about issues of multiple ROOs (Kawai and Wignaraja 2009). In contrast, smaller firms tend to export to a single market and hence do not have much basis for complaining. While inter-country and intra-firm size variations exist, there does not seem to be much variation in perceptions across sectors.

7.7   POLICY IMPLICATIONS ARISING FROM ASIAN FTAS

Asia's evolving trade policy architecture is likely to be increasingly anchored on FTAs for the foreseeable future. There are three reasons for this prediction. First, the multilateral negotiating function at the WTO seems broken as there is little end in sight for the longstanding WTO Doha Round trade talks.[12] Second, the momentum for further unilateral liberalization in Asia seems to have run out of steam, with import tariffs reaching historic lows by the early 2000s. Third, almost all Asian economies are currently pursuing FTAs to sustain the momentum for liberalization and to attempt to reduce more difficult behind-the-border regulatory barriers.

As the numbers of FTAs grow and business increasingly uses FTA preferences, we may expect more concerns about Asian FTAs to arise in the future. As with all economic policy choices, however, there are costs and benefits associated with the formation of FTAs. Accordingly, a realistic and pragmatic approach would be to encourage Asian economies to design and implement FTAs in such a way as to maximize benefits and minimize potential costs. This would involve complementary actions at the national, regional and global level.

7.7.1 National Level

Important elements of a realistic and pragmatic approach at the national level include the actions below.

Promoting comprehensive coverage of agricultural trade
Liberalizing agriculture through FTAs is a key element of the continuation of the liberalization agenda for trade in goods including encouraging greater coverage of agricultural products in Asian FTAs and supporting gradual increases in liberalizing agricultural-trade policies. Including some provisions on agricultural products in all prospective FTAs would serve as a signal for producers to adjust to competition and improve productivity. Over time, coverage could be extended to at least 85 per cent of agricultural product lines in a given agreement and exclusions minimized to no more than 150 product lines. Issues for the future would include a realistic tariff elimination schedule, a transparent sanitary and phytosanitary regime and subsidy reform.

Facilitating services trade liberalization
Radical liberalization of trade in services via the WTO or Asian FTAs seems unlikely in the foreseeable future for political economy reasons. With limited appetite for multilateral service trade liberalization, a modest way forward is for all future Asian FTAs to cover the five key sectors of the GATS (business and professional services, communications services, financial services, transport services, labor mobility/entry of business persons). Furthermore, such coverage should adhere at least to GATS

principles (such as market access, national treatment, transparency and mutual recognition agreements) and contain only limited exemptions. Over time, sectoral coverage can be extended and further GATS-plus commitments can be considered particularly in agreements encompassing more developed economies.

Increasing WTO-plus elements

The inclusion of WTO-plus provisions – particularly the four Singapore issues – would be desirable in all future Asian FTAs. For example, competition policy and investment provisions are integral ingredients in facilitating FDI inflows and the development of production networks. Inclusion of provisions on trade facilitation and logistics development would help lower transaction costs in conducting trade. Cooperation provisions – along the lines of the APEC economic and technical cooperation (ECOTECH) agenda – would stimulate technology transfer and industrial competitiveness. In their FTA negotiations, the US and EU prefer a single undertaking and the inclusion of these WTO-plus provisions. The US–Singapore, US–Republic of Korea and EU–Republic of Korea agreements are cases in point. The ASEAN Comprehensive Investment Agreement, which came into effect in March 2012, is in line with the goal of achieving an ASEAN Economic Community by 2015.

Improving use of FTA preferences

Use of FTA preferences can be encouraged by raising awareness of: (i) FTA provisions, including the phasing out of tariff schedules; (ii) margins of preference at the product level; and (iii) administrative procedures for rules of origin (ROOs). Business associations and governments could make information available on how to use FTAs more transparent, particularly for SMEs. Practical ideas include frequent seminars with SMEs, television programs directed at businesses, and dedicated websites and telephone helplines. More generally, institutional support systems for businesses, particularly for SMEs, need to be improved. Existing support systems for exporting under FTAs are of varying quality and take-up rates are inconsistent. Significant public and private investment is required in Asia to improve coverage of support services, upgrade service quality and reduce bureaucratic impediments to service use. Business and industry associations will have to play a greater role in providing members with support services for exporting under FTAs. Upgrading SME technical standards, quality and productivity could be useful so that they can participate more fully in regional production networks driven by large firms. Furthermore, a region-wide database on FTA use needs to be established and maintained so that FTA use can be tracked over time.

Tackling the Asian noodle bowl of ROOs

The finding of a limited burden imposed by multiple ROOs does not mean that policymakers should be complacent about the issue. As the number of concluded FTAs increases, it is possible that multiple ROOs may become more of a problem for firms. Supportive measures – such as encouraging rationalization of ROOs and upgrading their administration – are needed to mitigate the negative effects of the Asian noodle bowl in the future. Widespread gains are possible from pursuing a simplified approach to ROOs in Asia involving harmonized ROOs, cumulation of value contents and coequality of ROOs.[13] Likewise, it would be useful to adopt international best practices in ROO administration. These may include introducing a trusted trader program, as is the case with NAFTA, which would allow successful applicants to self-certify their own certificates of origin, switching to business associations issuing certificates of origin for a fee, increasing use of information technology-based systems of ROO administration, and training SMEs to enhance their capacity to use FTAs.

7.7.2 Regional Level

Multilateralization of regional FTAs – through liberal cumulation rules and eventually a merger of various overlapping FTAs in Asia into a large region-wide agreement – would provide notable economic benefits (Chia 2010; Baldwin and Kawai 2013). These include: greater market access for goods, services, skills and technology; larger market size permitting increased specialization and realization of economies of scale; easier foreign direct investment and technology transfer by multinational corporations and SMEs; simpler trade and investment rules; inclusion of small, low-income economies in the region's wider trade agreement; and insurance against protectionist sentiments.

A region-wide FTA in Asia could arise from a series of linked agreements covering varied issues and participants (Cheong and Tongzon 2013; Kawai and Wignaraja 2013). Two competing processes are emerging as the future basis for a region-wide FTA: a Regional Comprehensive Economic Partnership (RCEP) among the ASEAN+6 countries (the 10 ASEAN economies plus Australia, the PRC, India, Japan, Republic of Korea and New Zealand); and the Trans-Pacific Strategic Economic Partnership (Trans-Pacific Partnership, or TPP) agreement among the 12 economies (Australia, Brunei Darussalam, Canada, Chile, Japan, Malaysia, Mexico, New Zealand, Peru, Singapore, United States and Viet Nam) currently in negotiations.

To realize the RCEP, a trilateral FTA among the PRC, Japan and Republic of Korea should first be concluded and then connected with the existing ASEAN+1 FTAs – that is, ASEAN's five FTAs with Australia–New Zealand, the PRC, India, Japan and Republic of Korea. The TPP aims to achieve a high-quality agreement and includes four ASEAN members and Australia, Japan and New Zealand, from Asia. These two mega FTAs are key processes in creating a larger Asia-Pacific FTA, which, however, would require the difficult task of forging a US–PRC agreement to be successfully addressed.

These two processes are not mutually exclusive and will probably prove to be complementary. The changing center of global economic gravity – given the rapid economic rise of the PRC and India – suggests that a RCEP is attractive to many Asian economies, including developing ones. Countries that are ready to accept the high standards required for the TPP, and that wish to strengthen existing ties with the US, are likely to join the TPP.

Whichever path or paths may be taken, it will be important to accelerate the liberalization of goods and services trade and of investment, reduce behind-the-border barriers, and pursue domestic reforms. A harmonious Asia and Pacific region would be likely to see a convergence of the two processes being considered. This would be a win–win solution for the Asia and the Pacific community.

Asia's next step would be to strengthen its trade relationships with other parts of the world, starting with Europe. A mega Asia–Europe FTA would be an important building bock, along with the Asia–Pacific FTA, to connect Asia with the global economy and support global trade integration in a way to complement the WTO Doha Round trade talks.

7.7.3 Global Level

International trade rules and institutions can have profound effects on the shifts of trade relationships in Asia and globally. The responsibility for global trade governance has rested with the WTO since its creation in 1995 and its membership had grown to 159 countries by early 2013. The WTO's central function is to provide a forum for international trade negotiations which results in WTO agreements. The WTO's other functions include administering WTO agreements, monitoring national trade policies, and providing technical assistance and training for developing countries.

The slow progress in the WTO Doha Round trade talks means that new multilateral trading rules will take time to evolve amid calls for WTO reforms. Successful conclusion of comprehensive global trade talks would be an invaluable contribution to global, including Asian, prosperity (see Hoekman et al. 2009; Bhagwati and Sutherland 2011; and WTO 2011). The small Bali Package agreed in December 2013 is a useful step towards restoring the credibility of the WTO as a trade rule-making institution.

However, the outcome of the current Doha Round trade talks remains uncertain and the eventual result may be a significantly limited agreement.

The narrow negotiating agenda and slow progress of the WTO Doha Round may be partly due to the nature of the WTO's decision-making mechanism and its underlying principles of consensus and single undertaking. In this vein, an important initiative at the global level may be greater use of plurilateral agreements (which focus on rule making and liberalization on a single trade issue) within the WTO framework. An example is the Information Technology Agreement (ITA) with an open accession clause. Plurilateral agreements permit interested parties to freely choose the issue for an agreement and voluntarily participate in the negotiations. Well-designed issue-based plurilateral agreements can serve the needs of like-minded developed and developing countries, enhance the spread of foreign direct investment (FDI) driven by global supply chains, and complement WTO and FTA rule-making. Services, trade facilitation and electronic commerce may be candidates for future issue-based plurilateral agreements.

In the medium term, a WTO agenda on supply chains and FTAs would be necessary to encourage convergence of regional and global trading rules. Such a WTO agenda would tackle behind-the-border issues relevant to fragmented production systems and supply chains, particularly trade facilitation, investment policy and non-tariff barriers. It would also encompass relevant rules in FTAs, particularly those relating to the Singapore issues (investment, trade facilitation, competition, and government procurement). It has been argued that the WTO has not kept up with the need for new rules governing the intertwining of trade, investment, intellectual property and services (Baldwin 2011). Bringing these rules to the global level needs the creation of a new international organization – a "WTO 2.0".

7.8   CONCLUSIONS

This chapter has addressed important concerns associated with the spread of Asian FTAs. It has provided new evidence on the impacts of Asian FTAs on the region's evolving trade policy architecture through the analysis of such agreements and insights from enterprise-level surveys. Policy implications from the research were also explored at the national, regional and global level.

FTAs are assuming greater importance as tools of Asian commercial policy than ever before. The region's largest economies and Singapore are key to the growing Asian FTA activity while ASEAN, as an organization, is emerging as an integration hub for such efforts. The trade coverage of

Asian FTAs has increased, and broader issues than simply trade liberalization have been addressed.

With the large number of FTAs concluded and under negotiation, Asian FTAs are here to stay. Maximizing the benefits of these Asian FTAs while minimizing their costs would be highly pragmatic. Given the observations of this study, this chapter suggests a coherent approach to concordance of national, regional and global trade rules.

Some key elements of pragmatic responses to Asian FTAs at the national and regional levels may include:

- encouraging greater coverage of agricultural products in Asian FTAs and supporting gradual increases in liberalizing agricultural-trade policies;
- facilitating gradual increases in liberalizing services-trade policies through emphasis on key GATS sectors;
- including WTO-plus provisions – particularly the four Singapore issues – in all future Asian FTAs;
- increasing the use of FTAs through improved awareness and strengthened institutional support, particularly for SMEs, and creating a regional database on FTA use;
- addressing the Asian noodle bowl through greater rationalization of ROO and upgrading ROO administration to best-practice levels; and
- facilitating the creation of a region-wide agreement in Asia – through an eventual convergence of RCEP and TPP – with appropriate sub-sequencing and support for development gaps among members.

To strengthen global trade governance, such national and regional level actions might be accompanied by actions at the global level including:

- Building on the Bali small package, eventually concluding the WTO global trade talks would be a useful step towards restoring the credibility of the WTO as a trade rule-making institution. However, the outcome of the current Doha Round trade talks remains uncertain and the eventual result may be a limited agreement.
- Additional key actions for the WTO are enhancing surveillance of non-tariff measures to reduce tendencies towards protectionism in the global economy and a WTO agenda on supply chains and FTAs to foster convergence of global and regional trading rules.

Actual developments may well not be as orderly, neat or rational as those described above. The reality could easily become substantially more complex. The convergence between national, regional and global trade rules will take some time. Nonetheless, how Asia thinks and acts on these issues is likely to influence the world economy. As Pascal Lamy (former Director-General of the WTO) reminded us recently:

> Asia has been a successful model of development through trade, which has inspired many others around the world. There is no doubt that the region will continue to inspire the trade community in the next decades to come.
> With its significant economic and trade weight in the global economy, Asia is expected to shoulder more responsibilities and take the lead in the global trading system in the future. (Lamy 2013, p.18)

NOTES

*   We are most grateful to Menaka Arudchelvan for efficient research assistance.

1.   The Asia-Pacific Trade Agreement (APTA) of 1976 was the region's first agreement and the Association of Southeast Asian Nations (ASEAN) Free Trade Agreement (1993) was another prominent one among a very small number of Asia's early FTAs.

2.   The data set excludes FTAs involving the Pakistan–Indonesia and Viet Nam–Chile FTAs for which texts were not available.

3.   However, rice (a key sensitive sector) was excluded from the KORUS agreement.

4.   This approach, which draws on Wignaraja and Lazaro (2010) and Baldwin et al. (2013), can be readily applied to a large proportion of Asian FTAs. Future research can extend Fink and Molinuevo's (2008) more detailed review of key architectural choices in East Asian FTAs with a services component (e.g. scheduling commitments, treatment of investment, movement of natural persons and dispute settlement) to analyzing the 69 Asian FTAs.

5.   Namely, cross-border trade in services (Mode 1); consumption abroad (Mode 2); commercial presence (Mode 3); and temporary movement of natural persons (Mode 4).

6.   Six FTAs involved Singapore, which typically covered the five key services in its FTAs. A similar approach was followed in the Taipei,China–Panama FTA, the Japan–Mexico FTA, and the Thailand–Australia FTA. The ASEAN Framework Agreement on Services (AFAS) was signed in 1995/96 and the protocol to amend AFAS was launched in 2003. Thereafter, several rounds of negotiations have aimed at deepening AFAS.

7.   An early review of 11 Asian agreements concluded that "modern FTAs in Asia, some of which are the most sophisticated in the world, have tended to be more comprehensive in terms of coverage and of the "building bloc" rather than the "stumbling bloc" type, though there are some (minor) exceptions in terms of certain components" (Plummer 2007, p.1795). The study suggested a set of best practices to guide future FTAs.

8.   Data for the Republic of Korea–US FTA and Republic of Korea–EU FTA are for 2012. The rest are for 2011.

9.   In essence, experienced teams of researchers used a common questionnaire and random sampling methods to collect the firm-level data. The firm surveys of each country contained a mix of firms of different ownership (foreign and local) and size classes (large firms and SMEs), which were broadly representative of national industrial structures. The firms were drawn from the region's largest industries (such as electronics, automotives, textiles and garments) as well as an industry of national importance in each country (such as metals and machinery in the Republic of Korea and food in the Philippines).

10.   Others suggest that the depiction of Asian FTAs as a complicated noodle bowl is misleading. On the other hand, it has been argued that Asian FTAs may be creating

an order of a different sort by building the foundation for a stronger regional trading system (Petri 2008; Chia 2010).

11. Data for Malaysia and Indonesia were from the ADB/ADBI firm surveys, while data for other countries can be found in Kawai and Wignaraja (2011b).

12. A mini Doha Development Round deal called the Bali Package was reached in Bali in December 2013, covering trade facilitation, agriculture, and development issues. This is far smaller a deal than the one envisaged under the Doha Development Agenda. Even this modest deal may not be fully implemented due to concerns raised by India about food security.

13. Harmonized ROOs means the same ROO is applied across FTAs. Co-equal ROOs means alternative ROOs for the same product are available in an FTA and firms are free to choose between them. Cumulation allows the use of non-domestic inputs from a specific country or group of countries (with such inputs taken as originating in the FTA partner country claiming origin) as determining the product's origin. See Kawai and Wignaraja (2011b) and Baldwin and Kawai (2013).

REFERENCES

Baldwin, R. 2006. 'Multilateralizing Regionalism: Spaghetti Bowls as Building Blocks on the Path to Global Free Trade'. *World Economy* **29**(11): 1451–518.

Baldwin, R. 2011. '21st Century Regionalism, Filling the Gap between 21st Century Trade and 20th Century Trade Rules'. Center for Economic Policy Research (CEPR) Insights No. 56. London Center for Economic Policy Research.

Baldwin, R. and M. Kawai. 2013. 'Multilateralizing Asian Regionalism'. ADBI Working Paper Series No. 431 (August). Tokyo: Asian Development Bank Institute.

Baldwin, R., M. Kawai and G. Wignaraja (eds). 2013. *The Future of the World Trading System: Asian Perspectives*, London and Tokyo: Center for Economic Policy Research (CEPR) and Asian Development Bank Institute.

Banda, O.G.D. and J. Whalley. 2005. 'Beyond Goods and Services: Competition Policy, Investment, Mutual Recognition, Movement of Persons, and Broader Cooperation Provisions of Recent FTAs involving ASEAN Countries'. NBER Working Paper Series 11232 (March). Cambridge: National Bureau of Economic Research.

Bhagwati, J.N. 1995. 'US Trade Policy: The Infatuation with FTAs'. Columbia University Discussion Paper Series 726. New York: Columbia University.

Bhagwati, J.N. 2008. *Termites in the Trading System: How Preferential Agreements Undermine Free Trade*. Oxford: Oxford University Press.

Bhagwati, J.N. and P. Sutherland. 2011. 'The Doha Round: Setting a Deadline, Defining a Final Deal'. High Level Experts Group, Interim Report, Co-Chairs Jagdish Bhagwati and Peter Sutherland. Available at: www.number10.gov.uk/wp-content/uploads/doha-round-jan-2011.pdf.

Cheong, I. and J. Tongzon. 2013. 'Comparing the Economic Impact of the Trans-Pacific Partnership and the Regional Comprehensive Economic Partnership'. *Asian Economic Papers* **12**(2): 144–64.

Chia, S.Y. 2010. 'Regional Trade Policy Cooperation and Architecture in East Asia'. ADBI Working Paper Series No. 191 (September). Tokyo: Asian Development Bank Institute.

Drysdale, P. and S. Armstrong. 2010. 'International and Regional Cooperation: Asia's Role and Responsibilities'. *Asian Economic Policy Review* **5**(2): 157–73.

Feridhanusetyawan, T. 2005. 'Preferential Trade Agreements in the Asia-Pacific Region'. IMF Working Paper WP/05/149 (July). Washington, DC: International Monetary Fund.

Findlay, C., R. Ochiai and P. Dee. 2009. 'Integrating Services Market'. In J. François, P.B. Rana and G. Wignaraja (eds) *Pan-Asian Integration: Linking East and South Asia*. Basingstoke, UK: Palgrave Macmillan. pp. 245–350.

Fink, C. and M. Molinuevo. 2008. 'East Asian Free Trade Agreements in Services: Key Architectural Elements'. *Journal of International Economic Law* **11**(2): 263–311.

Fiorentino, R.V., J. Crawford and C. Toqueboeuf. 2009. 'The Landscape of Regional Trade Agreements and WTO Surveillance'. In R. Baldwin and P. Low (eds) *Multilateralizing Regionalism: Challenges for the Global Trading System*. Cambridge: Cambridge University Press.

Freund, C. and E. Ornelas. 2010. 'Regional Trade Agreements'. World Bank Policy Research Working Papers 5314. Washington, DC: World Bank.

Hoekman, B. and A. Mattoo. 2011. 'Services Trade Liberalization and Regulatory Reform: Re-invigorating International Cooperation'. World Bank Policy Research Working Papers 5517. Washington, DC: World Bank.

Hoekman, B., W. Martin and A. Mattoo. 2009. 'Conclude Doha: It Matters'. World Bank Policy Research Working Papers 5135. Washington, DC: World Bank.

JETRO. 2010 and 2012. *Global Trade and Investment Report 2010 and 2012*. Tokyo: Japan External Trade Organization.

Kawai, M. and G. Wignaraja. 2009. 'The Asian Noodle Bowl: Is it Serious for Business?' ADBI Working Paper Series No. 136 (April). Tokyo: Asian Development Bank Institute.

Kawai, M. and G. Wignaraja. 2011a. 'Asian FTAs: Trends, Prospects and Challenges'. *Journal of Asian Economics* **22**: 1–22.

Kawai, M. and G. Wignaraja. 2011b. *Asia's Free Trade Agreements: How Is Business Responding?* Cheltenham, UK and Northampton, MA, USA: Edward Elgar Publishing.

Kawai, M. and G. Wignaraja. 2013. 'Patterns of Free Trade Areas in Asia', *Policy Studies* No. 65. East-West Center: Honolulu.

Lamy, P. 2013. 'The future of the world trade system: Asian perspectives'. In R. Baldwin, M. Kawai and G. Wignaraja (eds) *The Future of the World Trading System: Asian Perspectives*, VoxEu e-book, available at: http://www.voxeu.org/sites/default/files/Future_World_Trading_System.pdf.

Manchin, M. and A.O. Pelkmans-Balaoing. 2007. 'Rules of Origin and the Web of East Asian Free Trade Agreements'. World Bank Policy Research Working Papers 4273 (July). Washington, DC: World Bank.

Petri, P.A. 2008. 'Multitrack Integration in East Asian Trade: Noodle Bowl or Matrix?' *Asia Pacific Issues* No. 86. Honolulu: East-West Center.

Plummer, M. 2007. 'Best Practices in Regional Trade Agreements: An Application to Asia'. *World Economy* **30**(12): 1771–96.

Ravenhill, J. 2010. 'The New East Asian Regionalism: A Political Domino Effect', *Review of International Political Economy* **17**(2): 178–208.

Tran Ba Cuong, 2012. 'FTA Utilization and How to Support SMEs: Vietnam'. Powerpoint presentation made at APEC Workshop on Increasing FTA Utilization by SMES, 7 August. Tokyo, Japan.

Tumbarello, P. 2007. 'Are Regional Trade Agreements in Asia Stumbling Blocks or Building Blocks? Implications for Mekong-3 Countries'. IMF Working Paper WP/07/53 (March). Washington, DC: International Monetary Fund.

Wignaraja, G. 2010. 'Are ASEAN FTAs Used for Exporting?' In P. Gugler and J. Chaisse (eds) *Competitiveness of the ASEAN Countries: Corporate and Regulatory Drivers*. Cheltenham, UK and Northampton, MA, USA: Edward Elgar Publishing.

Wignaraja, G. 2013. 'Regional Trade Agreements and Enterprises in Southeast Asia', ADBI Working Paper Series No. 442 (October). Tokyo: Asian Development Bank Institute.

Wignaraja, G. and D. Lazaro. 2010. 'North–South vs. South–South Asian FTAs: Trends, Compatibilities, and Ways Forward'. UNU-CRIS Working Paper W-2010/3. Bruges, Belgium: UNU-CRIS.

World Bank. 2007. 'Trade Issues in East Asia: Preferential Rules of Origin'. Policy Research Report. East Asia and Pacific Region (Poverty Reduction and Economic Management). Washington, DC: World Bank.

World Trade Organization. 2011. *The WTO and Preferential Trade Agreements: From Co-existence to Coherence*. Geneva: World Trade Organization.

APPENDIX 7A.1

Table 7A.1   Per capita income and trade policy in Asia

	Per capita income, PPP (current US$)		Share of world GDP, PPP (%)		Simple mean, MFN tariff rate (%)[a]		Concluded FTAs (no. of FTAs)		Trade coverage of FTAs (% of total trade)	
	2000	2012	2000	2012	2000	2012	2000	2013	2000	2012
Northeast Asia										
Japan	25 709	35 855	7.6	5.5	4.3	4.6	0	13	0.0	18.8
China, People's Republic of	2382	9055	7.0	14.7	17.0	9.6	1	14	8.2	30.5
Korea, Republic of	16 528	31 950	1.8	1.9	12.7	13.3	1	11	10.4	55.9
Hong Kong, China	26 778	50 936	0.4	0.4	0.0	0.0	0	4	0.0	53.6
Taipei,China	20 290	38 357	1.1	1.1	9.5	7.8	0	6	0.0	21.6
ASEAN										
Brunei Darussalam	43 386	54 114	0.0	0.0	3.8	2.5	1	8	33.9	94.1
Cambodia	909	2395	0.0	0.0	16.4	10.9	1	6	24.8	46.6
Indonesia	2433	4923	1.2	1.4	8.4	7.0	1	9	18.2	69.4
Lao PDR	1185	2847	0.0	0.0	9.5	9.7	3	8	65.0	87.5
Malaysia	9102	16 794	0.5	0.6	8.3	6.5	1	13	25.4	64.9
Myanmar	530	1612	0.1	0.1	5.5	5.6	1	6	35.8	91.8
Philippines	2446	4380	0.4	0.5	7.6	6.2	1	7	15.6	71.4

Singapore	33 195	60 799	0.3	0.4	0.2	0.2	1	1	21	26.3	57.9
Thailand	5015	9503	0.7	0.8	18.4	9.8	2	2	12	18.1	44.8
Viet Nam	1426	3788	0.3	0.4	16.5	9.5	1	1	8	23.5	59.5
India	1548	3843	3.7	5.7	34.6	13.7	1	1	13	6.1	20.1
Memorandum items											
US	36 450	51 704	24.0	19.5	4.1	3.4	1		20		39.1
EU-27	21 900	31 571	24.8	19.2	5.7	5.5	15		31		71.5

Notes:
[a] The MFN tariff data relates to the year 2012 except in the case of Brunei Darussalam (2011), Lao People's Democratic Republic (2008), Thailand (2011), PRC (2011) and Taipei,China (2009).
The EU-27 trade coverage of FTAs includes intra-EU trade. Excluding intra-EU trade, trade coverage of FTAs is 9.9%.

Sources: World Bank, World Development Indicators; ADB, Asia Regional Integration Center; IMF, Direction of Trade Statistics; IMF, World Economic Outlook Database; US Trade Representative (http://www.ustr.gov); and EU Trade (http://ec.europa.eu).

8. The emerging "post-Doha" agenda and the new regionalism in the Asia-Pacific

Michael G. Plummer

8.1 INTRODUCTION

As of 31 January 2014, the World Trade Organization (WTO) reports that, counting goods and services separately, it has received 583 notifications of regional trading arrangements (RTAs, defined by the WTO to be a reciprocal trading agreement between two or more countries), with 377 in force.[1] This number is up from 300 at the end of 2005 and 130 at the beginning of 1995 (Plummer 2007). Asia has been a major participant in this rapid increase in RTAs; in fact, apart from the ASEAN Free Trade Area (AFTA) in 1992, no Asian country had a significant RTA in place prior to 2000, whereas at the end of 2013 there were 113 Asia-related RTAs signed and in effect, and another 261 at various stages of negotiation.[2] Many of these arrangements are intra-regional; Appendix Table 8A.1 gives an inventory of these arrangements for the East Asian summit (ASEAN+8) economies. Clearly, Asia has embraced regionalism in a big way.

At the multilateral level, however, the situation is mixed. On the one hand, the WTO system itself is functioning well, with the rule-based system being respected, a much-improved dispute settlement mechanism (over the General Agreement on Tariffs and Trade, or GATT) in place, and rising membership (with the Russian Federation joining in 2012). The WTO continues to be the pre-eminent institution of global governance of trade. On the other hand, the multilateral liberalization process has borne little fruit, with any "single undertaking" agreement under Doha Development Agenda (DDA) negotiations still a long way off, despite some success at the 9th WTO Ministerial Meeting in Bali in December 2013, which produced a "mini-package" including trade facilitation and some development- and agriculture-related measures. Moreover, the WTO agreement itself has been criticized for not including (or covering insufficiently) a number of trade-related issues that, some argue, need to be addressed at the multilateral level in the twenty-first century, for example export restrictions, competition policy ("competitive neutrality"), environmental-related measures (e.g. "environmental" dumping), and, of course, issues related to exchange-rate "manipulation".

On the positive side, perhaps the Bali "mini-package" will breathe new life into multilateral liberalization, either under the form of a rejuvenated DDA or in other ways, but much will have to change (and some proposals could be problematic). We discuss these problems in section 8.2. Nevertheless, regionalism is the most important force in international commercial policy today and it will likely continue to be so in the foreseeable future. Hence, we consider whether regionalism is an inherent threat to the multilateral system (section 8.3) and anticipate what we believe will be the "new regionalism" in Asia and the Pacific (section 8.4). Section 8.5 offers some concluding remarks.

8.2 MULTILATERALISM AFTER THE 9TH WTO MINISTERIAL CONFERENCE

Relative to previous negotiating rounds, the DDA has been characterized by far greater participation of developing countries, which have raised their expectations as to what they hope to receive from developed countries in terms of liberalization of certain labor-intensive, but especially agricultural, goods.[3] Developed countries, on the other hand, pressed, *inter alia*, for deeper cuts in industrial tariffs in developing economies. This has given the impression of "North–South" tension at the DDA and has been blamed for the 2011 impasse, which continues to date.

No doubt the differences between the negotiating stances of the "North" and the "South" were in evidence throughout the entire DDA negotiations. This is, perhaps, quite predictable: negotiators focus on improving market access and facilitating the development of comparative advantage industries. For the North, this means concentrating on higher-value added manufactures; financial and other services; protection of intellectual property; and investment and trade facilitation, which facilitate foreign direct investment (FDI) flows. The South, on the other hand, naturally focuses on labor-intensive manufactures and resists liberalization of its most sensitive areas, as well as behind-the-border measures that may infringe on national sovereignty.

However, the situation is far more complex: negotiating stances are not completely dictated by North–South differences. Developing countries have become more active at Doha because most have now embraced an outward-oriented development strategy and depend on the international marketplace to enhance growth and development. In the past, these countries were not active at GATT rounds, as they generally chose to "free-ride" on commitments between developed countries from which they also received most-favored nation (MFN) benefits. The cost of this approach became evident in time: the sectors that were being liberalized were of principal interest to developed, rather than developing, countries. In order to include comparative-advantage sectors of the developing world, a proactive stance at the WTO was necessary, and these economies did have an overlap of interests vis-à-vis developed economies.

Still, the world is changing rapidly, and it is too simplistic to evaluate trends in commercial policy based on this traditional North–South divide. The share of emerging markets in global economic activity has been rising significantly; for example, Asian economies constituted 28 per cent of the global economy in 2010, up from 8 per cent in 1980, and this share is projected to rise to 40 per cent in 2030 and 52 per cent in 2050 (ADB 2011). Other key emerging markets, such as Brazil, Russian Federation and South Africa, have also been experiencing a much greater presence in global markets. Whereas in the past GATT rounds were dominated by Northern initiatives without a large role for the South, this is certainly no longer the case. In this sense, one might say that the impasse at the DDA has been a sign of maturity of the organization, with a more symmetric distribution of power – and responsibility.

In fact, there are also tensions across emerging market economies. Trade across the "BRICS" (Brazil, Russian Federation, India, the People's Republic of China [PRC] and South Africa) has been rising considerably and productive and export structures between most of them (in particular, Brazil, India and the PRC) are far more similar than, say, those of the key developed countries at the negotiating table at the DDA. *Ceteris paribus*, we would expect that political interests in these economies would be at least as sensitive (but, most likely, more sensitive) to competition due to liberalization under the DDA from fellow BRICS than from developed economies. A textile-producing country fears competition from another textile-producing country more than from a country that produces automobiles. Arguably, trade patterns are reinforcing these sensitivities. For example, the PRC's trade with other developing economies has been growing by leaps and bounds in recent years; indeed, the share of its trade with non-Asian developing economies is the most dynamic in its trade portfolio (ADB 2012). This trade tends to be dominated by the PRC's exporting manufactures in exchange for natural-resource-related goods. The reaction in other BRICS has at times been negative, with some fearing that this could be a new manifestation of "dependencia", which in turn has given wind to the sails of some domestic protectionist interests. Coupled with the fact that the BRICS are cast as leaders of the developing world and that standing up to developed economies may be perceived as a manifestation of leadership credentials, the DDA may have been facing more than just headwinds from economic issues.

If indeed these political-economy issues are important determinants of the emerging market negotiating stance, we might have to wait a long time for the DDA (or any other single-undertaking under the WTO) to be completed.[4] Perhaps recognizing this, policymakers have been exploring opportunities outside the single-undertaking, for example, in the area of "plurilaterals", or more modest practices such as the accord reached in Bali.

Currently, there are two prominent, quite successful plurilaterals under the auspices of the WTO: the Information Technology Agreement (ITA) and the Government Procurement Agreement (GPA).[5] The ITA has 70 participating parties that constitute 97 per cent of the pooled markets of WTO membership in included products. The ITA focuses exclusively on tariffs, which are bound at zero, and benefits are applied on an MFN basis. The GPA includes 15 economies (taking the European Union [EU] as only one member) and its benefits are not applied on a MFN basis but rather are only accorded to its membership, though any WTO member has a right to join (there are currently 22 observers, with nine currently negotiating accession, including the PRC).

As a single-undertaking has proven so difficult, it is only natural that policymakers are considering less ambitious approaches by focusing on sectors. To the extent that these accords grant MFN to all parties, there is no reason to believe that they could potentially damage the multilateral system. I note "potentially" because, arguably, an agreement such as the GPA does not create distortions related to "trade diversion"; prior to the agreement, preferences generally were given to domestic producers and, hence, the GPA increased competition between domestic firms and foreign (GPA-member) firms, rather than across foreign competitors (who were previously discriminated against anyway). However, to the extent that such a plurilateral could lead to new discrimination across members, it could create some serious problems.

To begin, if a plurilateral does not include substantially all goods (as required for the Article XXIV or the General Agreement on Trade in Services [GATS] Article V exceptions), it would violate Article I of the WTO. For example, there has been some talk of proposing an "ITA II", which would expand significantly product coverage, making it reciprocal without the 90 per cent minimum as required with the first ITA agreement. If the developed economies were to table an expansive list of additional products that would be considered excessive from the viewpoint of India and the PRC, a reciprocal ITA II would simply exclude them, with potential for trade diversion and arguably a violation of MFN. Some might note that they could join later if they wished, but an exception under Article XXIV does not allow for this. Moreover, these kinds of single-sector accords could have significant negative implications for effective rates of protection.

Another plurilateral approach would be to require reciprocity but to meet the "substantially all goods" requirement. Such an idea was tabled at the 8th WTO Ministerial in the area of service, where the GATS Article V would also require that most services sectors be included in any accord. In theory, this would be a very interesting approach; in practice, it could create problems. First, "substantially all goods" has never been appropriately defined. The GATT saw, for example, a number of FTAs in manufactures alone (arguably not "substantially all goods") and even bilateral free trade in one sector between the US and Canada: the 1965 agreement on auto parts. A limited set of services included in such an agreement would have the potential for negative, "second-best" ramifications and reflect poorly on the WTO itself. Second, who will join such an agreement? If it is only the Organisation for Economic Co-operation and Development (OECD) countries, it could exacerbate the impression of a North–South divide in the WTO. Currently, the momentum for a services plurilateral is coming from the 18 "Really Good Friends of Services", comprised mostly of OECD economies and including none from the BRIC group (*Geneva Watch* 2012).

In sum, the DDA is likely to be stalled for some time, and more modest approaches to multilateral liberalization will themselves probably be limited (and could, and least in principle, create worrying precedents). As the regionalism trend emerged in full force in the early 2000s side-by-side with DDA negotiations, we can expect that it will be the only game in town for at least the next few years (and, most likely, longer).

8.3　ON BUILDING BLOCS AND STUMBLING BLOCS

Disillusionment with progress at the DDA may be one reason for the proliferation of regional agreements in Asia and the rest of the world. The ambitious agenda of Doha, from both developed- and developing-country viewpoints, could be more easily managed bilaterally or between a small group of countries than in an organization of 160 highly-divergent economies. Hence, it is no mystery as to why many of the new regional agreements are between developed and developing countries: what is needed to integrate global markets further, from non-tariff barriers to behind-the-border issues, may be too much to handle at the WTO.

The WTO is cognizant of the regionalism trend and understands the problems that it could potentially entail for the global trading system (see, for example, WTO 2011). Indeed, the challenges of regionalism to the WTO are many, but two in particular stand out. First, the GATT/WTO was created with MFN treatment as its overriding principle, and Article XXIV was to be a conditional exception to this rule. With so many accords in place and every major economy participating in at least one FTA (and most in many), what happens when the exception becomes the rule? How valid is the coveted MFN, a birthright of WTO membership, when regional trading arrangements erode it and, in essence, force countries into regional trading arrangements in order to *retain* MFN status? Second, as we will argue below, regionalism is not necessarily in conflict with multilateralism, subject to the principle of openness and the minimization of the inefficiencies and potential discrimination inherent in regional agreements.

In this section, I will first discuss some of the problems associated with the "regionalism debate", beginning with some introductory observations and followed by a summary of the "building blocs versus stumbling blocs" debate itself.[6]

8.3.1 Introductory Comments Regarding Regionalism versus Multilateralism

It is important to note first of all that, while WTO accords do impose a certain symmetry, they do not guarantee it. For example, the WTO sets out rules of behavior in terms of anti-dumping that are no doubt superior to a system void of rules. But they do not harmonize all anti-dumping practices. Member states continue to have a great deal of flexibility in this regard (and probably always will have, at least in the context of the WTO). Moreover, the lack of across-the-board inclusion of sectors and asymmetric liberalization within the context of GATT/WTO liberalization could create distortions that exacerbate effective rates of protection; that is, while regionalism discriminates across *countries*, the GATT/WTO discriminates across *sectors*, and, to the extent that this is the case, both are second-best. The existence of a WTO Valuation Agreement on customs is extremely useful but there continues to be considerable variation in terms of adopted practices across WTO member-states. The same can generally be true of "Singapore issue"-related topics, intellectual property rights (IPR) protection, and the like, in which the WTO often has little or incomplete jurisdiction. A salient disadvantage of the multilateral approach under the WTO is that harmonization of such rules and policies has proven to be extremely difficult, and progress highly limited, due to the diversity of its membership, as well as disagreements as to how comprehensive the mission of the WTO should be. Given that the organization of the international economy (e.g. via production networks) has become more complicated and reaches ever-deeper into the very fabric of domestic policy and legislation, behind-the-border issues are becoming increasingly important. These, though, are even more difficult to include in negotiations among a membership with widely-diverging interests and positions regarding an outward-oriented development strategy.

The usefulness of regional agreements – and certainly one reason for their popularity (see World Bank 2005; Kreinin and Plummer 2002; Frankel 1998) – lies in their ability to drive integration and cooperation in areas that have hitherto been neglected by the WTO, for example in terms of sensitive tariff, non-tariff and behind-the-border measures. Thus, while it is true that a multilateral approach would dominate a bilateral/regional strategy if all the same measures are included and harmonized/liberalized to the same extent, it is not a dominant strategy once we relax this (unrealistic) assumption of symmetry in liberalization and coverage.

In fact, critiques of FTAs relative to free trade can easily fall into "straw man" analysis. For example, the rules of origin constraints under North American Free Trade Agreement (NAFTA) in automobiles (62.5 per cent) and certain textile products (effectively 100 per cent) do not fit the criteria for "open regionalism" under any definition of this term. However, these are probably among the most obvious out of relatively few such divergences in what is in reality a liberal agreement. Besides, for NAFTA, the effective benchmark should be the status quo, not *free trade*. Would auto and textile imports to the US have been much less restrictive without NAFTA? Not necessarily. In fact, certainly trade diversion does have costs, but we cannot say that NAFTA closed those markets, since failure to meet NAFTA rules of origin meant recourse to the status quo. The status quo did not become more protective; in textiles and apparel, the US market has become *more* open with the expiration of global import quotas on 1 January 2005 (under Uruguay Round commitments). Again, Mexican textiles receive preferential treatment and, hence, trade diversion is a cost to be borne by non-partners and US consumers, but there still is an associated trade creation effect that would have not occurred had there been no NAFTA. Net gains have been estimated to have been positive.[7]

Many American economists supported NAFTA not for general support for regionalism per se or their belief that it would have great effects on allocative efficiency in North America through the liberalization of tariff and non-tariff barriers, which were, after all, low in the aggregate.[8] Effects on the US and, especially, Canada, were estimated to be positive but small. Rather, it was supported in the main because it would lock in the Mexican economic reforms leading up to NAFTA and would set the stage for further liberalization. Given the history of economic volatility in Mexico, NAFTA as a "policy anchor" was deemed to be extremely useful. Once NAFTA began to be implemented in full force (i.e., after the Mexican crisis in December 1994, which had little or nothing to do with NAFTA directly), the net effect on macro performance in Mexico has been very positive (Kose and Rebucci 2005). In 2005, the US government gave a high priority to an FTA with Central America ("CAFTA") in hopes that it would have the same stabilizing effect.[9] And while the percentage of total Mexican trade has risen to somewhat over three-quarters (from two-thirds) in the wake of NAFTA, a result of both trade creation and diversion, one cannot say that Mexico has been "captive" in NAFTA. In fact, Mexico now has negotiated 44 FTAs.[10] Moreover, the openness of the Mexican economy has allowed non-partner countries to benefit; the financial sector in Mexico, for example, is characterized by a considerable European presence. Again, this is not to argue that restrictive rules of origin and other inward-looking clauses in regional trading arrangements do not constitute a problematic aspect of RTA. A consistent, liberal, across-the-board rules-of-origin policy is the least distortionary in a second-best world (Plummer 2007). But we should not exaggerate its absolute importance in the regionalism debate.

Moreover, time *and* depth matter. Many protagonists of a purely multilateral approach to economic cooperation tend to present arguments without a well-defined time horizon. But time is important when considering the present discounted value to national welfare of a regional trading accord compared to multilateral free trade. A heuristic example may help underscore this point. Suppose Indonesia has an option to create an FTA with the US, but its leaders know that this will have some costs in terms of trade diversion. The "first-best" (global free trade) policy, its leaders might reckon, would ultimately be the best deal for Indonesia, as non-discriminatory free trade would have no trade diversion and could maximize trade creation. But since Indonesia is unable to benefit from global free-trade (no such option exists at present), timing becomes an essential factor in the policy decision. If global free trade were an option in the very short term, then, *ceteris paribus*, free trade would be better than the deal with the US. But what if the FTA with the US were possible today, and yet global free trade would take five more years? Which would be better? It would depend on what the Indonesia–US deal would look like (relative to the global deal), but nevertheless, it could be that free trade would still be worth the wait. But what if free trade were to take more like 20, 30 or 40 years? After all, the GATT/WTO has existed for over a half century, and global free trade is nowhere in sight. Of course, this type of analysis will be a function of the type of regional accord, in particular if it is inward-looking or outward-looking. If it were the former, the deal with the US could end up being very much to the detriment of Indonesia. As we shall see in terms of the "building bloc versus stumbling bloc" debate, the type of agreement is of the essence. But it would also be important to know what the multilateral deal would be. If a regional accord entailed far more reforms vis-à-vis market-friendly, efficient policies at macro and micro levels whereas global free trade meant merely the abolition of tariff barriers, the former could still potentially be as good as, or better than, the latter.

Herein lies the attraction and, in many ways, advantage that regionalism holds over multilateralism: *it allows like-minded countries to address far more issues and in a shorter period of time.* By choosing one or several like-minded partners, countries are able to make more progress in terms of deep integration than they could in the extremely diverse WTO context. Rising interest in regionalism on the part of OECD countries that traditionally had shunned them (the US, Japan, the Republic of Korea) derives from their desire to address these many issues and their understanding that they cannot accomplish them in the context of the WTO, or at least not in the short/medium run. A successful conclusion to DDA would, perhaps, have had an impact on the momentum behind the regionalism movement, but this is not guaranteed: the incentives for new bilateral/plurilateral accords, as well as for deepening existing ones, would remain. Besides, the DDA is stalled and, as noted above, may well be so for some time in the future.

What is guaranteed through successful multilateralism is a reduction in the potential negative effects of these regional agreements and overall less risk to the integrity of the international trading system. Moreover, to the extent that a multilateral accord can, indeed, make Article XXIV more effective in ensuring that these new regional agreements will be outward-looking and consistent with a WTO approach, the risks associated with regionalism could be significantly mitigated (Plummer 2007). Economists should continue to support a "deep" DDA.

Hence, the obvious question emerges as to how regional agreements themselves can work in favor of global free trade. The traditional approach is to view it from the "building blocs versus stumbling blocs" lens, which we do below.

8.3.2   Building Blocs versus Stumbling Blocs: Theoretical Considerations

Does regionalism support unilateral/multilateral reform goals, or does the discrimination inherent in a trade bloc lead to a "second best" outcome at best, or an inward-looking one at worst? This is the essence of the "building blocs" versus "stumbling blocs" debate. The literature would suggest that several possible negative policy consequences could emerge from an FTA, that is, inherent "stumbling bloc" tendencies, while other tendencies would be consistent with multilateral goals and market-friendly domestic liberalization and could actually facilitate multilateral liberalization, that is, "building blocs". Briefly, these would include the following.[11]

8.3.2.1 Stumbling blocs

1. *Maximizing terms of trade.* Regional integration, particularly customs unions, increases the size of an economic zone and, as such, increases market power. The potential benefits of exploiting such an advantage by imposing an "optimal tariff" (i.e. maximizing the difference between the terms of trade gains from a tariff regime against its costs in terms of efficiency) are familiar from the international trade literature. Moreover, FTAs and customs unions, by "virtue" of the trade diversion effect, improve their terms of trade relative to the rest of the world; the larger the grouping, the larger the potential improvement in the terms of trade.

   In reality, the first effect is probably not particularly relevant, as even tariff regimes in the context of a customs union are not erected according to optimum tariff rules.[12] Moreover, in the cases of both customs unions and FTAs, changes in the external tariff regime cannot on average be more protective than the pre-integration status quo, according to Article XXIV. This does not mean that there will not be any potentially negative sectoral effects, but in this case GATT/WTO members are able to sue for compensation. The most famous case in this regard is, perhaps, "Turkey: Restrictions on Imports of Textile Products", in which India initiated a GATT panel against Turkey in the wake of the harmonization of its external tariff with the EU when it formed a customs union in manufactures (Herzstein and Whitlock 2005).[13] Of course, this effect would be even less important with improved rules within the context of Article XXIV.

   With respect to the terms of trade effect, since trade diversion undeniably results from preferential trading arrangements, it is certainly a concern. But trade diversion is actually a one-time price effect and, hence, static in nature. In fact, it is *the* static cost of preferential trading accords.

2. *Manipulation of the contents and scope of the agreement by special interests.* This concern obviously also manifests itself in the context of domestic policy formation. Deardorff (2003) stresses that this is especially a problem in the context of developed–developing country

accords, in which the former obviously have the upper hand, as special interests tend to be far better organized and funded. The lack of rigor and coverage in Article XXIV makes this a particular problem, as the flexibility allowed in an FTA tends to give considerable liberty to special-interest influences. Of course, this could also have a positive effect: special interest groups in developed countries no doubt push for better IPR protection, competition policy, treatment of FDI and better trade and investment facilitation, but these arguably could have important positive effects on efficiency and policy formation in developing countries.[14]

3. *Waste of scarce negotiating resources.* Particularly (but not exclusively) in the case of developing countries, the scarcity of well-trained and well-experienced experts on trade negotiations imply that the opportunity cost of resources devoted to regional agreements is the allocation of less talent to multilateral deals. Critics of regionalism suggest that such a capacity constraint can only be detrimental to multilateral liberalization, and even well-developed domestic policy reform. For example, after Viet Nam joined the Association of Southeast Asian Nations (ASEAN) in 1995, it worked not only to enter into AFTA (due for completion in 2006) but also to implement a number of other accords, including an extensive Bilateral Trade Agreement with the US in 2001. On top of that, it was working on ASEAN+3 initiatives and, eventually, the AEC. Given its human-capital capacity constraints, this could very well have delayed its drive to join the WTO.

Or, perhaps, not. A counter-argument would be that Viet Nam has been able to ready its economy for the WTO through the outward-oriented policies adopted because of its membership in ASEAN, and the Bilateral Trade Agreement itself was essentially a means of preparing Viet Nam for WTO entry, including legal and administrative reforms that would in any event be necessary. The agreement is replete with references to WTO protocols and WTO-consistent reforms, from services liberalization to TRIPs-plus. These negotiations have also sharpened the expertise of Vietnamese negotiating authorities. The US also allocated a relatively large project (the "STAR Project") to assist Viet Nam in reforming its legal system to be more compatible with international norms, as well as to train officials.

8.3.2.2 Building blocs

1. *Lock in policy change.* We have referred to this effect fairly frequently in previous sections, using in particular the case of Mexico in NAFTA. But there are many others, including the case of Viet Nam,

mentioned above, which has been able to use regional integration as a blueprint for market-friendly reform to become more competitive in the international marketplace. Without ASEAN (and eventually the Bilateral Trade Agreement), one can easily argue that Viet Nam would not have made as much progress (and its joining the WTO would no doubt have been further delayed).

2. *Improve negotiating power for smaller units.* Traditionally, the possibility of small countries joining together and working as one cohesive unit in trade negotiations has always been recognized: even Harry Johnson, who was an avid critic of regionalism, acknowledged this potential benefit. This would apply both to smaller countries as well as larger units, such as the EU. Hence, in theory, ASEAN should be able to have much more power in influencing WTO negotiations, or bilateral/regional/plurilateral deals in general, as a group: the whole could be greater than the sum of its parts.

   The EU has certainly been effective in this regard from its beginning as the European Economic Community. But it began as a customs union, not merely an FTA, in which national commercial policy vis-à-vis third countries can differ (often substantially). ASEAN, however, has never been very effective at projecting its power as a unified group, even after AFTA. In the past, the region was just too diverse and the interests of individual countries diverged too much, something that should change with the AEC. Thus, we could probably conclude that this potential "building bloc" is theoretically a possibility, but in practice can be somewhat difficult, being a function of the type of accord (FTA or customs union) and the interests of the component states. The move toward greater "ASEAN Centrality", for example in the context of the Regional Comprehensive Economic Partnership (RCEP, discussed below) is an attempt to augment the regional influence of ASEAN (Petri and Plummer 2014).

3. *A dynamic weeding process as a first step toward free trade.* It could very well be that the process of structural adjustment unleashed by a regional trading arrangement through trade creation could, in effect, make multilateral accords easier. As the weakest (and, hence, more resistant to any international competition) are weeded out due to, say, an FTA, the stock of opposition to trade falls in importance, thereby making multilateral initiatives easier.

   Perhaps an example would illustrate the point. Suppose that the trade policies of a country (let's call it "home") are determined by domestic firms, and "home" trades with two other countries: "partner" (i.e. the country that would ultimately form an FTA with "home") and "rest of world". Furthermore, assume that, in autarky, there are six industries, with linear cost structures of the firms in the home country being such that two are globally competitive (goods A and B), two (goods C and D) are competitive only regionally (in a potential FTA with "partner"), and two would never be competitive with trade (goods E and F). Now, assume that the "home" government puts to vote whether or not the country should move to free trade. Firms producing A and B will vote yes, as they would benefit from a larger market, but the other four firms would vote against it, as they would be put out of business. We remain in an autarkic equilibrium. But suppose now that the home country votes on whether or not it should have an FTA with "partner". Goods A, B, C and D will vote in favor, and E and F against. The FTA would pass. Eventually, competition from the partner country will force out production of goods E and F in the home country (trade creation), and there will be no trade diversion (as we began in autarky). The remaining firms in the home country will, therefore, eventually only produce A, B, C and D. Next, assume that the home country votes once again on whether or not it should have free trade. The votes will now be two in favor (A and B) and two against (C and D). Assuming that consumers have even a little say would be sufficient to usher in free trade, and this would be due to the FTA "stepping stone" process.

4.   *Competitive liberalization to attract international capital, as well as a positive "threat".* Regional integration can be used as a means of rendering the component economies more efficient, competitive and market friendly. While a grouping may or may not adopt global "best practices" in regulatory, legal and other issues, it can reduce the stock of divergences across countries (thereby making it easier to integrate globally). By reducing transaction costs across countries, an FTA can enhance its attractiveness to multinationals. As policy externalities become increasingly important as an FTA "deepens", the incentive to internalize them through monitoring, sharing information and closer cooperation increases. Because trade and financial links are becoming increasingly appreciated, countries within an FTA soon find it useful – or even necessary – to further financial and macroeconomic cooperation.

It may also be true that regional agreements can be used as implicit and explicit "threats", particularly since FTAs seem to have a tendency to grow over time. An obvious example was the boost that President Clinton gave to Asia-Pacific Economic Cooperation (APEC) in 1993, when it invited leaders to Blake Island, Washington, for the first APEC Heads of State summit. Strengthening the organization was supported at Blake Island, and the political will to move forward on economic cooperation, especially in trade, was obviously in evidence (in the following year, in Indonesia, this would manifest itself in the "Bogor Vision" goals of open trade and investment by 2010 for developed economies and 2020 for developing economies). Prior to Blake Island, the Uruguay Round had failed to be approved twice (in 2000 and again in 2002) essentially because the EU and the US, backed by the Cairns Group, could not reach an agreement on agriculture. After the Blake Island summit, the Europeans decided to sign the agreement. Some experts have stressed that Clinton deliberately used APEC as a "threat" to Europe, that is, if the Uruguay Round didn't go through, the US was perfectly willing to move forward on free trade with Asia. Rather than face trade diversion in the world's most rapidly growing market by far, the EU opted for the GATT.

Each of these arguments has *theoretical* merits. But in practice, the inclination of the regional accord tends to be extremely important. Clearly, if the group is being formed as a means of enhancing inward-looking development strategies or as a way of isolating the region from global competition, this initial policy thrust would set in motion many of the problems discussed above. In fact, this approach has led to the downfall of many regional trading agreements in the past, especially in Latin American (e.g. the Latin American Free Trade Area).[15] Yet, if outward-looking economies form a regional grouping, it is likely that regionalism will serve to promote the goals of domestic policy reform and multilateral liberalization. This is due to at least four factors: (1) it is unlikely that a country wishing to promote outward-looking policies, including extensive unilateral liberalization and active participation at the WTO, would contradict this stance in favor of a regionally-closed system; (2) reductions in trade barriers within a preferential trading arrangement make it more attractive for a country to reduce external barriers, in effect "MFN-izing" regional concessions, because the most important cost of regionalism is trade diversion and lower external barriers will reduce associated costs; (3) the "weeding out" of least competitive industries (discussed above) and making the political economy of trade liberalization more favorable over time seems to have been important empirically;[16] and (4) the membership of RTAs tends to expand and to become more diverse over time, thereby reducing regional sources of support for protectionism in a particular country and industry, as well as reducing the overall potential for trade diversion. One might add to this the list of non-traditional benefits for developing countries in regional trading agreements such as enhanced macroeconomic stability via cooperation, greater FDI inflows and attendant technology transfer, structural policy change and reform, and state-of-the-art harmonization. The lion's share of empirical estimates of the economic effects of regional trading agreements in East Asia, for example, using either computable general equilibrium (CGE) modeling or econometric methods, reveals net trade creation.

In sum, while the risks of regionalism are real and, as with any real-world second-best policies, costs exist, it would appear that what is driving the regionalism movement since the early 2000s, particularly in Asia, is based on an outward-looking approach to integration and that the implications have been positive for the region. AFTA and other expressions of ASEAN integration are exemplary of this. Still, minimizing costs is of the essence. In Plummer (2007), I suggest a framework under which this might be done; additional ideas are found in WTO (2011) and "multilateralising regionalism" work forthcoming from the OECD.

8.4 THE NEW REGIONALISM IN THE ASIA-PACIFIC

There have been many excellent surveys of regional economic integration in Asia (e.g. ADB 2008, 2012; Kawai 2005). Several factors influencing the regionalism trend in East Asia stem directly from the Asian Financial Crisis, including: (1) the obvious contagion relationships, which demonstrated the policy externalities across countries in ASEAN and the NIEs; (2) major disappointment with respect to the Western reaction to the crisis, leaving the feeling of "being in it alone together"; (3) disappointing progress in APEC in achieving closer trade and financial cooperation, as well as development assistance cooperation; (4) Japan's offer to create an Asian Monetary Fund during the crisis – opposed by the IMF and the US – gave the impression that Japan wanted to be proactive in the region; (5) arguably, the PRC's decision not to devalue during this period also created a sense of solidarity; (6) the "New Miyazawa Plan", launched in October 1998 which dedicated US$30 billion to help spur recovery in East Asia (and deemed highly successful) (Kawai 2005); and (7) the policies promulgated by the IMF to solve the crisis were deemed inappropriate, giving greater credibility to the "Asian approach".

Hence, the crisis itself set the stage for serious and durable East Asian regionalism. There are many other internal and external forces at work that have expedited the process, such as the rise of regionalism globally and its potential negative effects on the region; the successful example of the Single Market Program in Europe; general pessimism regarding what can be achieved at the WTO in light of failure to move forward at the Seattle and Cancun WTO Ministerials; and the potential inherent benefits of FTAs. Importantly, bringing down barriers to economic interaction in order to lure FDI and promote production networks has certainly been a key factor in the ever-expanding intra-regional (Appendix Table 8A.1) and extra-regional (www.aric.adb.org) agreements. Nevertheless, I would suggest that the next wave of regionalism will be in favor of regional accords, rather than the plethora of bilateral FTAs that constitute the "Asian noodle bowl".

A strong majority of the RTAs concluded or initiated by Asian economies were bilateral FTAs, which tend to be easier to negotiate than, say, larger memberships or deeper accords such as customs unions. Moreover, a majority of these FTAs are with economies outside of Asia. Thus, when Asian governments consider bilateral accords, they think globally, rather than just regionally. These priorities reflect the driving forces behind regionalism in Asia, which tend to be *economic* rather than political, though obviously the political context is always important. Indeed, this might distinguish Asia from bilateral and regional accords elsewhere, which tend to be politically dominated. For example, early integration initiatives in Europe, beginning with the Coal and Steel Community and the European Economic Community, had strong political backing (integrating France and Germany after the World War II, Cold War exigencies), even though the economics were somewhat dubious at the time. Even monetary union in the EU was made possible due to political reasons, that is, post-Cold War incentives and, in particular, facilitating the political integration of East and West Germany. In fact, the need to support economic integration in Asia is even helping to overcome some of the most difficult obstacles to cooperation in the region; a decade ago few, if anyone, could have foreseen that the PRC, the Republic of Korea, and Japan would be able to improve relations sufficiently to sit down and negotiate an FTA. Yet that is exactly what was agreed to at their May 2012 summit. Recent political disputes have put the trilateral FTA negotiations on hold; however, they did sign an investment agreement and are negotiating partners in RCEP.

If this thesis that Asian regionalism is based on economics is correct, then the creation of regional accords would certainly emerge as a more efficient approach than bilateral FTAs. While the vast majority of empirical studies on bilateral FTAs in Asia would suggest that these accords have had (or will have) a positive effect on the welfare of their member-states, with small negative effects on the rest of the world in terms of trade diversion, they clearly have important shortcomings (as noted above). But most importantly: *if the driving force behind regionalism in Asia pertains to international and regional production networks, bilateral FTAs will tend to fall short.* Regional FTAs would be needed to optimize regional production networks and lower costs associated with, for example, rules of origin (via cumulation), and outward-oriented regional FTAs that minimize discrimination against non-partners and have open membership clauses would facilitate international production networks.

We might call the realization of the need to create regional FTAs the "new regionalism" in Asia. Creating these regional institutions that will facilitate the integration of the region over the medium to long term will no doubt be high on the agenda of most Asian policymakers in years to come. We might consider two "pathways" in this regard: one East Asian, the other Pacific Rim.

To begin, in 2004 the ASEAN+3 Economic Ministers commissioned a study of the feasibility of an East Asia FTA, and the idea of an Asia-wide FTA gained momentum particularly when negotiations for the Trans-Pacific Partnership (TPP) began in 2008. Ultimately, the chosen unit of cooperation became RCEP, which was launched in November 2012 with "ASEAN centrality" explicitly at its core; indeed, members of RCEP must have an FTA in place with ASEAN (in addition to the 10 ASEAN members, this includes PRC, Japan, Republic of Korea, India and Australia–New Zealand). While it is not yet clear what form RCEP will take, it is intended to be "ambitious", covering, *inter alia*, trade in goods and services, investment, intellectual property and competition policy, as well as flexibility for least-developed members. The Third Round of RCEP negotiations took place in Kuala Lumpur in January 2014.

The TPP builds on a high-quality FTA between four small, open economies (Brunei Darussalam, Singapore, New Zealand and Chile), known as the "P4", and in addition to these negotiators the TPP includes the US, Australia, Malaysia, Viet Nam and Peru (the "TPP"), later joined by Mexico, Canada and Japan in 2012 and 2013, with the Republic of Korea currently undergoing preliminary negotiations with the view to possibly joining the talks. The TPP negotiators had hoped to come to an agreement by the end of 2013 but negotiations have continued into 2014.

The TPP is distinct not only in terms of the large differences in levels of development (from low-middle-income developing countries such as Peru and Viet Nam to high-income, advanced OECD members such as the US and Japan) but in terms of its ambitions to become a "twenty-first century" agreement that would embrace a wide-variety of areas, from trade in goods and services to science and technology and small- and medium-sized enterprises, including many difficult-to-negotiate behind-the-border measures. Its membership is technically open to any APEC member; indeed, its ultimate goal is the creation of a "Free-Trade Area of the Asia Pacific" (FTAAP) that would include all APEC members. Both the RCEP and TPP "tracks" were cited by APEC at its 2010 summit in Yokohama as paths to the creation of an FTAAP. Clearly, there is a good deal of membership overlap between the RCEP and TPP economies.

Petri et al. (2011) use an advanced CGE modeling approach to estimate the economic impact of the "Asian track" and the "Trans-Pacific track" (TPP) as pathways to the FTAAP. The Asian track assumes a PRC, Japan, Republic of Korea FTA in 2012 and then an ASEAN+3 FTA in 2015; for the Trans-Pacific track, they assume a TPP9 agreement in 2012 and an expansion in 2015 to include Japan, the Republic of Korea, Canada and Mexico. They assume that both tracks eventually lead to an FTAAP that would begin in 2020. They estimate fairly large gains for both tracks: the effects on the world economy would be small initially but by 2025 the annual welfare gains would rise to US$104 billion on the TPP track, US$303 billion on both tracks, and US$862 billion with an FTAAP.[17] Interestingly, the biggest gains accrue when the two tracks are consolidated; in effect, this results from both the PRC and the US being included in the same agreement.

As of this writing, the outlook for the RCEP and TPP agreements in the near future is mixed, with the latter having progressed further than the former. Should each of these tracks begin implementation in the short run, the medium-term goal of an FTAAP would seem much more within reach. The literature is replete with arguments as to why the FTAAP will not be reached for various reasons, prominent among them being US–PRC trade relations. But it is worth underscoring that the PRC and the US are big economic winners in the FTAAP scenario in Petri et al. (2011). Success in this regard would be consistent with the diplomatic and political goals of both countries, and eight years is a long time in trade policy.

8.5 CONCLUSIONS

We can summarize the main conclusions of this chapter as follows:

1. A strong, vibrant WTO is essential to the prosperity of the international trading system.
2. Still, it is important to note that the prospects for significant liberalization scenarios under the WTO in the near future are not bright. The decade-plus DDA single-undertaking is on hold (again) and at present there are no plans to restart negotiations; other possible liberalization approaches (e.g. "plurilaterals") are possible but, again, difficult and fraught with potential problems, depending on how they develop.

3. While a multilateral approach to trade policy is best *ceteris paribus*, regionalism does have a number of advantages in that it is able to achieve more progress in a shorter period of time within the context of a group of like-minded countries. Global free-trade is not an option at present (or likely in my lifetime, and I hope to live a long time), and even if it were what could be tackled at the multilateral level with 160 (and growing) diverse economies in the WTO context would be far less than what can be achieved within a regional grouping.

4. Of course, if regionalism is "closed" it will be detrimental to the global trading system. We survey the issues related to the "stumbling bloc versus building bloc" debate and suggest that, while FTAs do have potential drawbacks and that the essence of the agreement will be a key determinant, FTAs can, indeed, be building blocs, particularly if the orientation of the integrating economies is outward in nature, as in the case of Asia. A continued emphasis on outward orientation, minimizing discrimination, inclusiveness and embracing the first-best needs to be made in order to ensure that regionalism in Asia (and elsewhere) serves to enhance competitiveness and support global free markets, rather than detract from them.

Finally, we also note that while regionalism is usually compared to multilateralism in the literature, insufficient attention is, perhaps, placed on the inefficiencies of bilateral FTAs relative to regional ones. We stress that regional arrangements are of the essence in the Asia-Pacific region for economic (e.g., regional production networks) as well as diplomatic political goals. This "new regionalism", which has been supported by APEC, will lead to significant reductions in the costs associated with bilateral FTAs (e.g. lower costs associated with rules of origin, improved utilization rates) and seems to (rightly) be receiving a good deal more attention.

A successful conclusion to the TPP negotiations will be likely to increase the incentives to push forward in the RCEP. If both of these Asian and Asia-Pacific tracks are concluded, the Asia-Pacific region will be well on its way to a Free-Trade Area of the Asia Pacific (FTAAP) beginning in 2020, which was articulated at the November 2010 Yokohama APEC summit as the ultimate goal of the region's trade cooperation. This process could also potentially draw in other economies, for example in South Asia (India) and in Latin America.

Now, an APEC-only FTAAP itself, with over 60 per cent of global GDP – let alone an FTAAP that includes additional members – would be sufficient to create concerns as to the future of the global trading system.

Such concerns need to be allayed by emphasizing in word and deed that Asia-Pacific cooperation is about open regionalism and supporting the global system, rather than creating a competitor to it. That might take some doing. But in the meantime, it could well be that, as in the case of the Uruguay Round and the Blake Island summit of APEC in 1993, the successful Asia-Pacific integration process could revitalize global negotiations well before 2020. All that is certain is that trade policy over the next decade will be interesting.

NOTES

1. WTO website, www.wto.org, accessed 19 March 2014.
2. www.aric.adb.org, accessed 19 March 2014.
3. Part of this section draws from Plummer (2012).
4. Hufbauer and Schott (2012) are also skeptical of future progress at the DDA and propose moving away from a single-undertaking toward a "Grand Bargain" as a more effective way of moving the process forward.
5. The third WTO plurilateral relates to trade in civil aircraft.
6. Some of this discussion is adapted from Plummer (2006).
7. See, for example, Hufbauer and Schott (2005).
8. These were higher in the case of Mexico, but as Mexico is a small economy compared to the US and Canada, the net effects could not be large.
9. It is interesting to note that CAFTA was passed in the US only after personal lobbying by the President himself, and then the pact passed by only a two-vote margin in the House of Representatives. But Congressional opposition was not due to a dislike of regionalism per se but rather a dislike of trade liberalization, that is, it was generally opposed on traditional protectionist grounds.
10. The NAFTA office of Mexico in Canada, http://www.nafta-mexico.org/ls23al. php?s=501&p=3&l=2, accessed 19 March 2014.
11. See the classic piece by Frankel (1997), from which some of these topics are adopted.
12. Nor are they at the country-level. While the optimum tariff argument is one of the three classic economic arguments in favor of protection (the others being the infant-industry argument and strategic trade policy), it is well recognized to be a theoretical argument. Tariffs are generally implemented for political and political-economy-related reasons, not as a means of trying to extract terms of trade gains.
13. The Turkey case may be the most famous but there are others. For example, while Spain's external tariff regime became more liberal after it joined the EC, the country did raise protection on agricultural imports in order to harmonize its policies with the EC's Common Agricultural Policy. The US was able to extract compensation from the EC in the feed-grains sectors in compensation for the associated trade diversion.
14. It should be noted that IPR is probably the most controversial in terms of the ultimate effect on economic efficiency.
15. It is not clear that much has changed in Latin America: MERCOSUR, which is a customs union between Brazil, Argentina, Paraguay and Uruguay, has often been reluctant to open certain markets domestically (e.g. automobiles) and the customs union itself has over 1000 exemptions.
16. Perhaps it would be more accurate to say "anecdotally", as the empirical literature on this subject is not well developed.
17. For additional cooperative scenarios see www.asiapacifictrade.org.

REFERENCES

Asian Development Bank (ADB). 2008. *Emerging Asian Regionalism*. Manila: ADB.
Asian Development Bank. 2011. *Asia 2050: Realizing the Asian Century.* Manila: ADB. Available at: http://www.adb.org/publications/asia-2050-real izing-asian-century.
Asian Development Bank. 2012. *Asian Economic Integration Monitor*. Manila: ADB.
Deardorff, A.V. 2003. What might globalisation's critics believe? *The World Economy* **26**(5): 639–58.
Frankel, J.A. 1997. *Regional Trading Blocs in the World Trading System.* Washington, DC: Institute for International Economics.
Frankel, J. (ed.). 1998. *The Regionalization of the World Economy*, Chicago: University of Chicago Press.
Geneva Watch. 2012. Pursuing an ambitious services plurilateral agreement. *Geneva Watch* **12**(19), June: 1. Available at: http://www.chep-poic.ca/pdf/ Geneva_Watch/2012/Geneva%20Watch_June%201%202012.pdf, accessed 18 July, 2012.
Herzstein, R.E. and J.P. Whitlock. 2005. Regulating regional trade agreements: A legal analysis. In: P.J. Macrory, A.E. Appleton and M.G. Plummer (eds) *The World Trade Organization: Legal, Economic and Political Analysis*. New York: Springer.
Hufbauer, G.C. and J.J. Schott. 2005. *NAFTA Revisited: Achievements and Challenges*. Peterson Institute for International Economics. October.
Hufbauer, G.C. and J.J. Schott. 2012. Will the World Trade Organization enjoy a bright future? Peterson Institute for International Economics Policy Brief No. PB12–11. May.
Kawai, M. 2005. East Asian economic regionalism: Progress and challenges. *Journal of Asian Economics* **16**(1).
Kose, M.A. and A. Rebucci. 2005. How might CAFTA change macroeconomic fluctuations in Central America? Lessons from NAFTA. *Journal of Asian Economics* **16**(1): 77–104.
Kreinin, M.E. and M.G. Plummer. 2002. *Economic Integration and Development: Has Regionalism Delivered for Developing Countries?* Cheltenham, UK and Northampton, MA, USA: Edward Elgar Publishing.
Petri, P.A. and M.G. Plummer. 2014. ASEAN centrality and the ASEAN-US economic relationship. *Policy Studies* No. 69. Honolulu: East-West Center.
Petri, P.A., M.G. Plummer and F. Zhai. 2011. The trans-Pacific partnership and Asia-Pacific integration: A quantitative assessment. Working Paper. Peterson Institute for International Economics and the East-West Center. October.
Plummer, M. 2006. Toward win–win regionalism in Asia: Issues and challenges in forming efficient free-trade agreements, ADB Working Paper on Regional Economic Integration No. 5. Manila: ADB. Available at: http://aric.adb.org/ publications/workingpaperseries.
Plummer, M.G. 2007. Best practices in regional trading agreements: An application to Asia. *The World Economy* **30**(12): 1771–96.
Plummer, M.G. 2012. Transatlantic economic relations in a changing global

environment. Invited paper prepared for the European Parliament and presented 30 May in Brussels. Mimeo.

World Bank. 2005. *Global Economic Prospects: Trade, Regionalism, and Development*. Washington, DC: The World Bank.

World Trade Organization (WTO). 2011. *World Trade Report: The WTO and Preferential Trading Agreements: From Co-Existence to Coherence*. Geneva, Switzerland: WTO.

APPENDIX 8A.1

Table 8A.1   FTA partnerships in East Asian summit countries

	Australia	New Zealand	ASEAN	Brunei Darussalam	Cambodia	Indonesia
Australia		CERTA/ AFTA/SPECA	AFTA	AFTA	AFTA	AFTA
New Zealand	CERTA/ AFTA/SPECA		AFTA	AFTA/ TSEPA	AFTA	AFTA
ASEAN	AFTA	AFTA	AEC	AEC	AEC	AEC
Brunei Darussalam	AFTA	AFTA/TSEPA	AEC		AEC	AEC
Cambodia	AFTA	AFTA	AEC	AEC		AEC
Indonesia	AFTA	AFTA	AEC	AEC	AEC	
Lao PDR	AFTA	AFTA	AEC	AEC	AEC	AEC
Malaysia	AFTA	AFTA/FTA	AEC	AEC	AEC	AEC/ PTA-8*
Myanmar	AFTA	AFTA	AEC	AEC	AEC	AEC
Philippines	AFTA	AFTA	AEC	AEC	AEC	AEC
Singapore	AFTA/FTA	AFTA/TSEPA/ CEP	AEC	AEC/TSEPA	AEC	AEC
Thailand	AFTA/FTA	AFTA/CEP	AEC	AEC	AEC	AEC
Viet Nam	AFTA	AFTA	AEC	AEC	AEC	AEC
North-East Asia						
PRC		FTA	ACECA	ACECA	ACECA	ACECA
Japan			ACEPA	ACEPA/FTA	ACEPA	ACEPA/ EPA
Republic of Korea			ACECA	ACECA	ACECA	ACECA
India			ACECA	ACECA	ACECA	ACECA
US	FTA					
Russian Federation						

Lao PDR	Malaysia	Myanmar	Philippines	Singapore	Thailand	Viet Nam
AFTA	AFTA	AFTA	AFTA	AFTA/FTA	AFTA/FTA	AFTA
AFTA	AFTA/FTA	AFTA	AFTA	AFTA/TSEPA/ CEP	AFTA/CEP	AFTA
AEC	AEC	AEC	AEC	AEC	AEC	AEC
AEC	AEC	AEC	AEC	AEC/TSEPA	AEC	AEC
AEC	AEC	AEC	AEC	AEC	AEC	AEC
AEC	AEC/PTA-8*	AEC	AEC	AEC	AEC	AEC
	AEC	AEC	AEC	AEC	AEC/ PTA	AEC
AEC		AEC	AEC	AEC	AEC	AEC
AEC	AEC		AEC	AEC	AEC	AEC
AEC	AEC	AEC		AEC	AEC	AEC
AEC	AEC	AEC	AEC		AEC	AEC
AEC/PTA	AEC	AEC	AEC	AEC		AEC
AEC	AEC	AEC	AEC	AEC	AEC	
ACECA/ APTA	ACECA	ACECA	ACECA	ACECA/FTA	ACECA/FTA	ACECA
ACEPA	ACEPA/EPA	ACEPA	ACEPA/ EPA	ACEPA/EANP	ACEPA/EPA	ACEPA/ EPA
ACECA/ APTA	ACECA	ACECA	ACECA	ACECA/FTA	ACECA	ACECA
ACECA/ APTA	ACECA/ CECA	ACECA	ACECA	ACECA/CECA	ACECA	ACECA
				FTA		

New global economic architecture

Table 8A.1   (continued)

	PRC	Japan	Republic of Korea	India	US	Russian Federation
Australia					FTA	
New Zealand	FTA					
ASEAN	ACECA	ACEPA	ACECA	ACECA		
Brunei Darussalam	ACECA	ACEPA/FTA	ACECA	ACECA		
Cambodia	ACECA	ACEPA	ACECA	ACECA		
Indonesia	ACECA	ACEPA/EPA	ACECA	ACECA		
Lao PDR	ACECA/APTA	ACEPA	ACECA/APTA	ACECA/APTA		
Malaysia	ACECA	ACEPA/EPA	ACECA	ACECA/CECA		
Myanmar	ACECA	ACEPA	ACECA	ACECA		
Philippines	ACECA	ACEPA/EPA	ACECA	ACECA		
Singapore	ACECA/FTA	ACEPA/EANP	ACECA/FTA	ACECA/CECA	FTA	
Thailand	ACECA/FTA	ACEPA/EPA	ACECA	ACECA		
Viet Nam	ACECA	ACEPA/EPA	ACECA	ACECA		
North-East Asia						
PRC			APTA	APTA		
Japan				CEPA		
Republic of Korea	APTA			CEPA/APTA	FTA*	
India	APTA	CEPA	CEPA/APTA			
US			FTA*			
Russian Federation						

Notes:
* Signed but not yet in effect.
ACECA   ASEAN-Comprehensive Economic Cooperation Agreement (ASEAN-PRC,
         ASEAN-Rep. of Korea, ASEAN-India).
ACEPA   ASEAN Comprehensive Economic Partnership Agreement.
AEC   ASEAN Economic Community.
AFTA   ASEAN–Australia and New Zealand Free Trade Agreement.
APTA   Asia-Pacific Trade Agreement.
CECA   Comprehensive Economic Cooperation Agreement.
CEP   Closer Economic Partnership.
CEPA   Comprehensive Economic Partnership Agreement.
CERTA   Closer Economic Relations Trade Agreement.
EANP   Economic Agreement for a New-Age Partnership.
FTA   Free Trade Agreement.
PTA   Preferential Trading Agreement.
PTA-8   Preferential Tariff Arrangement – Group of Eight Developing Countries.
SEPA   Strategic Economic Partnership Agreement.
SPECA   South Pacific Regional Trade and Economic Cooperation Agreement.
TSEPA   Trans-Pacific Strategic Economic Partnership Agreement.

9. The World Bank and the Asian Development Bank: should Asia have both?

Vikram Nehru

9.1 INTRODUCTION

The World Bank and the Asian Development Bank (ADB) face three sets of challenges: those that are common to others in the official development finance community; those that are common to the World Bank's relations with other multilateral regional development banks (the European Bank for Reconstruction and Development, the African Development Bank and the Inter-American Development Bank), several multilateral subregional development banks, and multilateral financial institutions (MFIs);[1] and finally, those related to operating as multilateral development banks in the most dynamic region in the world: Asia.

This chapter examines all three challenges and asks whether it may be an opportune time to rethink the configuration of the world's multilateral development banking system. The current configuration – like the rest of the global aid architecture – has grown organically, responding to emerging challenges with new institutional and procedural "fixes". The result is a complex and unwieldy set of institutions that, despite their best efforts at coordination and cooperation, sometimes work against each other and often add to the administrative burden of the member governments they serve.

The chapter begins with an overview of how a rapidly changing world is altering development priorities and giving rise to new development challenges that are stretching the capabilities of the development community, including development finance institutions. Section 9.3 describes the roles of the World Bank and ADB in Asia, provides some comparisons, notes their overlapping responsibilities, and explains current approaches to coordination and cooperation. Section 9.4 examines the issues and options confronting the two institutions, and Section 9.5 concludes by asking if Asia can afford both.

9.2   THE WORLD OF – AND AROUND – DEVELOPMENT FINANCE IS CHANGING

Output, Trade and Finance

The global economic landscape is undergoing a profound transformation. The structure of world output, trade and finance is shifting rapidly. The rise of Asia, especially the People's Republic of China (PRC) and to a lesser extent India, is inexorably shifting the global economy's center of gravity away from Europe and the United States. This trend was clearly visible in the 1990s, accelerated in the 2000s, and has been amplified by the 2008–09 global financial crisis. As a result, emerging economies have become an influential force in the global economy. The share of developing countries in global trade has climbed from 30 per cent in 1995 to 45 per cent in 2010. Much of this increased trade has been among developing countries. Similarly, over a third of foreign direct investment in developing countries now comes from other developing countries. Indeed, since the global financial crisis, the investment risk premium in many emerging economies is below that in some European countries. Reflecting the strong external payments position in many developing countries, international reserves held by emerging economies reached US$7.4 trillion in 2010, well over three times the US$2.1 trillion in reserves held by advanced economies (World Bank 2011).

Capital Flows

Another dimension of change in the global economic landscape has been the level and volatility of capital flows. International trade in financial assets has grown much more rapidly than international trade in goods and services. Indeed, the volume of assets traded internationally climbed over 15-fold in the two decades prior to the financial crisis – with bank loans, bonds and portfolio flows growing at roughly the same pace as each other while derivatives grew much faster. This growth is likely to accelerate as global savings is expected to rise rapidly because savings will rise in advanced countries and there will be little corresponding decline in savings in developing countries. The size of the foreign asset market has already significantly complicated macroeconomic management, especially in emerging market economies where capital inflows and outflows tend to be particularly volatile – and the size and volatility of such flows is only likely to increase.

Multiple Growth Poles and Global Governance Mechanisms

Going forward, emerging economies are expected to outperform advanced countries and become important drivers of global growth and trade. By 2030, global economic projections show emerging economies are likely to contribute two-thirds of global growth, half of global output, and will be the main destinations of world trade. Just as the rise of the United States in the late nineteenth century altered the balance of power and influenced the course of events in the twentieth century, so too will the rise of emerging economies affect the distribution of global economic and geopolitical power in the twenty-first century.

The emergence of multiple growth poles and centers of economic power will need to be reflected in global governance mechanisms responsible for the management of global economic affairs including global economic and financial stability, economic development and global trade in goods and services. While there has been considerable discussion on how these shifts should be reflected in the world's governance arrangements, agreement has been difficult to reach and progress has been slow.

Global Public Goods

Notwithstanding the global financial crisis and the increased risk of protectionism, especially in developed countries, the forces of globalization will remain irresistible. As a result, global public goods – a global agreement for trade of goods and services, climate change mitigation, international financial stability, anti-money laundering and countering the financing of terrorism, food and energy security, intellectual property rights, a legal framework for commercialization of space and the sea bed, among others – are only going to increase in value. There is little doubt that the world's demand for these global public goods will increase. The major question is whether there is sufficient global will for collective action that will ensure their supply.

International Aid Architecture

It is within this global context that the current international aid architecture will need to evolve. Official aid flows to developing countries peaked in 1991, driven in large part by bilateral aid. Multilateral aid grew only modestly, at about 4 per cent a year in the two decades before 1991. Aid flows slowed after 1991, again largely owing to bilateral aid, falling by as much as 22 per cent by 1997. But this period also saw increased poverty in sub-Saharan Africa and an expanding group of fragile states. In 2002, spurred by the Millennium Development Goals, the international community committed to doubling aid by 2010. Actual aid flows have since climbed by more than 50 per cent, but the amount of aid that recipients can actually use is barely above the level of 1991 (Kharas 2007).[2]

While multilateral aid has climbed steadily in nominal terms, its composition shifted in two ways. First, the share of IDA and regional banks fell from 47 per cent of total multilateral aid in 1995 to 36 per cent in 2005, while the share of UN agencies fell from 25 per cent to 17 per cent over the same period. The European Commission, which became the largest source of multilateral aid in 1997, largely filled the gap (Kharas 2007). Second, the last two decades have seen the birth of an increasing number of vertical funds – such as the Global Environmental Facility (GEF), the Global Vaccines Alliance (GAVI) and the Global Fund to Fight AIDS, Tuberculosis, and Malaria (GFATM) – some of which have themselves become bewilderingly complex.

Perhaps the most significant development in recent years has been the rise of non-traditional donors: non-DAC (Development Assistance Committee of the Organisation for Economic Co-operation and Development) bilateral donors, foundations, non-government organizations (NGOs), religious organizations and private voluntary organizations. Non-traditional donors are the fastest growing component of aid flows. Of these, private giving (by foundations, NGOs, religious organizations and private voluntary organizations) is by far the most significant, surpassing official aid flows in recent years. Non-DAC bilateral donors include Brazil; the People's Republic of China (PRC); India; Taipei,China; Turkey; and Thailand. Of these, aid from the PRC has grown the fastest.[3]

In summary, the international aid architecture has become a complex behemoth. Some 37 bilateral donor countries report their aid to DAC and many others do not; there are 233 multilateral agencies, more than there are bilateral donors and recipient countries (155) combined. Dozens of international NGOs receive funds from bilateral donors, and thousands of private organizations have joined the aid community, some of them, such as the Gates Foundation, rivaling the largest bilateral and multilateral organizations in size and reach.

More donors have meant greater fragmentation of aid. In 1996, DAC bilateral donors financed 15 750 new aid activities with an average size of almost US$3 million. By 2008, this had climbed to 84 764 activities, and the average size had shrunk to US$1.35 million – with a median size of only US$87 499 (Kharas and Fengler 2011).

Notwithstanding the rapid growth in aid from private givers, the prevailing view is that overall official development assistance (ODA) flows fall significantly short of what is desirable. But there are differing views on how much incremental ODA should flow to developing countries. Estimates range from US$50 billion (United Nations 2002) to US$200 billion (by those who argue that aid should reach the 0.7 per cent of GDP target of developed countries). Detractors, however, respond that further aid will only spawn additional corruption, and unless aid effectiveness is increased, channeling additional aid will do little for promoting sustainable and inclusive development.

The challenge for the international aid community is to improve the current system (starting from a clean slate is not an option) and configure it in a way that channels aid through the most efficient organizations, ensures that it is provided for optimal-sized programs, projects and activities with high development impact, and to deliver it to countries where need is greatest.

One way to do this would be to tailor aid in accordance with a country's circumstances. To achieve this will require country ownership of aid-financed projects and the discipline of supporting country priorities and strategies. Another way is to better coordinate aid so donors don't work at cross-purposes or add to the administrative burden of the recipients. This will require acceleration in implementing the Paris Declaration on Aid Effectiveness and expansion of it to cover non-traditional donors. Finally, national development agencies should insist on rigorous evaluations that identify successful projects for scaling up and delivering systemic change, while ensuring unsuccessful ones are discontinued or redesigned.

9.3 ADB AND THE WORLD BANK: FUNCTIONS, STRUCTURES, ROLES AND RESPONSIBILITIES

The previous section showed that ADB and the World Bank operate within a rapidly evolving and increasingly complicated global aid architecture. This section examines the institutions in greater detail and compares them along different dimensions.

ADB was established in 1966 "to foster economic growth and co-operation in the region of Asia and the Far East . . . and to contribute to the acceleration of the process of economic development of the developing member countries in the region, collectively and individually" (ADB 1966, p. 4). Its initial focus was on food and rural development projects but it quickly diversified its operations to include education, health and infrastructure development. During the 1970s oil crisis, ADB began financing energy projects to increase energy security in the region. It financed its first equity investment in the 1980s and was a major player, together with the

International Monetary Fund (IMF) and the World Bank, in responding to the Asian Financial Crisis in the late 1990s by supporting financial sector development and strengthening social safety nets. It was during this period that ADB made poverty reduction its key objective. Starting with 31 members in 1966, ADB now has 67 members, of which 48 are from Asia and the Pacific and 19 are from outside this region (ADB Annual Reports, various issues).

The World Bank was created in 1944 to extend finance for the reconstruction of Europe following World War II and subsequently to overcome obstacles facing developing countries trying to access international capital for development purposes. It now consists of five separate entities: the International Bank for Reconstruction and Development (IBRD); the International Development Association (IDA); the International Finance Corporation (IFC); the Multilateral Investment Guarantee Agency (MIGA); and the International Centre for Settlement of Investment Disputes (ICSID). IBRD and IDA constitute the core of the World Bank Group and provide financial and technical assistance for development in low- and middle-income countries through a suite of loans and grants across the entire range of development challenges facing poor countries – including health, education, infrastructure, agriculture, public administration, macroeconomic management, institutional development, governance, financial and private-sector development, environmental protection, and natural resource management (World Bank Annual Reports, various issues).

Both the World Bank and ADB are actively involved in every low- and middle-income country in Asia and the Pacific, except the Democratic People's Republic of Korea. There is a similar overlap in sectoral involvement.

Coordination is therefore a key issue. At the Group of Twenty (G20) summit in Pittsburgh in September 2009, leaders called for greater coordination and a clearer division of labor between the World Bank and the regional development banks. They further stated that the World Bank and regional development banks take into account their comparative advantage, while improving coordination and efficiency and minimizing overlap with other international financial institutions and private financial institutions (World Bank 2010).

Notwithstanding this, coordination between the World Bank and ADB in Asia has not been a simple matter. ADB has to coordinate country strategies with three different regional vice presidents of the World Bank (East Asia and the Pacific, South Asia, and Europe and Central Asia) as well as the country directors in each country. Previously it also had to coordinate sector strategies with the World Bank's three major networks: poverty reduction and economic management; sustainable development; and

Table 9.1   ADB and the World Bank: selected financial indicators (US$ billion)

	ADB	World Bank[b]
Lending in 2010[a]	8.2	44.2
Disbursements in 2010[a]	5.3	28.9
Outstanding loans[a]	43.6	129.5
Authorized capital	163.8	278.3
Outstanding debt	51.8	135.2
Total assets	100.2	312.8
Net income	0.6	0.9

Notes:
[a]   To sovereign borrowers only.
[b]   Excludes IFC.

Sources: ADB Annual Report (2010); World Bank Annual Report (2010).

human development. That coordination will now become more complex after the reorganization of the World Bank's knowledge networks into 14 global practice groups and five cross-cutting areas. While procedures for coordination will of necessity need to be more elaborate and institutionalized, the quality of coordination will continue to depend on personalities in both institutions and, occasionally, the role of the country authorities.

The recent tripling of ADB's authorized capital from US$55 billion to US$165 billion has significantly increased its financial strength (ADB Annual Report 2010). It is now, by far, the largest of the regional development banks and some of its financial indicators are approaching those of the World Bank. ADB's authorized capital is some 60 per cent of the World Bank's, its net income in 2010 was two-thirds, and its total assets about a third (Table 9.1). The chief difference between the two institutions is that ADB's sustainable lending is significantly above its current level, while that of the World Bank is trending downward.

It is more difficult to do a detailed comparison of ADB's lending indicators with those of the World Bank's Asian operations. Comparisons could only be made for two variables: commitments and disbursements (Figure 9.1).[4] These show that ADB's commitments and disbursements declined in 2010 while those of the World Bank increased. But the World Bank's lending levels will not be sustainable without fundamental reforms aimed at increasing net income significantly (a difficult task), while ADB's commitment levels are likely to remain at about US$10 billion a year. Thus ADB will continue to challenge the World Bank as the dominant multilateral development bank lender in Asia.

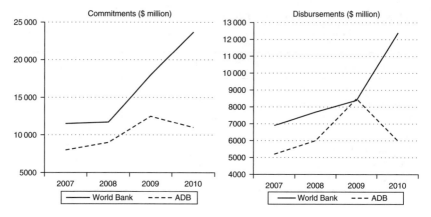

Note: To sovereign borrowers only.

Source: Aidflows (http://www.aidflows.org/).

*Figure 9.1   ADB and World Bank: comparisons of commitments and
disbursements (2007–10)*

*Table 9.2   Institutional profile of private sector operations: comparisons
between ADB and IFC, 2010 (US$ million)*

	ADB	IFC
Investment portfolio	4284	38841
New commitments	1918	12664
Advisory services/technical assistance	3	188

Note: IFC = International Finance Corporation.

Source: Multilateral Development Banks' Common Performance Assessment System
(2010). Annex 2.

There are no head-to-head comparisons of operational performance
indicators between ADB and the World Bank's Asian operations.[5] Even
head-to-head staffing comparisons are not available, although one analysis
of the PRC operations of the two institutions found that despite the much
larger lending and non-lending (analytical and advisory) activities of the
World Bank, the staffing numbers were virtually identical (ADB 2007).

There is available, however, a comparison of the institutional profile
of private sector operations prepared by the Multilateral Development
Banks' Common Performance Assessment (Table 9.2). But even this is of

limited use, because there is little regional breakdown available on IFC's private sector operations.

Comparisons of the quality of aid by agency – bilateral and multilateral – tend to give the World Bank (mainly IDA) and ADB (mainly Asian Development Fund or ADF) high marks. In four studies, the World Bank appears in the top five agencies in all four, while ADB appears in two of the four (Knack et al. 2010; Easterly and Pfutze 2008; Roodman 2006; Birdsall and Kharas 2010). The latest of these studies measures the quality of aid on four different dimensions: maximizing efficiency; fostering institutions; reducing burdens; and transparency and learning (Birdsall and Kharas 2010). It finds that IDA is the only multilateral agency that ranks in the top 10 in all four indicators (Ireland is the only bilateral aid agency to do so). ADB appears in the top 10 for two of the four measures. In a fifth study that includes ADF and IDA, both institutions were rated "very good", with ADF better on partnerships, strategic management,

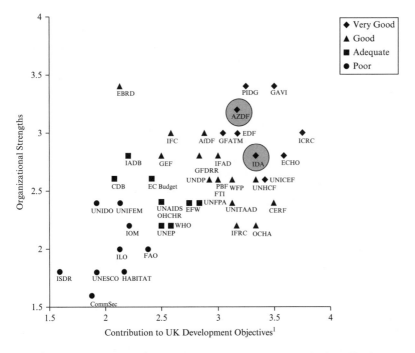

Note: [1]Contribution to UK development objectives includes humanitarian objectives.

Source: DFID (2011).

Figure 9.2   Comparison of effectiveness of aid agencies (UK perspective)

Table 9.3   Comparison of the publications record of the World Bank and ADB

	Articles		
	Mentioning a developing country	In 16 top development economic journals	In 27 specialized development journals
World Bank	1757	1343	1702
ADB	69	–	56

Source: Ravallion and Wagstaff (2010).

and operations in fragile contexts, and IDA better at focusing on poor countries (Figure 9.2) (DFID 2011). Similarly, in studies using a common performance assessment methodology, both institutions emerged with high performance ratings in the strategic, operational, relationship and knowledge management areas (MOPAN 2009, 2010).

Unfortunately, there is no head-to-head comparison of the two institutions for the quality of knowledge services provided to client countries – arguably the most important contribution these two institutions make to development efforts. The closest there is to such an indicator is the publications record of the research of the two institutions (Table 9.3). The World Bank now ranks second only to Harvard University in terms of the volume of journal articles it publishes each year on development economics (Ravallion and Wagstaff 2010).

In East Asia, it is not just the volume of the World Bank's research output that has been important, but also its relevance. A Gallup poll conducted in East Asia found that the World Bank's knowledge, research and data outputs were given higher ratings compared to international universities and private consulting firms in all the countries surveyed (Figure 9.3).

9.4   ISSUES AND OPTIONS CONFRONTING THE WORLD BANK AND ADB

Going forward, there are three issues that confront the World Bank and ADB in Asia that are more broadly symptomatic of the role of the World Bank and its relationships to all the regional development banks.

The first is the very fundamental issue of relevance. Given the declining role of official development assistance in overall capital flows to developing countries, and the diminishing role of multilateral development banks within that space, the World Bank and ADB should constantly re-evaluate

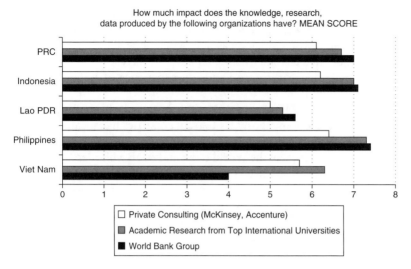

How much impact does the knowledge, research,
data produced by the following organizations have? MEAN SCORE

☐ Private Consulting (McKinsey, Accenture)
◨ Academic Research from Top International Universities
■ World Bank Group

Note: 10-point scale; 10 is high level of impact and 1 is no impact at all.

Source: World Bank (2008).

Figure 9.3 Impact of knowledge and research in East Asia

the value they bring to developing countries through their operations. While there are biting critiques of aid in general (Easterly 2006; Moyo 2009), within the international aid community, the overall assessment of the World Bank and ADB remains broadly positive.

Nevertheless, the two institutions face competition from two directions. The first is the growing importance of non-traditional donors, some of whom provide resources without the strings that come attached to World Bank and ADB lending. But the two institutions argue that their resources also come packaged with development knowledge and global experience – and this contention is backed by surveys of client countries on the effectiveness of the two institutions.

The development knowledge space is becoming increasingly crowded with regional and international think tanks and consultancy organizations, academic institutions with centers focused on development issues, specialized agencies, bilateral technical agencies, and organizations such as the OECD–DAC. Although the World Bank and ADB continue to enjoy unique access to policymakers in many Asian developing countries, their comparative advantage is rapidly diminishing – especially in middle-income countries which have less need for their financing (and, therefore, feel less pressure to engage in policy dialogue), and in any case can afford to access the best technical knowledge available in the world wherever it may reside. Sometimes, this knowledge may reside in the World Bank and ADB, but often it does not. Moreover, increasingly Asian policymakers and their staff are just as qualified as their World Bank or ADB counterparts, sometimes more so, and often with more hands-on experience of policy issues and policy implementation.

In Asia, the World Bank and ADB face a particularly challenging situation. The rapid economic growth of Asian countries has meant that many have moved from low-income to middle-income status and consequently need fewer resources from the World Bank and ADB while demanding more responsive and more sophisticated knowledge inputs. In many instances, policymakers in these countries look to examples and experience of the developed countries, not just in policy formulation but also in policy implementation. But such expertise is less likely to reside in ADB and the World Bank and is more likely to be found in government departments and implementing agencies of developed countries. True, ADB and the World Bank could act as conveners, matching demand for knowledge with those who have the best expertise available on the subject. But this space is highly contestable too, and other agencies – private and public – are increasingly providing these services, sometimes more efficiently than the World Bank or ADB.

The second key issue confronting both institutions is governance. This is perhaps more keenly felt in the World Bank, where there has been considerable concern that the voting structure does not represent the increasing influence of developing countries. Recent increases in the voting rights of some developing countries, particularly the PRC, have raised the combined voting share of developing countries from 42.6 per cent to 44.1 per cent in 2008 and then to 47 per cent in 2011, still short of parity with the developed (Part I) countries.[6] In addition, African countries were given an additional seat at the World Bank's Executive Board to bring the total number to 25.

The reality remains, however, that the voting power in the World Bank does not truly reflect the relative importance of member countries in the global economy. To boost its legitimacy, the World Bank will need to further revise its voting shares to bring the share of developing countries closer to their contribution to the global gross domestic product (GDP). A study has shown that whether a country has a seat on IBRD's board of directors appears to be important not just because it confers prestige but also because it increases its normal loan allocation by nearly US$60 million on average (Kaja and Werker 2010). The analysis shows that this does not stem from voting rights but could result more from the informal powers that executive directors and their alternate directors exert on the institution's staff and management. Interestingly, the same result does not hold for IDA, suggesting that less discretionary mechanisms for allocating resources could overcome such governance problems.

Interestingly, ADB seems to face fewer criticisms on account of governance – even though the economy of the largest shareholder of the institution, Japan, is now smaller than that of the PRC, which has far fewer voting rights.

Moreover, in the selection of the heads of the two institutions, the United States has come under considerable criticism for continuing to push for its nominee to become the President of the World Bank even when the United States is both the largest economy in the world and is the World Bank's largest shareholder. Yet Japan has not been subjected to similar criticism, even though it is no longer the largest economy in Asia and yet remains the largest Asian shareholder, and the President of ADB has always been a Japanese national.[7]

The third challenge confronting the World Bank and ADB in Asia is their relationship with each other in operational matters and in advising their Asian clients on development policies and strategies. Some would suggest that the comparative advantage of the World Bank and ADB differs. The former has a clear comparative advantage of working on global public goods (climate change, global trade negotiations, global migration, among others). The latter has an advantage in delivering regional public goods, such as the development of the Greater Mekong Subregion, the Chiang Mai Initiative, and support for the formation of the ASEAN Economic Community.

Clearly, the two institutions can and must coordinate on all these issues, in part to reduce the cost of operations and the burdens of Asian clients, and to increase their development impact. The G20 made this point at the 2009 Pittsburgh summit. To achieve better coordination, both institutions can leverage each other, make sure their support for Asian client countries is aligned and mutually reinforcing, and ensure they do not duplicate services.

In reality, however, coordination and cooperation between the two institutions masks a hidden and unrecognized subtext of competition. Where the two have coordinated, the results have been impressive – such as when they worked together with the IMF during the 1997–98 Asian Financial Crisis. Indeed, in all East Asian countries, ADB and the World Bank have agreed to carve out "areas of primacy" in which one or the other institution takes the lead in crafting a country sector strategy jointly with the client government and the other institution accepts the policy framework in its future operations. But friction remains between the two institutions, especially if they take different positions on the adequacy (or lack thereof) of policy reforms sufficient to meet tranche conditions for budget support operations, or when they have differences on sector strategies. But such differences are healthy if they are acknowledged openly and there are mechanisms in place to resolve them amicably. Unfortunately, there is a tendency to mask such differences in the interest of showing a common front vis-à-vis the client and in ensuring that shareholders – most of whom are the same in both institutions – see the two institutions as working closely together.

9.5   CAN ASIA AFFORD BOTH INSTITUTIONS?

Notwithstanding Asia's rapid economic progress, its growing access to capital markets and development expertise, and its own rapidly evolving capabilities, the reality is that the region still needs the presence of one – or more – multilateral development banks. For Asia's low-income countries, these banks will continue to be an important source of long-term finance, implementation know-how, and development knowledge based on global experience. In addition, middle-income countries have constantly expressed their appreciation for the objective policy advice and analytical insight the two institutions provide and continue to use their services even though they may have increased access to development knowledge from other sources.

The challenge is how the two institutions can offer these services in the most efficient manner so that there is genuine value added in development support and that the burden for Asian client countries of dealing with these institutions is minimized.

So what would be the optimal configuration of multilateral development banks supporting Asia? There are a number of ways to approach this question: through the theory of clubs, the theory of fiscal federalism, or through the theory of cooperatives (Kawai and Petri 2010; Casella and Frey 1992). All of them broadly lead to the same conclusion. The World Bank and ADB should provide critical public goods that are partially (or wholly) non-excludable and non-rivalrous in nature.[8] As such, the services they provide must not be replicable by private sector organizations. At the same time, these institutions, being cooperatives (formed by members to serve members and thereby achieve economies of scale), need to function in accordance with rules that ensure that the governance arrangements are acceptable to all members. The larger the number of members, the greater the economies of scale become, but also the greater is the likelihood of divergent interests among the membership and the greater the difficulty in fashioning a consensus.

In the case of the World Bank and other regional development banks such as ADB, the natural specialization would be for the World Bank to focus on removing barriers to global agreements on the most important global issues – such as trade, climate change, international migration, global financial stability, disaster management (including health pandemics and natural hazards) – working in tandem with the specialized global agencies responsible for each of these areas. At the same time, the World Bank, using the advantages of economies of scale could also be responsible for development research and global knowledge management, as well as mobilization of development resources for itself and the family of regional development banks. ADB, on the other hand, could focus on crafting regional agreements on public goods and services, such as support for the ASEAN Economic Community, regional infrastructure corridors, the Asian Bond Markets Initiative, and the Chiang Mai Initiative.

But such a division of labor has a fundamental problem. It is silent on financing operations in countries and responsibility for the policy dialogue. Clearly, neither one nor the other institution could become solely responsible for this important role. If ADB were responsible, then countries would be deprived of the global knowledge and research findings of the World Bank. But if the World Bank were to be made responsible, then countries would be deprived of ADB's regional expertise and its understanding of the relationship between regional initiatives and country development strategies.

Furthermore, the reality is that without lending operations, neither institution has the business model to pay for its non-lending activities. Yet it is in this area where the greatest duplication and overlaps exist. The World Bank has for many years expressed its intentions of becoming a "knowledge bank", but it continues to be a "lending bank" because it has been unable to find a business model that could financially support knowledge activities in the absence of lending.

There are two possible business models that would permit the World Bank to specialize in being the world's premier development research agency and the key agency to push through global agreements on the delivery of global public goods and services. The first would be if the World Bank were to receive a financial endowment, the investment returns on which would finance knowledge activities. While this approach may sound appealing, it is impractical. There is, after all, the problem of mobilizing such an endowment and the probability of success in the current (and likely future) fiscal and financial environment appears next to negligible. Moreover, without development operations in its client countries, the World Bank would merely become like any other think tank with no direct involvement in development operations where it could draw insights into development constraints and opportunities and apply proposed solutions in country settings.

The second possible business model would be to formalize the links between the World Bank and ADB, effectively making them one decentralized bank in which the headquarters would be responsible for addressing global issues, knowledge management and research, and financial mobilization and allocation; while the regional "hub" would be responsible for lending operations and crafting regional agreements on regional public goods and services. Such an arrangement would follow an organizational structure of successful cooperative associations where the center uses economies of scale in providing overarching financial, research and knowledge support, while individual cooperatives provide retail services to their members.

While such an arrangement may appear optimal from a theoretical perspective, its practical and political economy objections in the current global economic environment appear prohibitive. First, there is the possible concern that the resulting World Bank – which would be a combination of the current World Bank and all the regional development banks – would be too large and could exhibit diseconomies of scale. Second, it has proven to be very difficult to engineer minor adjustments in the voting structure of the World Bank (and the IMF); it is hard to believe that there is sufficient political appetite or collective will among either Part I or Part II countries to push through a wholesale merger of the World Bank and the regional development banks. Third, it is unclear if the benefit–cost ratio of a merger would be worthwhile, but this will require further empirical analysis. Fourth, some observers may argue that healthy competition between the World Bank and ADB (and other regional banks) actually improves the services of both.

There is, of course, a third way forward which is that the two institutions will continue to "muddle through" under the current arrangement while tinkering at the margins to sharpen specialization and reduce overlap. This is the most likely scenario to unfold. Vested interests that have accumulated behind the existing institutional configuration in the developing regions and in the developed countries will almost certainly be in favor of inertia. The current system, while imperfect, seems to satisfy a variety of stakeholder interests and there appears little urgency among the membership of either ADB or the World Bank to change the current order. Moreover, performance assessments rate both institutions highly, suggesting that both are providing value to their stakeholders, giving credence to the view that "if it isn't broken, don't fix it". Within the broader perspective of the global financial system, there is a more urgent priority to focus attention on global financial stability and develop global financial institutions that encourage sound financial management and apply effective measures to minimize contagion. Next to these daunting challenges, the task of improving the multilateral development banking system, while important, pales in comparison.

NOTES

1. The multilateral development bank system is composed of the World Bank, the multilateral regional development banks, and the multilateral sub-regional development banks. Multilateral sub-regional development banks include Corporación Andina de Fomento; Caribbean Development Bank; Central American Bank for Economic Integration; East African Development Bank and West African Development Bank. Multilateral financial institutions include the European Commission and the European Investment Bank, International Fund for Agricultural Development, the Islamic Development Bank, the Nordic Development Fund, the Nordic Investment Bank, and the OPEC Fund for International Development.
2. A significant amount of aid is composed of administrative costs of aid agencies, humanitarian and emergency relief, food aid, and technical cooperation, none of which is a transfer of resources to recipient governments for development purposes.
3. Recent press reports noted that the PRC's foreign aid had surpassed that of the World Bank, but the PRC does not issue a definitive estimate of foreign aid and some PRC "aid" projects, executed as turnkey investments by the PRC state enterprises, have characteristics more akin to foreign direct investment.
4. I am grateful to Raymond Lu (Junior Fellow, Carnegie Endowment for International Peace) for putting together some of the numbers for this graph. The data include all Asian countries (East Asia, South Asia and Central Asia) and cover all commitments of grants and loans by the two institutions. Lending to the Pacific island economies has not been included.
5. Conducting fresh research for the purposes of this chapter was not possible, given time constraints.
6. The World Bank Part I and Part II countries are defined at: http://web.worldbank. org/WBSITE/EXTERNAL/EXTABOUTUS/EXTANNREP/EXTANNREP2K7/0,,co ntentMDK:21508940~menuPK:4245276~pagePK:64168445~piPK:64168309~theSite PK:4077916,00.html.
7. Some observers argue that Japan's leadership of ADB is unquestioned because it is the largest contributor to the Asian Development Fund. By this measure, the US leadership of the World Bank should also be unquestioned as it is the largest contributor to IDA.
8. Non-excludability of a good or service implies that the property rights on them cannot be enforced, such as fish in the sea; non-rivalrous implies that consumption of the good or service does not diminish its availability to others (such as knowledge or clean air).

REFERENCES

Asian Development Bank (ADB). 1966. Agreement Establishing the Asian Development Bank. Available at: http://www.adb.org/Documents/Reports/ Charter/charter.pdf#page=4.
Asian Development Bank. 2007. *Country Assistance Performance Evaluation: The People's Republic of China: Success Drives Demand for More Innovative and Responsive Services*. Manila: ADB.
Asian Development Bank. Various issues. *ADB Annual Report*. Manila: ADB.
Birdsall, N. and H. Kharas. 2010. *Quality of Official Development Assistance*.

Washington, DC: Brookings Institution and the Center for Global Development.
Casella, A. and B. Frey. 1992. Federalism and Clubs: Toward a Theory of Overlapping Jurisdictions. *European Economic Review*. **36**: 639–46.
Department of International Development of the United Kingdom (DFID). 2011. *Multilateral Aid Review*. Available at: http://www.dfid.gov.uk/Documents/publications1/mar/multilateral_aid_review.pdf.
Easterly, W. 2006. *The White Man's Burden: Why the West's Efforts to Aid the Rest Have Done So Much Ill and So Little Good*. New York: Penguin.
Easterly, W. and T. Pfutze. 2008. Where Does the Money Go? Best and Worst Practices in Foreign Aid. *Journal of Economic Perspectives*. **22**(2): 29–52.
Kaja, A. and E. Werker. 2010. Corporate Governance at the World Bank and the Dilemma of Global Governance. *The World Bank Economic Review*. **24**(2): 171–98.
Kawai, M. and P. Petri 2010. Asia's Role in the International Financial Architecture. ADBI Working Paper 235. Tokyo: Asian Development Bank Institute.
Kharas, H. 2007. Trends and Issues in Development Aid. Wolfensohn Center for Development at the Brookings Institution. Working Paper No. 1.
Kharas, H. and W. Fengler. 2011. Delivering Aid Differently: Lessons from the Field. Economic Premise No. 49, Poverty Reduction and Economic Management Network. World Bank. February.
Knack, S., H. Rogers and N. Eubank. 2010. Aid Quality and Donor Rankings. World Bank Policy Research Working Paper 5290. May.
MOPAN. 2009. *MOPAN Common Approach: World Bank 2009*. Available at: http://www.mopanonline.org/upload/documents/World_Bank_Final_February_19_issued.pdf.
MOPAN. 2010. *MOPAN Common Approach: Asian Development Bank 2010*. Available at: http://www.mopanonline.org/upload/documents/ADB_Final-Vol-I_January_17_Issued1.pdf.
Moyo, D. 2009. *Dead Aid: Why Aid Is Not Working and How There Is a Better Way for Africa*. New York: Farrar, Straus and Giroux.
Overseas Development Institute. 2011. Climate Finance Fundamentals. *The Evolving Global Climate Finance Architecture*. London: Overseas Development Institute.
Ravallion, M. and A. Wagstaff. 2010. The World Bank's Publication Record. World Bank Policy Research Working Paper No. 5374. July.
Roodman, D. 2006. An Index of Donor Performance. Center for Global Development Working Paper Number 67. Data set updated 2009.
United Nations. 2002. Recommendations of the High-level Panel on Financing for Development. Available at: http://www.un.org/esa/ffd/a55–1000.pdf.
World Bank. 2008. 2008 World Bank Group Global Poll. East Asia/Pacific: Full Results (data provided by Gallup Consulting).
World Bank. 2010. New World, New World Bank Group: Post-Crisis Directions. Paper prepared for the Development Committee of the World Bank. 20 April.
World Bank. 2011. *Global Development Horizons 2011*. Washington, DC: World Bank.
World Bank. Various issues. *The World Bank Annual Report*. Washington, DC: World Bank.

10. World Bank, Inter-American Development Bank, and subregional development banks in Latin America: dynamics of a system of multilateral development banks

Fernando Prada

10.1 INTRODUCTION

This chapter is a summary of the working hypothesis and main conclusions of an ongoing research program at FORO Nacional Internacional. The main objective of the program is to identify long-term trends and dynamics of the system of international development finance (Bezanson et al. 2005).

Among the actors that participate in this system, the multilateral development banks (MDBs) are an innovative institutional model to channel finance and knowledge to developing countries. They are international financial intermediaries whose shareholders include both borrowing developing countries and non-borrowing donor countries. MDBs have three functions: (i) to mobilize resources from private capital markets and from official sources to make loans to developing countries on better-than-market terms; (ii) to generate knowledge on and provide technical assistance and advice for economic and social development; and (iii) to furnish a range of complementary services, such as international public goods, to developing countries and to the international development community (Sagasti with the contribution of Prada 2002; Sagasti and Bezanson 2000).

MDBs operating in the Latin America and Caribbean (LAC) region have formed a dense network of institutions, where competition and complementation have been the main drivers of their evolution during the last 50 years. In a previous document (Sagasti and Prada 2006), we argued that the LAC region has great potential for decentralization compared to other regions because of the strength of its regional and subregional institutions. Certain dynamics contribute to realizing this potential: (i) the interaction between MDBs and other sources of development financing; (ii) the division of labor between MDBs and their search for comparative advantages; (iii) an improved financial situation and capacity to mobilize financial resources; (iv) innovation in financial instruments and customization of their interventions; and (v) patterns of allocating net income in concordance with negotiations among stakeholders and institutional decisions.

This chapter focuses on the analysis of statistical data from MDBs to describe these trends in the LAC region. In general we prioritize the dynamics between the World Bank and the Inter-American Development Bank (IDB), but recognize the growing importance of three subregional institutions: the Andean Corporation of Finance (CAF); the Central American Bank for Economic Integration (CABEI); and the Caribbean Development Bank (CDB), as facilitators of South–South cooperation and platforms for triangular cooperation (Prada et al. 2010). The chapter is organized as follows:

- The first section presents the relative position of MDBs in the LAC region regarding their financial role and how they offer a set of instruments to channel resources and knowledge to countries in the region.
- The next section analyzes the dynamics that are contributing to deepening the process of decentralization, with three questions in mind: (i) what are the main trends identified from observable variables? (ii) How have the most relevant institutional guidelines evolved recently? (iii) What are the main areas for future research?
- The third section presents recommendations and conclusions about MDBs in the LAC region, and how they can increase collaboration and promote collective action.

10.2   THE RELATIVE POSITION OF MULTILATERAL DEVELOPMENT BANKS IN LATIN AMERICA AND THE CARIBBEAN

Financing development in the LAC region has radically changed in the last forty years and, as Figure 10.1 suggests, the importance of official flows has decreased relative to other sources of financing. First, net private flows now represent more than 90 per cent of total financial flows. Despite periods of upsurge of official flows in the wake of financial crises – the debt crisis in the mid-1980s, the United States rescue after the Mexican

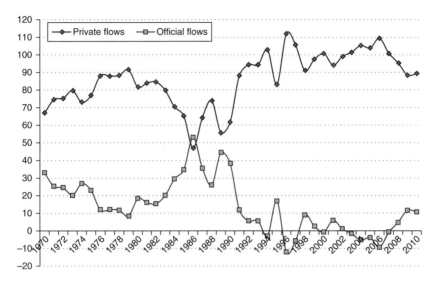

Source: Own elaboration with World Bank's DataBank.

Figure 10.1   Financial flows to countries in Latin America and the Caribbean as a percentage of total financial flows, 1970–2010

Tesobonos crisis in 1995, the Asian and dot.com crises, and the beginning of the global financial crisis in 2008 – the LAC region mostly relies on foreign direct investment, equity investment, remittances, and, to a lesser extent, official sources – particularly MDBs – to finance development.

Before 2008, official financial flows became negative due to prepayments to MDBs and debt relief operations with bilateral and multilateral creditors. Moreover, most countries in the region have been reducing their external debt–gross domestic product (GDP) ratio, and some of them have been able to diversify their access to other financial sources, including issuing bonds in international capital markets. The case of Peru is an example of such diversification and of how the relative position of MDBs has changed as a consequence (Appendix 10A.1).

Second, the capacity to mobilize domestic resources to finance a country's development is growing rapidly. On the one hand, the public sector collects more fiscal revenues and takes debt from domestic capital markets. Fiscal revenues grew 60 per cent between 2005 and 2011 for all countries in the region, while in Brazil, Bolivia and Peru they doubled. Domestic public debt increased 45 per cent on average in the same period, while in Brazil, Mexico, Peru and Uruguay domestic debt doubled. On the other hand, domestic credit to the private sector as a percentage of GDP increased from 27 per cent in 2000 to 42 per cent in 2010, mainly due to a 40 per cent growth in domestic credit to the private sector in Brazil, Chile, Colombia and Mexico between 2000 and 2010.

With more financial sources and domestic resources available, financial flows from MDBs to LAC countries have declined. Net flows from the World Bank and IDB became negative after 2003 (Figure 10.2a), partially as a consequence of prepayments from countries such as Argentina, Brazil and Mexico. This trend reversed after the global financial crisis as these two banks increased their lending to the region. Although there is no comparable data of net financial flows from all subregional development banks (SRDBs), the CDB increased net flows to Caribbean countries from US$50 million in 2007 to US$240 million in 2010, while IDB net flows to the same countries grew seven times to US$700 million in the same period (Figure 10.2b). The CAF has also increased its lending and thus contributed to the surge of MDB flows to the region after the global financial crisis. As Figure 10.3 indicates, commitments to the region increased during 2008 and 2009 as a consequence of the financial crisis, and then fell slightly in 2010. Preliminary data for 2011 and the first quarter of 2012 suggest that commitments will be lower than 2008–09 levels.

A paradoxical situation emerges for the next 10 years regarding the position of MDBs in financing development in the LAC region. On the one hand, most LAC countries have been able to diversify their access to financial sources. Moreover, financial needs have eased as the fiscal and current account positions of most LAC countries have remained strong throughout the global financial crisis. On the other hand, MDBs are increasing their capacity to serve the region; most MDBs operating in the region – the Central American Bank for Economic Integration (CABEI), CAF, CDB and IDB – have increased their lending capacity, and the World Bank board authorized capital increases in the five years to 2012. This new capacity is not only about taking the precaution of having additional funding in case the international context worsens; we argue it is also about real confidence in the region's long-term prospects and the ability of the MDBs to find niches to continue supporting the region through a sustainable business model.[1]

The innovation capacity of MDBs and the growth prospects of the region have the potential to generate a virtuous circle in the coming years in favor of LAC countries. The global financial crisis only temporarily moderated the trends regarding the relative position of the MDBs in the region, and, as a consequence, several questions and debates that took place in a pre-crisis context are back in 2012. The first group of questions relates to what precisely to do with increased MDB lending capacity in relation to countries' absorptive capacity and access to other financial sources; the second

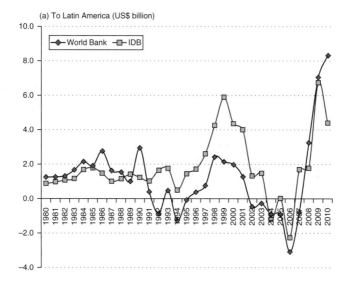

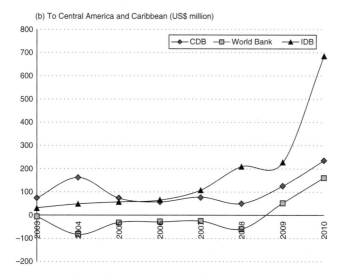

Note: CDB = Caribbean Development Bank; IDB = Inter-American Development Bank.

Sources: World Bank's DataBank, Global Development Finance and annual reports from institutions.

Figure 10.2   Net flows from multilateral development banks to countries in Latin America and the Caribbean

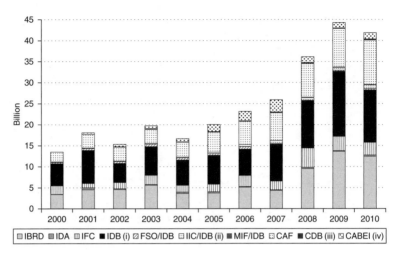

Notes:
IBRD = International Bank for Reconstruction and Development of the World Bank Group;
IDA = International Development Association from the World Bank Group; IFC = International
Finance Corporation from the World Bank Group; IDB = Inter-American Development Bank
(Ordinary Capital); FSO/IDB = Fund of Special Operations from the IDB; IIC/IDB = Inter-
American Investment Corporation from the IDB; MIF/IDB = Multilateral Investment Fund
from the IDB; CDB = Caribbean Development Bank; CABEI = Central American Bank for
Economic Integration.
(i) IDB annual reports 2003, 2010; loans and guarantees approved.
(ii) Operations approved from IIC annual reports (AR). AR2010 shows US$374.80 million
approved in direct loans and investments, and US$536.00 million in co-financing operations;
AR2009 shows US$299.00 million approved in direct loans and investments, and US$342.00
million in co-financing operations; AR2008 shows US$300.50 million approved in direct loans
and investments, and US$300.60 million in co-financing operations; AR2007 shows US$470.00
million approved in direct loans and investments, and US$273.00 million in co-financing
operations; AR2006 shows US$337.68 million from the IIC plus US$173.00 million from other
sources.
(iii) CABEI reports: AR2003 and AR2006 consider net loan approvals, which result from
deducing debt obligations from gross approvals, and other years' figures correspond to total
approvals.
(iv) Loans, grants and equity are included.
(*) Figures are not comparable since not all multilateral development banks have operations in all
countries: IDB has operations in all 26 countries of the Latin America and Caribbean region; the
CAF in 16 countries (Argentina, Bolivia, Brazil, Chile, Colombia, Costa Rica, Ecuador, Jamaica,
Mexico, Panama, Paraguay, Peru, Dominican Republic, Trinidad and Tobago, Uruguay and
Venezuela); CABEI in Belize, Costa Rica, the Dominican Republic, El Salvador, Guatemala,
Honduras, Nicaragua, Panama; and Argentina and Colombia outside the subregion; and CDB
in Anguilla, Antigua and Barbuda, the Bahamas, Barbados, Belize, British Virgin Islands,
Dominica, Grenada, Guyana, Haiti, Jamaica, Montserrat, St Kitts and Nevis, St Lucia, St
Vincent and the Grenadines, Trinidad and Tobago, and the Turks and Caicos Islands.

Source: Global Development Finance World Development Indicators from World Bank Data
and Annual Reports.

*Figure 10.3 Annual commitments of multilateral development banks,
2000–10 (by institution, US$ billion)*

group of questions relates to what is an adequate balance between the three MDB functions for the region, and whether MDBs can offer financial and non-financial services to perform these functions. Our response to both questions is that having a decentralized and financially healthy network of MDBs that compete and collaborate at different levels gives the region a comparative advantage to deal with these issues.

The number of MDBs operating in the LAC region is higher than in any other global region, and most of them have been operating there since before 1980 (Figure 10.4). Along with the World Bank and IDB groups of institutions, which are on a regional scale and serve all countries in the region, there is a group of SRDBs and extra-regional MDBs that cover only a limited number of countries. Combined, these institutions form an MDB system that serves a variety of clients from the private and public sector. All developing countries in the region, except Cuba, work in parallel with the World Bank, the IDB and at least one SRDB. This feature gives the system competition at the country level: MDBs need to find comparative advantages and differentiation from other MDBs, other sources of financing (e.g. domestic and international capital markets), and other development institutions (e.g. bilateral donors, private foundations, and social responsibility and non-government institutions).

This system of MDBs has been slowly consolidating in the LAC region, while successful but isolated cases of collaboration and collective action between MDBs are emerging and becoming more frequent. Nevertheless, a description of such a system 10 years ago is still accurate:

> far from functioning as an integrated system, it must be said that the MDBs currently behave more like a dysfunctional family, primarily in the field. Relations between the World Bank and the regional development banks are strained in several regions and in many countries, while most sub-regional MDBs have little interaction with the World Bank. Differences in management styles, extent of field presence, relations with borrowers, technical competence, knowledge of the region and countries, among others, combine to create sources of tension that could and should be reduced by taking a more systemic approach to the operations of MDBs. (Sagasti and Bezanson 2000, p. 68)

As we indicate in the next section, the system of MDBs in the LAC region has benefited from subregional dynamism and strength – a unique feature of the LAC region compared to other regions. This generates forces for competition, particularly at the country level, but at the same time also generates opportunities for regional collaboration. On the one hand, there are more and more cases of pool-funding and shared projects between MDBs throughout the region (e.g., pool-funding for Haiti reconstruction, where the IDB had a lead role in catalyzing additional financ-

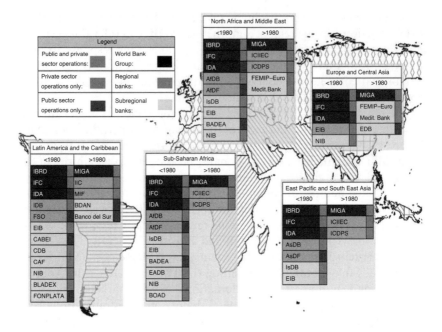

Notes:
IBRD = International Bank for Reconstruction and Development of the World Bank Group; IDA = International Development Association from the World Bank Group; IFC = International Finance Corporation from the World Bank Group; MIGA = Multilateral Investment Guarantee Agency from the World Bank Group; IDB = Inter-American Development Bank (Ordinary Capital); FSO = Fund of Special Operations from the IDB; IIC = Inter-American Investment Corporation from the IDB; MIF = Multilateral Investment Fund from the IDB; EIB = European Investment Bank; CDB = Caribbean Development Bank; CABEI = Central American Bank for Economic Integration; CAF = Development Bank of Latin America; NIB = Nordic Investment Bank; BLADEX = Foreign Trade Bank of Latin America; FONPLATA = Financial Fund for the Development of the River Plate Basin; BDAN = North American Development Bank; AfDB = African Development Bank; AfDF = African Development Fund; AsDB = Asian Development Bank; AsDF =Asian Development Fund; BADEA = Arab-African Development Bank; BOAD = West African Development Bank; EADB = East African Development Bank; EDB = Eurasian Development Bank; FEMIP = Facility for Euro-Mediterranean Investment and Partnership; ICDPS = Islamic Corporation for the Development of the Private Sector; ICIIEC = The Islamic Corporation for the Insurance of Investment and Export Credit; IsDB = Islamic Development Bank.

Source: Author's elaboration.

Figure 10.4   The global system of multilateral development banks

ing from a large variety of development institutions). On the other hand, the IDB has also taken a proactive approach to supporting development banks at the subregional level. For example, it supported the CDB with institutional credit of US$20 million in 1996 for capital strengthening, and it has recently provided technical assistance to the Financial Fund for the Development of the River Plate Basin (FONPLATA), which has resumed its credits to the common market of the Southern South American region (MERCOSUR). However, how countries benefit from these dynamics of collaboration and competition between MDBs depends on specific country cases.

Using a systemic approach, we indicate that the diversity of MDBs is positive, given the diversity of countries in the region. The fact that almost every country in the region is a middle-income country according to World Bank categorization hides deep differences between them. We have recently updated our index of capacity to mobilize external and domestic resources (Figure 10.5), which is an alternative to income-based rankings.[2] Most LAC countries are well positioned among the top, but some groups of countries can be distinguished: Argentina, Brazil and Mexico (due to the size of their economies); Caribbean islands such as Dominica; other South American countries; and Central America (except Mexico).

MDBs in the LAC region are becoming more responsive to these signals and are moving towards customizing their interventions on a country-by-country basis, thus enforcing a client-oriented culture of MDBs in the region. The World Bank's updated strategy for the region (World Bank 2011) is clustering different sets of interventions and services to four groups of countries according to income and additional dimensions such as the size of economy and particular vulnerabilities. The IDB has made significant investments to decentralize operations during its "realignment" process, and nowadays its country offices have more responsibilities, resources and personnel. Having strong SRDBs also allows for a degree of specialization and a diversity of approaches at the country level.

A working hypothesis of our research program indicates a strong relationship between the capacity to mobilize domestic and external resources, and the structure of sources of development financing that countries choose. Our case study on Peru (Appendix 10A.1) presents evidence on how the capacity to mobilize external resources has evolved, and how the related financial structure of its capital account has changed over 40 years.[3] Therefore, the position of MDBs relative to other financial sources changes as countries increase their capacity to mobilize domestic and external resources to finance development.

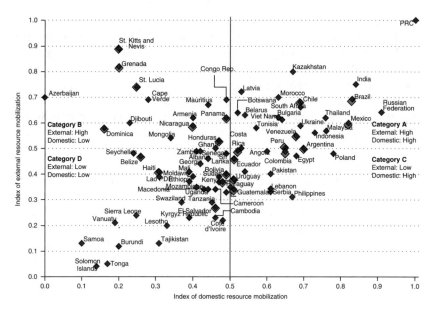

Source: Sagasti and Prada (2012, p. 266).

Figure 10.5   Capacity to mobilize external and domestic resources, 2010

As a response, MDBs have had strong incentives to extend and improve the set of instruments through which they channel financial resources and knowledge to the LAC region. Sagasti and Bezanson (2000) argue that MDBs enjoy a strategic position in the field of development finance and this increases their potential to innovate in development approaches and financial instruments. Not only do MDBs in the region operate within the international financial system but they also partner with a number of institutions such as United Nations agencies, bilateral assistance agencies, private foundations, the International Monetary Fund, and emerging donors such as the People's Republic of China (PRC).

MDBs offer a set of financial instruments for diverse demands (Figure 10.6). In addition to traditional loans and grants, the World Bank and IDB have introduced: (i) results-based loans that disburse tranches conditional on achieving improvements in agreed indicators on social or policy outcomes; (ii) a set of financial instruments such as guarantees, equity investments, and small and medium-sized enterprise (SME) support to mitigate risks for private investors; and (iii) fast-disbursement

C A B E I	1. Administrations of funds and trusts 2. IFACIL advances and guarantees 3. Letters of credit 4. MYPIMES Green Initiative 5. Tenders 6. Pre-investment and technical cooperation 7. Loans: A/B and syndicated 8. Programs: educational, SMEs, technical and financial cooperation, municipal infrastructure funding, financial intermediation for housing 9. Specific projects	**C A F**	1. Medium- and long-term loans 2. Sovereign loans 3. Programs and investment projects 4. Programmatic and swaps arrangements 5. Non-sovereign loans 6. Credit lines to companies and banks 7. Partial credit guarantees 8. Contingent lines of credit 9. Shareholdings 10. Cooperation funds
		C D B	1. Long-term loans 2. Equity and quasi-equity investments 3. Guarantees 4. Technical assistance

I D B	1. Sovereign guarantee loans:
	   • Investment loans: specific loans and predefined activities, such as innovation, training, equipment
	   • Policy-based loans: for institutional and policy reforms
	   • Emergency loans: for financial crises and natural disasters
	2. Non-sovereign guarantee loans
	3. Grants: trust fund grants, multilateral investment fund grants, and social entrepreneurship program
	4. Guarantees:
	   • Public sector guarantees
	   • Private sector guarantees: credit guarantees and political risk guarantees
	5. Equity investments: multilateral investment fund, International Investment Corporation
	6. Flexible financing (ordinary capital): flexible financing facility and local currency financing		

Source: Annual reports of institutions.

Figure 10.6 Multilateral development banks and financial instruments

loans and grants for disaster relief. SRDBs in the region are also part of this innovative trend. The CAF has a comparative advantage in structuring financing for large infrastructure projects by catalyzing funds from multiple private investors and investment funds due to its closeness to international capital markets. Other SRDBs are introducing innovations in microfinance and SME financing with instruments such as loans to financial intermediaries, financial support to productive chains and producer associations, and creation of domestic capital markets.

In summary, three main forces will shape the future of MDBs in the LAC region:

● the capacity of MDBs to innovate in approaches and financial instruments to address the diversity of demands of their member countries and clients from the private sector;

● the capacity of countries to mobilize domestic and external resources that impact the relative position of MDBs in the development financing landscape; and

- the balance between competition and collaboration among MDBs in their quest to find niches and their comparative advantages.

10.3   THE DYNAMICS OF MULTILATERAL DEVELOPMENT BANKS IN LATIN AMERICA AND THE CARIBBEAN

There are no common metrics to assess the level of decentralization of the MDB system in each region. Our hypothesis is that an MDB system is more decentralized as it shows more strength and dynamism at the subregional level in dimensions that are comparable across institutions and regions. We are analyzing three dimensions in this section: (i) division of labor; (ii) financial strength and institutional capacity to provide services at affordable costs for countries and clients; and (iii) managing net income to address specific needs of member countries, clients and stakeholders.

10.3.1   Division of Labor: Finding Niches and Comparative Advantages

To provide services to member countries, MDBs need to acquire specific skills, make available financial and human resources, and establish institutional guidelines that connect their mission with their activities at the country and regional level. Most of the studies about this issue, particularly those describing the operations of the World Bank and regional development banks, coincide in two ideas: (i) that the individual institutional missions are very broad and have tended to increase over time, a feature known as "mission creep"; and (ii) a significant part of MDB missions is shared with other MDBs, which tend to work in parallel with little coordination or harmonization of their procedures at a country and regional level. If this diagnostic is entirely correct, then the prospects of a division of labor based on comparative advantages among MDBs within a region are unpromising.

   This framework has been popular at describing the relationship between Bretton Woods system institutions, such as the World Bank and the International Monetary Fund, and other institutions such as the organizations of the United Nations system and, to a lesser extent, regional development banks – SRDBs have been generally excluded from this debate. Nevertheless, we argue that a country-level perspective on division of labor provides a more accurate picture of the forces that drive competition and collaboration between MDBs in the LAC region.

   During the 2000s, MDB operations were more concentrated in sovereign borrowers and, therefore, the debate was centered on whether the borrowing capacity of their clients would become a limit for the sustainability of MDBs' business model. This scenario has not materialized because countries have been able to increase their absorptive capacity as their economies have grown. Therefore, there has been room to maneuver and SRDBs have been able to find their own niches. Figure 10.7 shows that the CABEI, CAF and CDB are able to mobilize resources to LAC countries on a scale comparable to the World Bank and the IDB, representing a bigger percentage of total commitments.

De la Torre and Ize (2010) posit an interesting argument about the comparative advantages of MDBs regarding their lending role: since MDBs

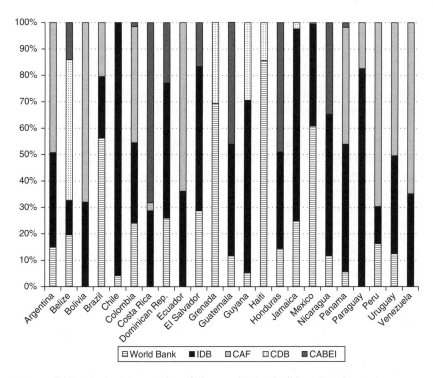

Notes: CAF = Andean Corporation of Finance; CDB = Caribbean Development Bank; IDB = Inter-American Development Bank; CABEI = Central American Bank for Economic Integration.

Source: Annual reports of institutions.

Figure 10.7   Multilateral development bank lending commitments to selected countries, 2010 (share of total, %)

are neutral to risk, they are able to spread risk more efficiently compared to risk-averse private sector lenders. As a consequence, they can expand the credit frontier by innovating in different sectors and experimenting with new approaches. This argument can be extended to the different attitudes to risk between MDBs and helps explain the logic behind the dynamics of the sector division of labor of MDBs in the LAC region.

Figure 10.8 shows how SRDBs tend to focus on infrastructure, power, energy and water, while the World Bank and the IDB concentrate on social services and support to the public sector and civil society. During the 1980s, there was a similar division of labor between the World Bank and the IDB: the IDB started its operations in the 1960s with a heavy focus on the productive sector that represented only a small percentage of the World Bank's lending to the region, which was more focused on infrastructure during that period (Sagasti 2002, p. 14). For example, the environment and support to the public sector are areas that SRDBs have not fully entered, while the World Bank and the IDB are investing heavily.

Therefore, as MDBs consolidate in the LAC region, they are progressively designing more complex interventions and venturing into sectors where they are willing to take more risks. However, SRDBs are often able to catch up, innovate, and create a niche for themselves even in sectors such as infrastructure. For example, the CAF has been able to take advantage of its flexible decision-making process and has gained expertise in catalyzing financing for large infrastructure projects. In the case of the CDB, it has been able to allocate emergency funding for disaster relief in a subregion frequently hit by hurricanes (multisector in Figure 10.8).

There are sectors where competition is intense as MDBs are willing to expand their client base and move away from their sovereign focus. This applies to operations with the private sector and, to a lesser extent, the new financial instruments, such as public–private partnerships, to mobilize resources from capital markets for infrastructure. Even though the World Bank and the IDB have specialized agencies to work with the private sector, they have funded operations with ordinary capital – a normal procedure in the case of SRDBs.

The International Finance Corporation (IFC) of the World Bank lent US$3.1 billion in financial year (FY) 2011, up from US$1.9 billion in FY 2000, but lending has not since reached the FY 2008 peak of US$4.5 billion during the global financial crisis. The IFC allocates 25 per cent of its total lending to the LAC region. The IDB has two specialized agencies for its private sector operations: the Multilateral Investment Fund (FOMIN) and the Inter-American Investment Corporation (IIC). During its 2011 annual meeting in Calgary, the IDB presented its new strategy for development of

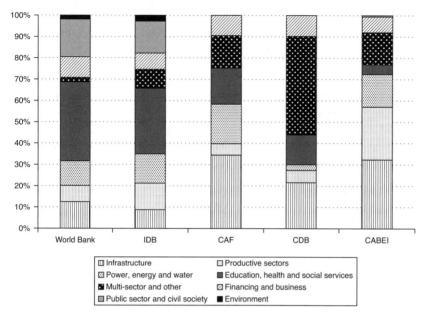

Notes:
CAF = Development Bank of Latin America; CDB = Caribbean Development Bank; IDB = Inter-American Development Bank; CABEI = Central American Bank for Economic Integration.
(i) Classification for World Bank and IDB are based on CRS sectors: transport and storage and communications are Infrastructure; agriculture, forestry, fishing, industry, mineral resources and mining, trade policies and regulations, and tourism are Productive Sector; water supply and sanitation and energy are Power, Energy and Water; education, health and population policies and programs, and reproductive health are Education, Health and Social Services; other multisector, reconstruction relief and rehabilitation, and disaster prevention and preparedness are Multisector and Other; banking and financial services, and business and other services are Financing and Business; and government and civil society – general and conflict, peace, and security are Public Sector and Civil Society.
(ii) CAF: Agricultural infrastructure and transport, storage and communications are Infrastructure; mining and quarrying and manufacturing are Productive Sector; development institutions and other are Multisector and Other; and commercial banking is Financing and Business.
(iii) CDB: Transportation and communication are Infrastructure; agriculture, forestry, fishing, manufacturing and tourism are Productive Sectors; social and personal services are Education, Health and Social Services; and financial is Financing and Business.
(iv) CABEI: Infrastructure, municipal infrastructure, transport, storage, communications and hotels are Infrastructure; trade, manufacturing, agriculture, ranching, fishing, hunting and forestry, oil and gas, and productive sectors are Productive Sector; education, social services, and health are Education, Health and Social Services; computing, other services, regional body and multisector are Multisector and Other; real estate and financial intermediation are Financing and Business; and public administration is Public Sector and Civil Society.
World Bank, IDB, FSO/IDB and CABEI amounts are commitments; CAF are loan portfolios; and CDB are net loans, secondary mortgages, equity, and grants approved.

Source: Credit Reporting System (Organisation for Economic Co-operation and Development (OECD)) and annual reports.

Figure 10.8   Division of labor by sector, 2000–10 (share of total, %)

the private sector, with the aim of streamlining its operations. The strategy includes several programs to develop capital markets in less-developed countries, increase funding to SMEs, promote financial inclusion, finance "bottom of the pyramid" initiatives, support microfinance and micro-insurance institutions, and help companies transition to a lower-carbon mode of production. The IDB allocated US$2.9 billion to the private sector in 2011, the IIC allocated US$465.0 million, and FOMIN allocated US$108.0 million.

SRDBs are also innovating and competing in these areas and complementing the operations of other MDBs. The CAF has been very active and is currently providing support to *multilatinas*,[4] providing capital to companies to initiate operations in other countries, and acquiring equities from companies to finance their expansion. In 2010, the support to private sector operations was US$2.8 billion, representing 20 per cent of the IDB's total allocations. CABEI has been focusing on supporting the private sector in Central America and promoting private investment, and this now represents 25 per cent of its annual commitments (US$300 million). The CDB has a small Private Sector Development Division (5 per cent of total commitments), which has been directed to support the development of mortgage markets and loans to institutions to provide student financing.

There is a strong case for collaboration between MDBs in specific areas. First, their research on development issues is becoming an important source of reference, but duplication of efforts in some areas should give rise to more collaborative efforts, peer-reviewed studies, and joint publications and evaluations. Second, although there is only anecdotal evidence, regional epistemic communities are emerging as a consequence of knowledge exchange. Each MDB is making efforts to create capacities in the public sector and support managers and consultants in organizing seminars to exchange information and provide technical cooperation. Harmonizing approaches and coordinating areas of support could increase the capacities of public officers through a more efficient use of resources. Third, MDBs are part of a financial innovation that is still strong, but the changes in the international system of financing development are posing several threats to their operations: they could be carrying out several exercises to think together about their future and their position regarding topics such as regional development, support to the private sector, and their countercyclical role.

There are other relevant topics regarding division of labor that are starting to become part of the debates about the future of MDBs. There is anecdotal evidence that some countries have been able to take leadership of their relationship with donors (Wood et al. 2011) and effectively manage their negotiations with MDBs. However, this information has been poorly systematized, but it could provide interesting insights into patterns of countries managing their relationship with MDBs and assess how client-oriented the regional MDBs are. It is frequently claimed by MDBs in the LAC region that competition from other international financial institutions creates an environment conducive to a more client-oriented behavior from these institutions; but again, this claim is only supported by anecdotal evidence and not by analytical studies.

Another area of research relates to epistemic communities that MDB contributions are consolidating through technical assistance support. The communities are important because they have contributed to generating strong consensus in public policies in certain areas such as macroeconomic management, and could be crucial in improving the skills of public officers. Understanding this dynamic could provide insight into how to improve the role of generating and providing knowledge to countries through technical assistance.

A third area of research is the role of MDBs as platforms for regional integration and international cooperation, particularly the case of South–South cooperation and triangular cooperation. MDBs in the LAC region are unclear about their specific role in this area, and are engaging in a series of reflections on these topics. MDBs have advantages in channeling cooperation between developing countries because of their networks and presence in countries, and can contribute to advancing the agenda of the Paris Declaration on Aid Effectiveness by helping new donors to design and implement cooperation programs.

10.3.2 Delicate Balances: Financial Strength, Low-cost Lending and Services, and Development Effectiveness

MDBs have been building a strong financial position, and years of responsible management are reflected in their financial statements. Table 10.1 presents the risk-bearing capital ratios (RBCR)[5] of MDBs and the World Bank in the LAC region, and three trends emerge that point to a healthy dynamism at the subregional level.

First, the IDB and SRDBs have expanded their net outstanding loans to the region, but those of the SRDBs have grown at a faster pace. While IDB net loans to the region grew 42 per cent between 2002 and 2010, net loans from SRDBs grew steadily and more than doubled: the CAF's loans expanded by 145 per cent, CDB's by 115 per cent, and CABEI's by 108 per cent. The IDB experienced a slowdown after 2003, and its net loans to the region only recovered after the global financial crisis. Second, retained earnings have followed a similar trend: they are growing for all MDBs in the region, but those of SRDBs are growing at a faster pace.

Table 10.1 Financial indicators of multilateral development banks (US$ million) and their risk-bearing capital ratios (points), 2002–11

	2002	2003	2004	2005	2006	2007	2008	2009	2010	2011
World Bank Group										
Net loans	116075	111762	105626	100910	100221	95433	97268	105698	120103	132459
Paid-in	11476	11478	11483	11483	11483	11486	11486	11491	11492	11720
Retained earnings	22227	27031	23982	27171	24782	27831	29322	28546	28793	29723
RBCR	3.44	2.90	2.98	2.61	2.76	2.43	2.38	2.64	2.98	3.20
Inter-American Development Bank										
Net loans	46397	50472	49643	47960	45842	47903	51037	57933	62862	65980
Paid-in	4340	4340	4340	4340	4340	4340	4399	4339	4339	4399
Retained earnings	9883	12288	13437	14199	14442	14576	14647	15481	15771	15488
RBCR	3.26	3.04	2.79	2.59	2.44	2.53	2.68	2.92	3.13	3.32
Corporación Andina de Fomento										
Net loans	5806	6328	6863	7128	7849	9333	9990	11487	13572	14773
Paid-in	1171	1319	1499	1682	1871	2015	2176	2486	2814	3229
Retained earnings	771	888	1074	1316	1565	1878	2097	2262	2323	2382
RBCR	2.99	2.87	2.67	2.38	2.28	2.40	2.34	2.42	2.64	2.63

Caribbean Development Bank

Net loans	462	513	637	687	718	750	769	818	994
Paid-in	156	156	156	156	156	157	157	157	207
Retained earnings	234	256	277	296	314	349	423	408	449
RBCR	1.19	1.24	1.47	1.52	1.53	1.48	1.33	1.45	1.52

Central American Bank for Economic Integration

Net loans	2 226	2 758	2 680	3 057	3 545	3 808	4 153	4 161	4 638	2 226
Paid-in	372	372	372	384	404	420	427	447	451	372
Retained earnings	706	800	936	993	1 049	1 122	1 286	1 357	1 471	706
RBCR	2.07	2.35	2.05	2.22	2.44	2.47	2.42	2.31	2.41	2.07

Note: RBCR = Risk-Bearing Capital Ratio, which is the ratio between net outstanding loans and the sum of paid capital and retained earnings.

Source: Annual financial statements of institutions.

Third, the RBCR indicates that there is enough room for MDBs to increase their lending without compromising the strength of their financial ratios. A high RBCR indicates high leverage, and a low RBCR indicates additional room to increase lending compared to levels of operating capital. This ratio has followed a common pattern: RBCRs reached a peak around 2002 for most MDBs and have not since regained that level, even though MDBs increased lending due to the global financial crisis. The CAF, for example, has been increasing leverage and rapidly catching up to levels of the World Bank and the IDB. It is worth noting that commercial lending institutions normally have RBCR levels of 5–10, which is an indication of the prudential lending standards of MDBs.

Financial strength and prudential lending standards are key characteristics of the MDBs' model. Because of a combination of comfortable financial levels in MDBs and a higher capacity to mobilize resources in LAC countries, there is an opportunity to take more risks and experiment and innovate with new approaches. An extra opportunity is presented by historically low interest rates, and central banks such as the US Federal Reserve have indicated their willingness to maintain rates at these levels as the economies need additional support.

Figure 10.9 shows average lending rates of the World Bank and the IDB during 2003–11. The global financial crisis caused a structural change in the price of London interbank offered rate (LIBOR)-based instruments for both banks, which have been stable at around 1 per cent since 2008. In parallel, sovereign spreads (the difference between the interest rate of sovereign bonds and US Treasury bonds) have returned to pre-crisis levels, as has the Emerging Market Bond Index (EMBI+). Although they are not strictly comparable, margins between the lending interest rates of MDBs and the average cost of financing from international capital markets have returned to pre-crisis levels. As was the case before the financial crisis, some countries see no comparative advantage in MDB lending interest rates because they have cheaper options. Therefore this feature is also driving competition between MDBs and is providing MDBs with incentives to enter into more complex operations and expand their client base. SRDBs are experiencing similar pressures, but more data is needed.

Interest rates from other financial sources and MDBs were converging before the global financial crisis and most banks adjusted their internal costs so they could offer lower prices to their clients, for example they have adjusted front-end fees and lending spreads (Figure 10.9b shows these changes for the IDB). Nevertheless, this is not a sustainable strategy in the long term because development interventions tend to increase in cost as they become more complex. For example, the World Bank performs periodic analysis of its internal costs of lending instruments, and there is evidence that supervision costs for investment loans have increased over the years.[6]

Although there is no data to compare administrative costs between MDBs, it is safe to affirm that administrative costs are higher as operations become more complex and competition between institutions increases. For example, decentralizing operations at the IDB after the process of realignment has implied an important reallocation of personnel and, thus, higher administrative costs, at least in the short term. But these investments are crucial to improve operations. The challenge is whether smaller MDBs are able to follow this trend. The CAF has been able to mobilize resources from extra-regional partners such as the PRC and Brazil, and it is heavily investing in creating capacities for research in development topics and new approaches, attracting talent and decentralizing offices.

A similar argument for collaboration can be made in the case of the focus on development effectiveness that most MDBs are implementing. Having an impact on development indicators requires more complex operations, a stronger focus on evaluation and monitoring, enhanced institutional skills to measure internal operations, and trained personnel to carry out these tasks. It is clear that this focus relates to higher administrative costs and, so far, only the World Bank and the IDB have actively engaged in implementing these reforms (IDB 2012). Therefore, increasing collaboration and utilizing cost-sharing schemes of MDBs in this area, particularly at the country level, may contribute to reducing costs of implementing operations with a stronger focus on development effectiveness.

Some areas with strong potential for cost sharing to advance in the area of development effectiveness are: (i) discussing a common framework to assess development effectiveness at the country and institutional level to ensure adequate benchmarking; (ii) engaging SRDBs in furthering the development effectiveness agenda, such as agreeing on common country operation frameworks under the leadership of borrowing countries; (iii) investing resources in guaranteeing the "evaluability" of development projects; and (iv) promoting knowledge and discussions to disseminate evidence-based interventions that can be later implemented by several MDBs in their respective subregions. The IDB and the World Bank are already implementing periodic reviews of their development effectiveness role with adequate resources and broad analysis of their operations. SRDBs need to catch up and other banks can collaborate efficiently to achieve this aim.

Some areas of research emerge regarding the delicate balance that MDBs need to find between financial strength, innovation capacity to provide services at competitive costs, and their impact on development. First, there is almost no work on comparing unitary costs of providing

(a) World Bank

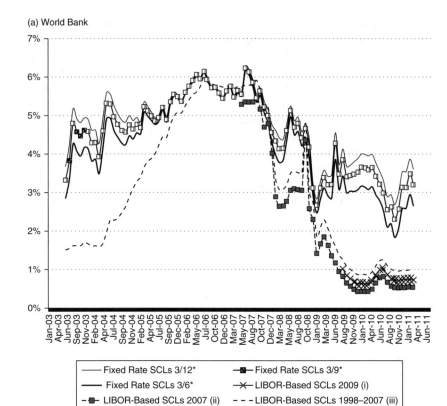

Notes:

SCLs = Fixed single currency loans (in months).

* Fixed-rate single currency loans (SCLs) for loans where invitation to negotiate was extended on or after 31 July 1998. The structure type indicates the grace period and final maturity for each disbursed loan amount, as approved in the loan agreement. Thus, a "3/12" structure means a grace period of 3 years and a final maturity of 12 years for each disbursed loan amount whose rate has been fixed.

(i) LIBOR-based SCLs for loans where invitation to negotiate was issued on or after 23 July 2009.

(ii) LIBOR-based SCLs for loans signed on or after 28 September 2007.

(iii) LIBOR-based SCLs for loans where invitation to negotiate was issued on or after 31 July 1998 and signed before 28 September 2007.

Source:　IDB and World Bank annual reports.

Figure 10.9　Average lending rates of multilateral development banks, 2003–11

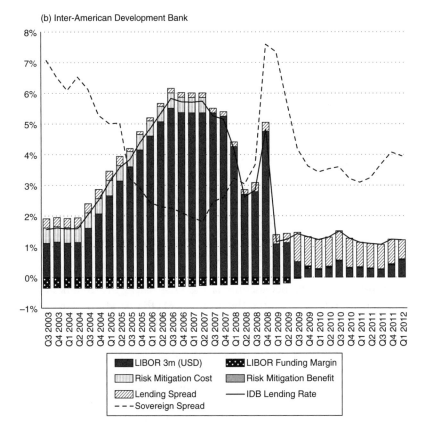

Figure 10.9 (continued)

certain types of services across banks. Second, MDBs need to systematize their knowledge of implementing development effectiveness in their institutions, estimate their costs to implement these reforms, and estimate changes in development effectiveness with comparable indicators across institutions. Third, more work is needed to systematize innovations in MDBs that contribute to reduced administrative costs or increased development effectiveness. SRDBs are generally catching up quickly, but further systematization and dissemination efforts of these innovations can increase collaboration between SRDBs and the main banks.

Table 10.2   Multilateral development bank net income, 2000–11 (US$ million)

	2000	2001	2002	2003	2004	2005	2006	2007	2008	2009	2010	2011
IDB	846	1021	709	2433	1176	762	243	134	(22)	794	330	(283)
CAF	107	113	127	136	208	283	321	401	311	235	166	153
CDB			27	22	19	7	18	35	85	40	38	
CABEI				137	56	57	73	81	83	71	114	

Notes: ( ) = negative; CAF = Andean Corporation of Finance; CDB = Caribbean Development Bank; IDB = Inter-American Development Bank; CABEI = Central American Bank for Economic Integration.

Source: Annual Reports.

10.3.3   Net Income Distribution: Where Policy and Politics Meet in Multilateral Development Banks

Decision-making over net income is the area where MDB stakeholders express their preferences about the future of MDB operations. Net income is the difference between income and expenses during a determined period of operations. In general, MDBs can choose to allocate their net income between: (i) improving the financial position of the institution by increasing reserves and strengthening lending capacity; (ii) providing grants, increasing concessional lending, or building fiduciary funds for specific purposes, particularly for providing international public goods, that will not generate additional income; and (iii) setting aside resources to invest in more complex operations, which tend to increase administrative expenses and, thus, reduce net income, or, in contrast, reducing fees or lending spreads to slash lending costs.

Table 10.2 shows that net income of MDBs operating in the LAC region have been highly variable and there is no common trend. Sagasti and Prada (2006) identified some patterns to allocate net income in regional MDBs, but the global financial crisis seems to have changed these patterns. For several years, MDBs in the LAC region have focused on strengthening their capital and lending base, and thus have prioritized building reserves and have allocated a greater share of net income to retained earnings. For example, the CDB and CABEI have consistently allocated 100 per cent of their net income to strengthening their capital base.

The situation is more complex in the case of the IDB, and the CAF is following this path and differentiating progressively from other SRDBs while expanding operations in non-Andean countries. Until 2007, the

IDB was allocating a significant part of its net income to retained earnings and a small percentage to increase resources of the Fund for Special Operations, the IDB's concessional lending window. This has radically changed as a consequence of two related events: the creation of the IDB Grant Facility in 2007; and the beginning of the IDB-9 negotiation process in 2009, the ninth capital replenishment that seeks to increase the IDB's capital by 70 per cent when the process finishes by 2015.

As part of the IDB-9 negotiation processes, the IDB board of governors has pledged a US$200 million per year allocation from the IDB's net income to strengthen the capital base of the Grant Facility until 2021. Currently, only Haiti is receiving funding from this facility, but any other poor country in the region under conditions of stress and vulnerability can apply for funding through this window. Moreover, following the catastrophic earthquake in Haiti in 2010, the IDB has mobilized extra resources from its net income: it provided full debt relief to Haiti and made a provision of US$484 million for this purpose.

For the IDB, these changes are an important sign of shifting roles and changing balances between the three functions of MDBs. With additional resources after the conclusion of IDB-9, the IDB will have extra room to expand lending without affecting its financial position. The IDB is now investing resources to increase its capacity to provide grants to countries under financial stress, and has chosen not to strengthen its concessional window. This extra capacity will add to several funds and special programs under IDB administration on behalf of member countries for specific purposes related to the production of international public goods such as research, technical cooperation, pre-investment and triangular cooperation.[7]

The CAF is also finding a balance between strengthening its financial position, making its operations more complex, and increasing resources to provide international public goods. The CAF's Constitutive Agreement requires that at least 10 per cent of net income should be allocated to increase reserves, but it tended to allocate slightly more before the global financial crisis. However, the CAF has been allocating almost half of its net income to special programs and funds for technical cooperation, research initiatives and the provision of grants. For example, in 2011 almost US$100 million was allocated for this from 2010 net income (55 per cent of total net income); in 2010 it allocated US$105 million of 2009 net income (45 per cent of total net income); and in 2009 it allocated US$70 million of 2008 net income (40 per cent of total net income).

Another area where politics and decision-making intersect is the decision to include non-regional partners in MDB operations. This can provide additional financial resources and new approaches, but can slightly alter the balance of power inside institutions. For example, the PRC, which joined the IDB as a member country in 2009, has pledged through its Eximbank a US$1 billion joint program to promote investment in the LAC region, but has committed 30 per cent of this to create a fund to combat violence in the region. The PRC is already a member country in SRDBs such as CABEI and CDB (Table 10.2), but it is also working closely with the CAF through the Chinese Development Bank and other PRC institutions to provide syndicated loans and support investment in the LAC region. Both institutions have launched research programs and joint initiatives to work more closely with the PRC, as this country is becoming the main trading partner of several LAC countries. Nevertheless, a growing influence of such an important player may add an extra layer of complexity to MDBs' affairs in the future.

The patterns of net income allocation contribute to understanding future directions that MDBs are willing to take. While the IDB (and the CAF to a lesser extent) is setting aside resources for more complex operations from its net income, other SRDBs are building their financial capacity to focus on their financial role. The IDB is taking the lead in the region to make resources available to countries in financial distress. It is thus creating precautionary funding options, such as the IDB Grant Facility, and working with multi-donor funds such as the Haiti Reconstruction Fund and others for specific purposes, such as FOMIN, as well as technical cooperation funds under its administration. As the CAF is expanding its original subregional focus and has started to provide financing to other countries such as Argentina, Brazil, Costa Rica, Panama and Uruguay, it is also investing heavily in creating additional capacity to work with new clients and more countries.

10.4 CONCLUSIONS

Dynamism and strength at the regional and subregional levels suggest that MDBs are part of a decentralized system in the LAC region. We have gathered several indicators about their interactions with other MDBs and other financial and development institutions, their relative position in the development financing landscape, and how they benefit from their comparative advantages such as different willingness and capacities to take risks. The evidence suggests that MDBs are actively looking for niches and competing with each other for relevance, financing and influence, particularly at the country level.

Most countries in the LAC region are benefiting from the competition between these institutions for two reasons. First, most of these countries have been growing (despite the global financial crisis), have improved their access to financial sources, and have comfortable room to maneuver in case the international context worsens. Secondly, they benefit from better services and customized interventions from MDBs, as well as additional insurance in case of a sudden reduction in financial flows due to a more complicated international situation. Therefore, there is a window of opportunity in the next 10 years to devote important resources to innovate in development approaches, scale-up investment to create institutional capacities in LAC countries, and improve the provision of regional public goods. MDBs have a crucial role to play in providing knowledge and mobilizing finance.

MDBs have traditionally prioritized their financial role and have built strong reserves to operate in the LAC region, and now there are strong signals that MDBs are investing in new approaches, increasing grant resources, decentralizing, and scaling-up their operations. But financial resources are scarce in the long term, and a rethink is required of how to allocate the additional resources that are a product of the current economic growth cycle. Here, a systemic approach could be important: MDBs should think together on how to find a balance between the three functions (providing that each MDB has space for specialization) and to benefit from their own comparative advantages.

There is enough anecdotal and systematized evidence about how dysfunctional the MDB system in the LAC region can be. For each example of collaboration between these institutions, there are several examples on how they duplicate efforts, engage in costly and ineffective interventions, and support initiatives and projects with politics in mind instead of applying an adequate project evaluation, among other valid concerns.

By taking a look at long-term dynamics and identifying patterns in available data about MDBs, we conclude that there is more room for collaboration between these institutions than the conventional wisdom suggests. One reason for this is that they are facing similar threats in the current international context and, thus, have incentives to find common ideas to maintain their relevance in the future. Another reason is that MDBs are important sources and promoters of knowledge and innovation in development thinking and ideas for intervention, and they are generating frequent (and poorly recognized) collaborations between their staff, between public officers in developing countries, and with the academic community. There are significant gains in having a dense network of MDBs that promote knowledge, provide technical cooperation, and function as platforms for collaboration.

NOTES

1. MDBs have been rethinking their relative position in the region, and most conclude that the current starting point offers great potential. For example, see Moreno (2012), CAF (2010) and World Bank (2011, 2012) on how these institutions have reassessed actions and strategies to support the region.
2. See Sagasti and Prada (2012, p. 266 and Appendix 2) for details of the index calculation.
3. Appendix 10A.1 presents partial results since we have only considered Peru's capital account data, that is, related only to its capacity to mobilize external resources. It is clear though that the Peruvian public sector in the 2010s relies more on domestic capital markets and public revenues to finance public investment, while before 1980 it relied on MDBs or syndicated loans from private banks (later converted into Paris Club debt).
4. This term refers to the main transnational companies from LAC countries.
5. The RBCR is the ratio between net outstanding loans and the sum of paid-in capital and retained earnings. It is an index to measure the leverage capacity of financial institutions.
6. World Bank (2009, p. 31) indicates that "between FY04 and FY09, expenditure on supervision of the IBRD portfolio increased at around 3.6 per cent a year, effectively flat in real terms; supervision costs for the IDA [International Development Association] portfolio increased by 9.2% a year over the same period. The net effect was to increase total supervision costs by $51.0 million".
7. For more details, see http://www.iadb.org/aboutus/trustfunds/fundsearch.cfm.

REFERENCES

Bezanson, K., F. Sagasti and F. Prada. 2005. *The Future of the Financing for Development System: Challenges, Scenarios and Strategic Choices*. Oxford: Palgrave.

De la Torre, A. and A. Ize. 2010. El papel crediticio de la banca de desarrollo en la post-crisis. Presentation at the Conference La Banca de desarrollo y el entorno internacional in Mexico City on 12 June 2010 organized by the World Bank – LAC office.

Development Bank of Latin America (CAF). 2010. *Visión para América Latina 2040: Hacia una sociedad más incluyente y próspera*. Panama: CAF.

Inter-American Development Bank (IDB). 2012. Marco de resultados del Banco para 2012–2015. Annex 2 in: IDB. 2012. *Panorama de la efectividad 2011*. Washington, DC.

Ministry of Economy and Finance of Peru. 2012. Statistics National Government Debt and Guarantees. Available at: http://www.mef.gob.pe/.

Moreno, L.A. 2012. *La década de América Latina y el Caribe: Una oportunidad real*. 2nd edn. Washington, DC: IDB.

Prada, F., U. Casabonne and K. Bezanson. 2010. Development resources beyond the current reach of the Paris Declaration. Copenhagen: Danish Institute of International Studies. Available at: www.oecd.org/dataoecd/1/14/46486829.pdf.

Sagasti, F. and K. Bezanson. 2000. *A Foresight and Policy Study of the Multilateral Development Banks*. Stockholm: Ministry for Foreign Affairs of Sweden.

Sagasti, F. with the contribution of F. Prada. 2002. *La Banca Multilateral de Desarrollo*. Santiago de Chile: CEPALC, Serie Financiamiento del Desarrollo No. 119.

Sagasti, F. and F. Prada. 2006. Regional development banks: A comparative perspective. In J.A. Ocampo (ed.). *Regional Financial Cooperation*. Washington, DC: Brookings Institution Press and the Economic Commission for Latin America and the Caribbean (ECLAC).
Sagasti, F. and F. Prada. 2012. The new face of development cooperation: The role of south–south cooperation and corporate social responsibility. In J.A. Alonso and J.A. Ocampo (eds). *Development Cooperation in Times of Crisis*. New York: Columbia University Press, pp. 250–315.
Wood, B. et al. 2011. The evaluation of the Paris Declaration Phase 2 – Final Report. Copenhagen: Danish Institute for International Studies.
World Bank. 2009. Moving ahead on investment lending reform: Risk framework and implementation support. Washington, DC: World Bank.
World Bank. 2011. Regional Strategy Update 2011: Latin America and the Caribbean region. Washington, DC: World Bank.
World Bank. 2012. Latin America copes with volatility: The dark side of globalization. Washington, DC: World Bank.

ADDITIONAL DATA SOURCES

Caribbean Development Bank (CDB). Annual Reports 2003–2010. Available at: http://www.caribank.org/.
Central American Bank for Economic Integration (CABEI). Annual Reports 2002–2010. Available at: http://www.bcie.org/uploaded/content/category/827774422.pdf and http://www.cabei.org/english/publicaciones/memorias_09.php.
Central American Bank for Economic Integration (CABEI). Products and Services. Available at: http://www.bcie.org/?cat=8&title=Product%20and%20Services&lang=en (accessed: April 2012).
Credit Report System (CRS) – Organisation for Economic Co-operation and Development (OECD) StatExtracts. Available at: http://stats.oecd.org/Index.aspx?datasetcode=CRS1 (accessed: May 2012).
Development Bank of Latin America (CAF). Annual Reports 1990 and 2001–2011. Available at: http://publicaciones.caf.com/corporativo?page=0.
Development Bank of Latin America (CAF). Products and Services. Available at: http://www.caf.com/view/index.asp?ms=19&pageMs=61974 (accessed: April 2012).
Global Development Finance (GDF). World Bank Data Catalog. Available at: http://data.worldbank.org/data-catalog (accessed: April 2012).
Inter-American Development Bank (IDB). Annual Reports 2000–2011. Available at: http://www.iadb.org/en/about-us/annual-reports,6293.html.
Inter-American Development Bank (IDB). Financing Solutions. Available at: http://www.iadb.org/en/idb-finance/english/financing-solutions,1978.html (accessed: April 2012).
Inter-American Development Bank (IDB). Interest Rates and Charges. Available at: http://www.iadb.org/en/idb-finance/interest-rates-and-loan-charges,2331.html (accessed: April 2012).
Inter-American Investment Corporation (IIC) Annual Reports 2000–2010. Available at: http://www.iic.org/en/promotion/2011-annual-report.
International Finance Corporation (IFC) Annual Reports 2001–2011.

Available at: http://www1.ifc.org/wps/wcm/connect/CORP_EXT_Content/
IFC_External_Corporate_Site/Annual+Report.

Ministry of Economy and Finance of Peru. 2012. Statistics National Government
Debt and Guarantees: External Debt (Historical Series for 1970–2011 Funding
Source and debt stock, disbursements and bond placements for 2000–2011).
Available at: http://www.mef.gob.pe/index.php?option=com_content&view=ar
ticle&id=273&Itemid=101338&lang=es (accessed: April–May 2012).

Superintendencia Nacional de Aduanas y de Administración Tributaria (SUNAT).
2012. Estadística y Estudios, Cuadro No.1: Ingresos del Gobierno Central
Consolidado, 1998–2012 (Millones de nuevos soles). Available at: http://www.
sunat.gob.pe/estadisticasestudios/.

World Bank Annual Reports 2000–2011. Available at: http://web.worldbank.org/
WBSITE/EXTERNAL/EXTABOUTUS/EXTANNREP/0,,menuPK:1397243~
pagePK:64168427~piPK:64168435~theSitePK:1397226,00.html.

World Bank Treasury. IBRD Lending Rates and Loan Charges. Available
at:http://treasury.worldbank.org/bdm/htm/ibrd.html (accessed: April 2012).

APPENDIX 10A.1 EXTERNAL FINANCIAL FLOWS TO THE GOVERNMENT OF PERU BY FERNANDO ROMERO[1]

Figure 10A.1 describes the evolution of net transfers to the government of Peru from external creditors: new loans minus payments of interest and principal of previous loans during the same period. The main trends can be summarized as follows:

- Annual average net transfers were positive by US$420 million during the 1970s and by US$150 million during the 1980s. Bilateral debt from Paris Club and non-Paris Club members and from other creditors (such as export credits, commercial banks and credit from suppliers) maintained positive net transfers with Peru during the 1970s. After the 1980s debt crisis, the financial structure changes as debt from multilateral development banks (MDBs) and Paris Club members increased to cope with the shortage of foreign currency.
- Net transfers became negative during the 1990s to an annual average of –US$670 million, and yet more negative and variable between 2000 and 2011: in 2007 they reached –US$3.7 billion due to large payments to Paris Club creditors and MDBs. The 2000s also coincided with sustained growth of fiscal revenues and a reduction of the debt–gross domestic product (GDP) ratio to 25 per cent in 2011 from 45 per cent in 2000. Central government tax revenue went from US$6.6 billion in 2000 to US$28.0 billion in 2011. Overall, this implies a structural reduction of external financial needs of the public budget.

The Peruvian debt profile has improved as a consequence and more financial options opened during the 2000s. New loans reached an average maturity of 13.4 years in 2010, while bonds reached 17.4 years. Moreover, almost 80 per cent of total public debt has fixed interest rates. This diversification of financial sources has allowed for better debt management: in 2010 almost half of new disbursements were utilized to prepay Paris Club and MDB debt. This debt replaces old and expensive debt with new debt arising from issuing global bonds in international capital markets; Peru has been issuing bonds at an average of US$1.5 billion per year during 2000–11. Meanwhile, Peru now relies more on domestic debt (a great percentage denominated in local currency), which currently represents almost half of the total liabilities of the central government.

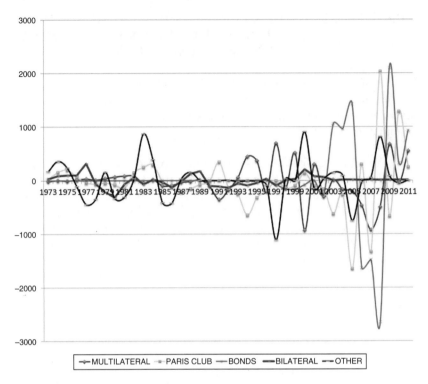

Notes: 'Bilateral' consists of creditors from Latin America, Eastern Europe and the People's Republic of China; 'Other' consists of international banks and suppliers; 'Paris Club' countries are Australia, Austria, Belgium, Canada, Denmark, Finland, France, Germany, Ireland, Italy, Japan, Netherlands, Norway, Russian Federation, Spain, Sweden, Switzerland, United Kingdom and United States.

Source: Ministry of Economy and Finance of Peru (2012).

Figure 10A.1   Net transfers of Peruvian public foreign debt, 1970–2011 (US$ billion)

The countercyclical role of MDB participation in central government financing is worth noting – an increment of net transfers has coincided with large increments during times of financial stress such as the 1980s debt crisis, the Asian Financial Crisis, the bursting of the dot.com bubble, and the recent global financial crisis. The three main MDBs in the region (the Development Bank of Latin America (CAF), the Inter-American Development Bank (IDB), and the World Bank) represent almost all financial transfers from MDBs in absolute terms to Peru.[2] Figure 10A.2 shows the interactions of these three MDBs during 2000–11.

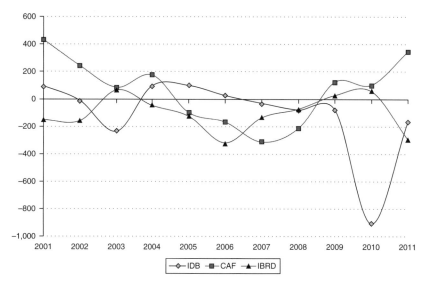

Notes: CAF = Andean Corporation of Finance; IDB = Inter-American Development Bank; IBRD = International Bank for Reconstruction and Development from the World Bank Group.

Source: Ministry of Economy and Finance of Peru.

Figure 10A.2 Multilateral development bank net transfers to the government of Peru, 2000–11 (US$ million)

Net transfers from the International Bank for Reconstruction and Development (IBRD) have been nearly constant with a tendency to become negative, even after the temporary surge during the global financial crisis. Transfers from the IDB have followed a similar pattern, except that the government of Peru has made large prepayments, such as in 2010, partially financed with global bond issues. In contrast, the CAF portfolio is increasing in Peru, particularly due to new infrastructure loans. Overall, MDBs channel important resources to the central government, but they are no longer the most relevant: domestic financing, bond issuing, and fiscal revenues are now central to public finances.

In summary, the central government structure of finances has changed dramatically during the 1970–2012 period. A look at net transfers gives a comprehensive view of such changes and how Peru has been able to diversify its access to financial sources. Looking at this evolution, it is clear that the capacity to mobilize domestic and external resources has had an impact on the structure of financing of the government of Peru.

Notes

1. Researcher of the Financing for Development program at FORO Nacional Internacional.
2. The European Investment Bank, International Fund for Agriculture Development, Nordic Investment Bank, and Organization of the Petroleum Exporting Countries represent less than 1 per cent of these transfers and thus have been excluded.

Index